THE WELFARE EXPERIMENTS

The Welfare Experiments

Politics and Policy Evaluation

ROBIN H. ROGERS-DILLON

Stanford Law and Politics
AN IMPRINT OF STANFORD UNIVERSITY PRESS
STANFORD, CALIFORNIA
2004

Stanford University Press
Stanford, California
www.sup.org

© 2004 by the Board of Trustees of the Leland Stanford Junior University.
All rights reserved.

Library of Congress Cataloging-in-Publication Data

Rogers-Dillon, Robin.
   The welfare experiments : politics and policy evaluation / Robin H. Rogers-Dillon.
      cip:Includes bibliographical references and index.
      ISBN 0-8047-4730-X (cloth : alk. paper)—ISBN 0-8047-4746-6 (pbk : alk. paper)
      1. Public welfare—United States.   2. United States—Social policy—1993–
3. United States—Politics and government—1993–2001.   I. Title.
HV95.R58 2004
361.6'0973'09049—dc22   2004001027

Printed in the United States of America on acid-free, archival-quality paper.

Original Printing 2004

Last figure below indicates year of this printing:
13   12   11   10   09   08   07   06   05   04

Designed and typeset at Stanford University Press in 10 / 12.5 Palatino.

Special discounts for bulk quantities of Stanford Law and Politics books are available to corporations, professional associations, and other organizations. For details and discount information, contact the special sales department of Stanford University Press. Tel: (650) 736-1783, Fax: (650) 736-1784

For Christopher

Contents

Figures

Acknowledgments

I received so much support during the research and writing of this book that attempting to acknowledge these contributions is daunting. I will fall short of the task. Since there is no way to quantify the generosity and importance of each contribution, I will order my thanks chronologically. First, I would like to thank the Women's Research and Education Institute (WREI) for giving me the opportunity to work as a Congressional Fellow for Congressman Charles Rangel in 1995/96—the height of welfare reform. It was an extraordinary opportunity. I also wish to thank Congressman Rangel and his staff, who permitted me to become involved in welfare reform at a level that went far beyond any of my expectations.

Next, I would like to thank the Manpower Demonstration Research Corporation (MDRC), particularly Dan Bloom and Judith Gueron. Although I critique the role that evaluation companies played in the 1990s, I have great respect for the people with whom I worked at MDRC and am personally grateful for the opportunities that they gave me. I also wish to thank the administrators and staff involved in Florida's Family Transition Program (FTP), particularly Shirley Jacques and John Bouldin. They are remarkable administrators and very generous people.

At the University of Pennsylvania, Robin Leidner, Harold Bershady, Jerry Jacobs, and John Skrentny provided me with great intellectual support and mentorship. At New York University, Lawrence Mead deserves special thanks for both the longevity of his support and its resilience. My interest in welfare was ignited in the late 1980s in his undergraduate class on poverty and social welfare. Since then, Larry has been a great mentor and critic. I like to think that we share a commitment both to rigorous research, about which we usually agree, and to the good society, where our differences emerge. I hope that as a teacher I bring the same critical support to my students that Larry has brought to me.

The Robert Wood Johnson Foundation and the Institute for Social and Policy Studies (ISPS) at Yale University provided me with a remarkable intellectual home from 1998 to 2000 as a Robert Wood Johnson Health Policy Scholar. At ISPS, I had not only the luxury of time for my research and writing but also the unique opportunity to engage in debate and discussion with outstanding scholars, both established and emerging. Ted Marmor and Mark Schlesinger in particular were generous with their time, which was limited, and their intellects, which appeared to have no limits at all. The Health Policy Scholars at ISPS, John Evans, Rogan Kersh, Taeku Lee, Gary McKissick, Eric Oliver, Mark Suchman, Ingrid Ellen, and Brian Gran contributed greatly to my thinking on health, poverty, public policy, and many others issues, and I thank them.

I would also like to thank my colleagues at Queens College, my intellectual home since 2000. Donald Scott, Dean Savage, Charlie Smith, and Hester Eisenstein helped me to find protected research time and provided me with great mentorship. Andy Beveridge, Bernard Cohen, and Charles Turner provided valuable comments on drafts of chapters in the manuscript. Victoria Pitts, my "senior" colleague by one year, has provided wise and often humorous counsel. I would like to make a special acknowledgment of four wonderful students from Queens College who contributed to the research for the Afterword, Sreekan Cheruku, Enge Ibrahim, Judith Rivera, and Michael Uvaydov. Shree, Enge, Julie, and Mike are proof that the City University of New York, particularly Queens College, attracts some of the best students in the world. David Humphries, a CUNY graduate student, provided me valuable editing and research assistance. I would have been lost without him.

I owe one of my greatest debts to Mary Jo Bane and David T. Ellwood of Harvard University, who agreed to talk with me and enriched this book immeasurably. Another great debt is to Steven M. Teles of Brandeis University. His intellectual generosity and insight are unparalleled, and his influence is woven throughout this book. Jill Quadagno read and commented on draft chapters of the manuscript. I am eternally grateful for her support of this project and remain in awe of her intellect. Anonymous reviewers of earlier drafts of the manuscript for Stanford University Press also provided incisive comments. I would also like to thank Lynne Haney of New York University, my co-investigator on another project, for graciously reading and commenting on material for the book. Jonathan Imber, the editor of *Society*, has given me the opportunity to write on issues of welfare policy in that outstanding publication. Some of the ideas that are explored in Chapter Seven of this book were initially raised by me in articles that appeared in *Society*. Finally, Amanda Moran, my editor at Stanford University Press, has energetically supported this book. An author could not ask for more.

I also received considerable personal support during this project. First and foremost, I want to thank my husband Chris, to whom this book is dedicated. Our son Nicholas was a year old when I began my residence at the Institute for Social and Policy Studies at Yale and spent the better part of each week away from my family in Brooklyn. Chris picked up the baby and helped me with my bags without a hint of dissent. Before and since, Chris has given me tremendous freedom—a room of my own as prescribed by Virginia Woolf—while still being his wonderful and highly original self. I am also indebted to my father, D. W. Rogers, who conveyed his respect for women's intelligence so thoroughly that I was shocked as a young adult to find that the sentiment was not universally shared. Finally, I would like to acknowledge my mother, Kay Rogers, who grew up in a time and a town where college education for women was considered unnecessary, and then sent her daughters off to graduate school. This book would not have been possible without her.

THE WELFARE EXPERIMENTS

CHAPTER 1

The Politics of Pilot Programs

> I think it is fair to say the debate is over. . . . We now know that welfare reform works.
>
> President Bill Clinton, 1997

The Personal Responsibility and Work Opportunity Reconciliation Act of 1996 (PRWORA) presents a riddle. For decades, substantial welfare reform had stalled at the federal level. The reform efforts that did pass, notably the Family Support Act of 1988, were watered down as they worked their way through the massive welfare bureaucracy. Efforts at reform had, at best, a slight impact on the majority of welfare recipients. Aid to Families with Dependent Children (AFDC) seemed to be a large bureaucracy that would withstand the most virulent political attacks by virtue of its sheer size and age. Then something odd happened. The system crumbled in the span of a few years. The demise of welfare was a matter of fact. Time-limited welfare, a radical departure from AFDC, was taken for granted as an obvious solution to a failed policy just a few years after even minor alterations to AFDC seemed to be a political impossibility. How did this happen?

To address this question, we need to look beyond the traditional actors in policymaking—the interest groups, members of Congress, and presidential administrations. All of these actors were important in welfare reform, but they do not fully explain the dramatic restructuring of the American welfare state that took place in 1996. President Clinton's pledge to "end welfare as we know it" in his 1992 presidential campaign laid the groundwork for radical reform of the welfare system.

The slogan "two years and you're off" famously, and unintentionally, paved the way for Temporary Assistance for Needy Families (TANF).[1] The Republican takeover of Congress in 1994 increased the momentum for welfare reform. In fact, welfare reform was one of the stated objectives in the Republican Contract with America, the platform on which many Republican members ran for office and won.

Yet even this constellation of factors fails to explain why such profound changes in the American welfare state passed with so little fanfare and why what had been an unthinkable policy idea became the obvious solution to reforming welfare in such a short period. To answer that question, we need to understand the political role of the experimental welfare pilot programs and how they became a part of the policy-making process.

The case of welfare reform in 1996 raises a set of larger questions: How is public policy made? How do we decide whether a new policy idea will work? Who determines which path to take when there are competing ideas? Historical institutional research has placed considerable emphasis on the role of overtly political actors—legislators and interest groups—in garnering support for favored policy ideas. In this book, I argue that there is a critical and largely unrecognized institutional channel in social policymaking—experimental pilot programs. Pilot programs are designed to test new policy ideas. They permit policy innovations to leave the realm of political debate and to come to life in programs that affect real people, programs that can be observed and whose results can be measured. They demonstrate to the public and policy elites whether or not a policy will work. Defining what works is a powerful political tool. It is particularly powerful if the definition of what works is framed as a scientific assessment objectively determined outside of the political realm.

Yet pilot programs, as this book demonstrates, are not neutral, and they are not outside of the political process. The very existence of a pilot program is often a part of a larger political strategy. Pilot programs can be used to send an idea "to committee" in order to placate advocates of a proposed policy even if the broader initiative is dead in the political waters. Similarly, pilot programs can postpone a political conflict, on the basis that "more research is needed," until a time when policy actors find more advantages.[2] Political actors can use pilot programs to claim credit on a policy issue that is not moving through normal legislative channels and thus avoid the consequences of failing to act on a popular policy issue. In the early 1990s, experimental welfare pilot programs were used by both Democrats and Republicans to claim progress as the federal legislative process stalled.[3] Evelyn Z. Brodkin and Alexander Kaufman have argued that pilot programs "have a tactical utility in the competition for space on the policy agenda."[4] As Wisconsin governor Tommy Thompson so brilliantly demonstrated with his highly visible welfare reform pilot programs, pilot programs can also define a policy idea and set the terms of a political debate.

Policy choices are about values and technical efficacy. Political rhetoric often emphasizes values. What do we want this country to do? What is the proper role of the government? What are America's fiscal and political priorities? The political realm is home to issues of values and priorities. Technical policy questions on the surface appear to be more concrete. Will a policy do what we want it to do? Will it work? Thus, policy questions are often understood to go through a process from the abstract, value-driven decision that the goal of a policy is desirable, to the specific, technical question of what means will attain that goal.[5] Policy specialists ostensibly have the task of making sure that legislation is technically sound and will promote the values and priorities promised in the original debate. Administrators, in the final stage of bringing a policy to life, are charged with effectively implementing the policy and sorting out the ground-level technical details.

In American culture, however, efficiency and effectiveness are often raised to the level of values themselves. Given this reality, is it then possible to separate the technical from the political? In the quote that began this chapter, Clinton hailed welfare reform by stating "the debate is over. . . . We now know that welfare reform works." Clinton did not claim that good had triumphed over evil, but rather that a system that *works* had replaced a broken one. American politicians often invoke the practicality of their ideas to gain popular support. In effect, they say: "My ideas work, my opponents' do not."

Technical questions, however, are not completely separate from political questions. Claiming that a policy idea works is politically powerful in itself. This is particularly true if the claim is based on evidence purported to be "scientific." As I will argue, such evidence often has little connection to social science. Nonetheless, Americans hold great faith in clinical tests. We believe that nearly all ideas can be scientifically tested and their value empirically proven. Americans are deeply suspicious of politics and scientific approaches appear, occasionally, to provide a viable alternative.

Deborah A. Stone has argued that America is engaged in a "rationality project." "The fields of political science, public administration, law, and policy analysis," Stone writes, "have shared a common mission of rescuing public policy from the irrationalities and indignities of politics, hoping to conduct it instead with rational, analytical, and scientific methods."[6] Even the language that we use to describe the study of politics and society reveals a faith that they can be rendered orderly. Our universities teach political *science* and policy *analysis*. Our studies of politics and society are housed in divisions of social science. The quest for rationality is particularly strong in the face of the disorder that normally characterizes politics. Americans diligently have sought to expand the former in order to minimize the latter. As Stone notes, "Inspired by a vague sense that reason is clean and politics is dirty Americans yearn to replace politics with rational decisionmaking."[7]

A faith in rationality is as central to American identity as is our distrust of politics. There is nothing inherently wrong with the American quest for rationality. Our constitutional structure, in one supremely noteworthy example of the triumph of rationality, has produced a stable, prosperous democracy that is to be marveled at more than criticized. And I am partial to a legal system based on, at least in principle, reason rather than authority. But there is a point at which the rationality project fails. Rather than encouraging knowledge and understanding, it obscures truths that do not fit within its rubric. The rationality project becomes procrustean.

In this book, I argue that this faith in the power of rationality to cleanse politics has caused us to overlook the political role of policy experiments. Testing policy ideas has not taken policy out of the political realm and placed it into the scientific realm; rather, it has created an institutional role for experimental programs in the policy-making process. Looking at the political role of policy experiments does not diminish the value of social science research or rationality. Instead, it takes away the blinders that social scientists put on in an attempt not to be distracted from empirical policy evaluation by passing political fashions. The desire to remove policy evaluation from politics is a noble one. The idea that "everybody's entitled to their own statistic" makes people who believe that the world does exist in some measurable way wince. We can do better than that. There is, however, an expanse of territory between the idea that research is nothing more than politics dressed up in fancy statistics and the idea that social research, particularly policy research, can ever fully be extracted from its political context.

In this book, I argue that researchers, particularly those involved in policy evaluation, have erred too far in the latter direction. The claim that research can be extracted from politics emanates from two related facts. First, trained and committed evaluation researchers believe that research can provide important and real results that are relevant to social policy. I believe that, too. Second, as policy evaluation became professionalized in the late 1960s and 1970s, it had to establish its own domain—what do evaluators do that is different from what other social scientists do? Why should the government listen to evaluators and, in fact, fund them? Here, I believe, evaluators began to stretch their ability to separate policy research and politics beyond the breaking point. In itself, this is not an unusual or particularly dangerous phenomenon. Professional groups often exaggerate the distinctiveness of their practices in order to make clear that only those within their fold are capable of providing particular services. In this case, however, the claims of evaluators had a ripple effect beyond the professional realm. The public accepted the fictitious divide between politics and policy evaluation.

The divide between politics and policy evaluation is inherently attractive. It fits with America's pragmatic bent toward politics—our taste for "what works" over ideological solutions. The best that social science can truly do, however, is to make clear what is involved in a particular program: the outcomes, how the programs actually functioned on the ground (not only as written), and the normative and value conflicts inherent within the program both on paper and in practice. Social science cannot tell us "what works" because "what works" is not solely an empirical question. It is a political one. In the 1990s, the professional claims making of evaluators obscured the political aspects of social experiments. Not surprisingly, politicians then put the fiction of apolitical policy experiments to their own political uses.

Pilot Programs and Welfare Reform

The 1996 Personal Responsibility and Work Opportunity Reconciliation Act would very likely not have passed without the pilot programs, which were also known as "waiver" programs because they required the federal government to waive AFDC requirements. Although it is impossible to rule out completely that some other political and institutional structure could have produced welfare reform, the evidence that the pilot programs played crucial roles in shaping the policy details of

PRWORA is compelling. It therefore merits looking beyond the conventional wisdom that policy experiments play a minor political role. In PRWORA, the *empirical results* from the numerous welfare reform experiments that preceded it were politically unimportant. However, the *existence* of the pilot programs reshaped the political landscape and made reform possible.

The pilot programs from 1992 to 1996 redefined what welfare means in the United States. They did not simply tinker with welfare-to-work programs or make small changes in the incentive structure within welfare. These programs redefined welfare as a temporary program rather than an entitlement. They abolished the entitlement to welfare in the public mind well before Congress ended it. More importantly, the pilot programs engaged the public through widespread media coverage. The previous pilot programs were in the domain of experts. The welfare experiments of the early to middle 1990s were in the public eye. Covered on the nightly news and in numerous newspaper articles, the welfare experiments changed the politics of welfare reform more visibly and dramatically than ever before.

Pilot programs are "shadow institutions" in the political process.[8] They are a way of taking policy ideas and publicly determining whether the ideas are viable. They are also fundamentally tied to the political process both in their administration, which is often filled by political appointees, and in their public role as an institutional channel through which the viability of a public policy is determined. Yet, they do even more than provide an institutional arena for policy ideas that buffers them from the political climate. Pilot programs show us whether the policy will "work" or not. They provide a glimpse of a newborn idea and shape our expectations of what the mature policy will look like well before the evaluation results are out. Arguably, pilot programs are most powerful before the evaluation research is complete, when they have been removed from politics but are not yet mired in empirical results.

Pilot programs can also serve the structural function of weakening policy legacies from below, as they did in the welfare reform experiments of the early 1990s. The structure of an existing program is often altered to permit a temporary experiment. By putting new administrative structures and procedures in place, even temporarily, the inertia of the old system is broken, creating an opportunity for permanent reform. Pilot programs, therefore, do not just test policy ideas; they play a political and structural role in the policy-making process. Pilot programs define the reality of the abstract ideas being debated. They change the bureaucratic structures of the institutions being targeted for reform. In the mid-1990s, pilot programs made time-limited welfare a reality and took away the argument that it could not be done.

This book is about the macro- and micropolitics that made time-limited welfare possible. By analyzing the political role of the pilot programs in an institutional framework, I hope to contribute to a stronger theoretical conceptualization of how and why welfare reform passed in 1996. More broadly, I aim to bring the experimental pilot programs—shadow institutions—out of the shadows and into mainstream political institutionalist theories of American policy development in sociology and political science. The role of the pilot programs in the welfare debate is a central feature of the book. Yet there is strong evidence that the pilot programs did more than shape the debate. These programs structurally changed the institutions that provide public assistance, the welfare offices themselves, which were notorious barriers to reform.[9]

The pilot programs eroded the institutional structures of AFDC and made it possible for a new welfare program to take a radically different direction without being dragged down by existing institutional structures and memory. To understand the street-level impact of pilot programs and welfare politics, it is important to look inside the "black box" of implementation. The public faith that policy experiments are removed from politics is what gives experimental programs their political power. Looking inside the "black box," it becomes clear that these programs are not removed from politics and, furthermore, that they *cannot* be removed from politics. Here I wish to make an important distinction. I do believe that policy experiments can and should be protected from overt political manipulation and "cooking the books." What cannot be removed from pilot programs is the political and administrative context in which they operate, which shapes program outcomes even without overt political manipulation or pressure. It is better for policy evaluation to recognize the inherently political nature of that which it studies than to obscure those aspects of pilot programs that do not fit cleanly into the framework of scientific experimentation. The refusal to acknowledge political dynamics that are plainly there has political implications of its own, often unintended, and violates the empiricism of social science research.

The metaphor of states as "laboratories of democracy" has dominated and distorted our view of pilot programs. The legitimacy of evaluation research appears to rest on its ability to render what is fundamentally political apolitical. Yet evaluation research can become more important, not less so, if it incorporates research on the political context of implementation more fully into its mandate. Evaluation research and research on welfare state development should not remain as distant as they are now. By developing a sophisticated understanding of the complex political and organizational contexts that create pilot programs and provide us with a vision of "what works" in social policy, evaluation research can demonstrate the ways in which street-level implementation creates and is created by larger political forces. In turn, political theorists can incorporate the shadow institution of pilot programs into their understanding of the structural and institutional factors that contribute to the development of the American welfare state. The story of how the 1996 welfare reform came to be shows why such broad considerations are important to our understanding of the politics of social policy and evaluation research.

Politics and Policy Evaluation

Much of contemporary policy evaluation grew out of the War on Poverty in the 1960s.[10] Ambitious new social programs begged the question: Do they work? If America was going to wage a war on poverty, it needed some way of measuring its gains and losses. The government required and funded evaluations as a part of many of the new policy initiatives, including education reforms and community health services. The rise of policy evaluation came out of a profound faith in the ability of science to make daily life better and more rational. Policy evaluation helped to build a body of knowledge concerning which policy ideas were effective and, perhaps even more importantly, which were not. Evaluation also served an auditing function, ensuring that procedures specified in the policy were actually followed. There was great optimism that the marriage of policy and research would produce and verify vastly improved social programs. Evaluations, however, often brought back dismal news. Few social policies, no matter how ambitious or eagerly anticipated, produced positive measurable results.

The aspirations for policy evaluation were not matched by their achievements, though there were moments of triumph for policy evaluators. The results from randomized policy experiments, for example, played a prominent role in shaping the Family Support Act of 1988. The manifest power of evaluation results in shaping public policy, however, has been limited by the mismatch between research and political timetables. Program outcomes take time to produce. Windows of political opportunity are short-lived. Moreover, evaluation results, when they do come in, are rarely dramatic enough to shift a political debate.

Experimental pilot programs, therefore, did not fulfill the dream of making public policy rational and scientific. For that reason many political scientists and even policy analysts dismiss them as having little to no impact on policymaking. In his otherwise excellent book on the politics of the 1996 welfare reform, *Ending Welfare as We Know It*, R. Kent Weaver limits his discussion of the role of pilot programs to the impact of the *evaluation results* on the policy-making process. He overlooks the pilot programs' structural and symbolic roles entirely. Perhaps because evaluation grew out of academia and, to paraphrase Henry J. Aaron, the Great Society's "politics of the professors," scholars have been surprisingly reluctant to examine the political role of policy experiments. Perhaps there is a fear that acknowledging the political dynamics of policy experiments will undermine their credibility and make the objective facts that social science can produce appear to be no better or worse than statistics generated by stridently ideological Washington think tanks. Yet fears that acknowledging the realpolitik[11] of pilot programs will diminish the purity of social science research is not sufficient justification to blind ourselves to the politics of policy experiments. Wishing for clean experiments and seeking objective truth should not obscure the messy political realities of policy evaluation. Otherwise, professional policy knowledge can obscure as many aspects of social policy as it illuminates.[12]

The Paradoxes of Welfare Reform

There are two key paradoxes of welfare reform. The first and more superficial paradox is how an almost universally despised social program resisted political reform for such a long time. AFDC, commonly known as welfare, had been unpopular since the late 1960s. By the late 1960s, it had come to be seen as a program that supported the "undeserving" poor. By the mid-1980s, it had become a lightning rod for political anger toward big government. Yet for years the program stood largely untouched by meaningful reform.

The paradox of an unpopular yet politically invulnerable AFDC is easily resolved. Public policies, as scholars such as Theda Skocpol and Paul Pierson have noted, create policy legacies that shape our future policy choices.[13] Simply put, once a policy is adopted it is difficult to veer too far away from that policy's direction. Social policy tends to move in small steps. We know from economists that we value a dollar that we lose more than a dollar we are given. This, too, has an impact on public policy. Once a benefit is given, it is hard to take that benefit back; constituents may exact their revenge at the next election. Public policies with large bureaucracies also become institutionally entrenched. Thousands of offices, hundreds of thousands of employees, computer systems, and funding streams all are a part of the administration of public programs. These programs not only support recipients but also fill buildings, create job ladders, and build pension plans. They create institutional memory. The rules of a program exist not only on paper but also in employees' memories, in their sense of how things are done, were done, and should be done. So it is perhaps not surprising that a social program as large and as old as AFDC resisted reform. The political institutionalism perspective helps to explain the paradox of a politically unpopular social policy that resisted change by pointing to the policy legacy and deep bureaucratic entrenchment of AFDC.

More difficult to explain is how welfare fell so quickly. Aside from cutbacks in the real value of welfare payments, the program was notoriously difficult to change. Gaining sufficient political support to pass reform was exceedingly difficult and the little reform that did pass was diluted in the vast bureaucracy. By 1993, the welfare program was deeply reviled but federal welfare reform efforts faced political gridlock. To understand the rapid demise of AFDC, we must look at the state-level welfare experiments of the early 1990s. Saddled with the strong policy legacy and entrenched bureaucracy of AFDC, welfare was all the more difficult to reform because most of its recipients were children. There was a political danger, and arguably real concern, that radically overhauling the safety net could harm children. In response to these obstacles, Clinton encouraged and promoted experimental state welfare programs to "test" new ideas.

Clinton's expansive use of waivers may have come from his own experience as governor of Arkansas. David T. Ellwood, a welfare expert from Harvard's Kennedy School of Government who served as assistant secretary for planning and evaluation at the Department of Health and Human Services (HHS) in the Clinton administration, noted that Clinton always brought a governor's perspective to welfare issues.

He was a governor, and he always viewed welfare through a governor's eyes. It was really interesting. . . . In general he felt, why should a bunch of federal bureaucrats decide what a state can and can't try to do? So, he was enormously sympathetic. He saw a political side as well. But I think it was much more visceral than that. . . . I just think that he fundamentally didn't think that the federal government should be getting in the way of states trying to do creative things and he was going to lean over backwards [to help the governors].[14]

It is not clear that Clinton used the waiver program as a part of an explicit strategy to force congressional action on reform or to circumvent Congress, although the waivers did both of those things. He was, however, aware that these experiments shifted policy-making—or at the very least policy-defining—power away from the federal government and to the states.

Mary Jo Bane, who served as assistant secretary for children and families at the Department of Health and Human Services until she resigned to protest Clinton's signing of the welfare reform bill, noted that Clinton's primary interest in the waiver process was in giving the states, particularly the governors, greater flexibility.

It was pretty clear that the president saw the waiver process as a way of letting the states do welfare reform. It wasn't that the president was opposed to the evaluations. He thought that that was great and almost always supported strict evaluation stuff. He was sort of a wonk at heart, or in one part of his heart. But the notion that these should be small experiments was not part of the way he thought about [the waivers]. And that became pretty clear early on. We would grumble about it, but it wasn't on the table.[15]

Clinton encouraged the governors to use the waivers to circumvent AFDC rules and to encourage innovation in state welfare programs. The waiver programs also built momentum for welfare reform while the Clinton Administration pursued other policy priorities, notably health care reform.

The ad hoc, governor-centered waiver process created its own momentum. In addition to loosening federal constraints and permitting state innovation, the pilot programs legitimated policy ideas. Officials at HHS were aware of this dynamic. As Ellwood explained, "Our fear was as soon as you were there in the waiver process, as soon as you had indicated that you had no line in the sand, no stopping point on waivers, that legitimated [those policy ideas] or made more difficult the process of drawing lines in the sand on welfare reform nationally."

According to Ellwood, President Clinton "didn't see nearly as much of the domino effect that we [at HHS] felt."[16] This political miscalculation by Clinton may be more responsible for sending welfare reform out of the administration's hands and into the hands of the governors and congressional Republicans than the Clinton team's use of the infamous slogan "Two Years and You Are Off" to describe a policy idea more accurately summarized as "Two Years and You Work." "There was," as Mary Jo Bane noted, "an interactive, almost a snowballing effect of one set of waiver approvals [that] would lead to a set of ideas."[17] Quickly, these ideas spiraled away from the work-oriented programs that the administration favored and toward the firm time limits that ultimately became law.

Governors found waiver programs to be politically popular and a good vehicle for national exposure. States quickly applied for permission to run their own experiments. Mary Jo Bane explained the political motivation for the governors.

Every governor saw it as something to run on. Back in that period, welfare was a huge political issue both at the national level and at many states. It was important in Bill Clinton's election that he said we would end welfare as we know it. Governors were picking that up. And especially once some governors started to do it other governors felt like they had to have—or state legislators, depending on who was the initiator—felt like they had to have their own welfare reform plan and if they didn't, they were somehow soft on welfare and could be vulnerable politically.[18]

Clinton and the governors were able to claim success at reforming welfare through waivers in spite of political gridlock at the federal level.[19] This method of credit claiming, however, did more than score political points with the public. It also altered the debate around welfare. In particular, it defined the meaning of time limits, which had been a popular but ambiguous concept in welfare reform.

Clinton had hoped to promote a "work-trigger" model of time-limited welfare, in which welfare recipients would receive cash benefits for a period of time (typically two to five years) and then have access to public jobs but not to continued cash benefits. Republican members of Congress soon were promoting a different welfare reform idea—"benefit-termination" time limits, also known as "firm" or "hard" time limits. Firm time limits restrict cash benefits to a specified period after which recipients lack access to public jobs or continued cash benefits. Confusingly, both models of time limits were known as "time-limited" welfare.

In the late 1980s, strong work requirements for welfare recipients were controversial. There was concern that some welfare families would not be able to handle even supported work, jobs and job training programs embedded into social services in order to ease recipients' transitions back into the labor market. By 1996, welfare reform with a firm time limit had passed, the states had regained their position as the locus of public assistance programs, and the federal entitlement to welfare had been eliminated. There are several competing theories about how this dramatic turn of events happened. None of the explanations, however, is sufficient without acknowledging the structural and political role of the pilot welfare programs.

Public Opinion, Public Values

One popular theory of why time-limited welfare passed with so little fanfare after years of stalling is that elected officials finally caught up with public opinion, which had been strongly opposed to AFDC for years. But is this true? Did public opinion support firm time limits? Can such dramatic political and institutional change really be attributed to policy actors "catching up" with what the public really knew all the time? It is clear that AFDC had been an unpopular program for years. The "Welfare Queen" rhetoric of the Reagan era conjured up images of lazy, immoral women raising dangerous children and living too well at the expense of taxpayers. It is a stretch to argue that most lawmakers discovered the public's distaste for AFDC only in the Clinton era. There was a well-mined trough of political capital in attacking welfare. If public opinion were truly the driving force behind welfare reform, why had it taken nearly thirty years of public disfavor to affect change? Perhaps public discontent had built up, like a pressure cooker, to finally compel change. R. Kent Weaver notes that public opinion by the 1990s *had* built up considerable power to pressure elected officials to reform welfare—but not in the direction that reform ultimately went.[20]

Public opinion on welfare in the mid-1990s was unambiguously negative. A 1995 Kaiser/Harvard survey showed that more than half of all Americans thought AFDC did more harm than good and only 7 percent thought the program should continue to exist as it was.[21] Another poll found that a full 93 percent of Americans favored work requirements for welfare recipients and 87 percent favored providing public-service jobs to those who could not find private-sector employment.[22] According to the Kaiser / Harvard poll, however, *only 16 percent* of Americans favored cutting off welfare benefits after two years even to recipients who were unable to find a job. These numbers clearly support the argument that the American public disliked AFDC and wanted reform. But they are not by any measure a clear mandate for firm time limits. They appear to support "work-trigger" time limits that place limits on cash benefits but then offer continued support in exchange for work.

Public opinion in the mid-1990s is best characterized as supporting what Lawrence Mead has termed the "New Paternalism."[23] Paternalists advocate a supervisory approach to poverty. In particular, there was strong support for the idea that welfare recipients should be required to work for their benefits. The New Paternalist arguments emphasize the obligations rather than the rights of welfare recipients and accept conditional intrusion into the lives of welfare recipients by government agents. The core of the New Paternalist argument is that there are obligations of citizenship, most fundamentally work and civil behavior, and that the state has a right to enforce these obligations among those who receive state benefits.

Mead's views on social welfare may have been more extreme than those of most Americans, but he did tap into widely held sentiments, at least toward recipients of need-based government programs. Few Americans in the mid-1990s seemed to be overly concerned about the work habits or civility of those who did not rely on any sort of public aid. Recipients of social insurance programs such as Social Security were not held to quite the same standards as recipients of need-based programs, although this may be because Social Security targets workers.[24] Regardless, the New Paternalists have a point—most Americans are not willing to help support others simply based on need or legal citizenship. There does seem to be a prevailing sense that some sort of social solidarity and enforceable reciprocal obligations should be the foundation for public support. The New Paternalism—although tending to be state-centered and authoritarian—draws from the liberal democratic values of equality and achievement. Proponents argue that assisting the able-bodied *without* reciprocal obligations goes against the core American values of work and independence.

Even if these feelings were particularly strong in the mid-1990s, it is difficult to prove that public values have ever been the primary force in motivating public policy. As John W. Kingdon suggests in *Agendas, Alternatives, and Public Policies,* national values most likely do influence the agendas of elected officials.[25] It is difficult, however, to make the case that they directly shape the specifics of policy choices. Theda Skocpol sums up the problems with a national values explanation of policy choices. She writes, "proponents of this [national values] approach have so far failed to pinpoint exactly how cultural values, intellectual traditions, and ideological outlook have concretely influenced processes of political conflict and policy debate."[26] This point can be illustrated by taking an example that should, on its face, be most reflective of public values: the referendum. Policies written and voted on by "the public" should reflect their values. And yet we know that referenda are highly sensitive to manipulations such as the phrasing of a question and the monetary resources of a proposal's backers. In fact, referenda arguably produce outcomes *less* in line with our national values than congressional votes.

Values and national mood may matter in terms of setting the tone and context of a debate, but ultimately individual actors in specific institutions have to put pen to paper to create a policy. By any reading of the public opinion polls of the mid-1990s, New Paternalism in welfare was what most Americans supported. And yet it is not what passed. TANF is based on firm time limits rather than on mandating work in return for assistance. As a policy, TANF is more in keeping with small government conservatism and the work of Charles Murray, though Murray advocates the elimination of public assistance altogether.[27] Despite this fact, there was little public outcry against terminating benefits and in favor of supported work. Public opinions and values did not translate directly into policy action.

A closer look at public opinion hints at why the public accepted the 1996 welfare reform law. The Kaiser / Harvard poll shows that in 1995 a majority of Americans, 52 percent, favored *experimenting with welfare reform at the state level*. In contrast, only 29 percent favored reform at the national level.[28] It is important to recognize that by 1995 many federal reform plans were entirely focused on giving the states the power to run their own welfare programs. National reform returning power to the states is not what the majority of people favored. They favored state-level *experimentation*.

Public opinion was unified in its disapproval of the AFDC program. To many Americans, work and limited cash benefits sounded like a good alternative to endless welfare, but the details of what a new program would look like were unclear. It appeared in 1994 and 1995 that both Democrats, particularly the president, and Republicans were supporting the same general welfare reform idea—time limits. Yet members of each party were hollering loudly that the other party's proposals would be catastrophic. Into this bizarre mix of surface consensus and partisan bickering stepped the governors and their experimental state waiver programs.

The waiver programs were (initially) small experimental welfare programs ostensibly designed to test new reform ideas. Most programs were authorized to run for five years. During the demonstration, a small group of people applying for public assistance would be placed in a model program that had new rules, such as a time limit on benefits. Most of the waiver programs had significant evaluation components. At the end of the experiment, the outcomes for participants, such as their incomes and marriage rates, could be measured and compared to a control group receiving the old AFDC program. In this way, the pilots could provide a "test" of radical new welfare ideas without dismantling the federal safety net.

The pilot programs were everyone's darling children. The president facilitated welfare reform through the state waiver programs, and predominantly Republican (and a few Democrat) governors took full advantage of the opportunities provided by the Clinton administration to advance their states' visibility as well as their own personal political careers through high profile welfare experiments. In the public eye, the pilot programs, steeped in politics from the beginning, were empirical tests of the new policy ideas. The pilot programs served many political masters and yet maintained a pristine image because they appeared to be scientific, empirical tests of new welfare ideas.

"What works?" is arguably our guiding national question. Here was a situation where the fundamentals appeared to be agreed upon: AFDC was broken, and time-limited welfare was the solution. Policy wonks were arguing over the technical details of what constituted a time limit. The different definitions of time limits were nearly incomprehensible to most ordinary people—no matter that the configuration of these "details" would amount to radically different policies. In this context, it makes sense that the public did not overtly back either the Clinton plan, which appeared to be more in line with public opinion but was potentially expensive and cumbersome, or the Republican plan, but instead backed the pilot programs. As the governors worked with state administrators and policy think tanks to develop various state pilot programs, the American people backed the idea of empirically testing welfare reform ideas and picking "what works."

Elite Politics

A second explanation for passage of the Personal Responsibility and Work Opportunity Reconciliation Act, which authorized TANF, centers on the role of elite political actors. The weakness of both the public opinion and the related national values explanations of policy change is that they are necessarily incomplete. Someone still had to put pen to paper and draft the legislation. Someone had to vote for it. Someone had to implement and administer the new program. Reform requires a vast and complex network of people operating within particular institutional frameworks. The effects of these networks and institutions cannot be accounted for simply by claiming that the policies we have are what the public wants.

Steven M. Teles, in the afterword of *Whose Welfare? AFDC and Elite Politics*, advances a compelling argument that old-style political machinery played a major role in PRWORA. Before the mid-1990s, Teles argues, welfare reform was primarily the concern of elite intellectuals and federal level politicians. Public opinion was against the program as it stood, but the politics of welfare reform was fundamentally intellectual-driven. When President George H. W. Bush and later President Clinton decided to use waivers to permit the states to experiment with welfare reform ideas, they brought a new and powerful group of political players into the welfare debate—the governors. The governors had good reason to want welfare reform. States were obligated to provide money for AFDC, but with the exception of setting benefit levels— which typically varied from $300 to $500 dollars a month for a family of three—the states had little power over AFDC. Many governors, including Clinton when he served as governor of Arkansas, resented the fiscal obligation and lack of power. Moreover, in the mid-1990s, many states had Republican governors who were ideologically committed to states' rights and local control. Midwestern states in particular played a leadership role in welfare reform. Tommy Thompson (R) of Wisconsin and John Engler (R) of Michigan were two of the most prominent governors in the welfare debate. Lawton Chiles (D) of Florida raced ahead of the midwestern Republicans to make his state the first in which welfare recipients reached a time limit. The waiver program afforded governors political power and they took it.

Governors are structurally much more invested in old-style machine politics than are members of Congress, and Teles is undoubtedly right in his assessment that part of what the waivers did was to open a political pathway for the governors to exercise their influence. This pathway was reinforced by Clinton's personal ties and network connections with the governors. As David T. Ellwood explains, "This was a cadre of people that had been friends throughout—from the 1980s. [Clinton] and Engler and Thompson and all these guys were buddies."[29] The increased power of the governors in welfare politics was a predictable outcome of having Clinton, a former governor who had been active in welfare reform issues, in the Oval Office.

One of the most persuasive pieces of evidence for the governors' power is the fact that PRWORA did in fact shift considerable power and money to the states. Devolution is a logical result of the governors' influence, particularly given the ideological sympathies of the Republican Congress at the time. So perhaps we can view PRWORA as the outcome of normal political channels that experienced a shift in elite networks. That is part of the story. Certainly, the governors, particularly Thompson and Engler, took full advantage of the opportunities for public grandstanding and political influence presented to them by the waivers. But noting that the waivers gave the governors an opportunity to expand their power and that the governors took this opportunity does not answer the question of how the expanded experimental waiver program changed welfare or how experimental welfare programs became a "shadow institution" in welfare reform.

The waiver process, though vastly expanded under Clinton, was not new. It had been in existence since 1962. In 1986, the Reagan administration expanded the range of experiments permitted under the waiver provision, arguably with the intention of slowly undermining AFDC. George H. W. Bush expanded the program in 1992 in order to claim credit for making progress in reforming welfare in his election campaign against then-Governor Clinton, who was making welfare reform a core campaign promise.[30] Once elected, Clinton opened the door to more numerous and radical waiver programs, but even more importantly, he changed the nature of the experimental programs. He put them onto the national stage as test cases. Governors rushed to have their state's program *win*. And they understood that winning or losing would be highly public events. Thompson and Engler were, as Carol Weissert writes, "[H]ighly visible leaders who relied on the mass media to persue their goals. Both identified welfare reform as a top priority, and both yoked their political success to it."[31]

Although the political opportunity presented by the waivers was critically important in welfare reform, the role of the waiver programs went beyond shifting the balance of power within official power structures. The programs themselves gained power because their outcomes publicly defined the success or failure of specific welfare reform policies. But why, if it is true that the waiver programs were critical to welfare reform, did waiver programs not topple welfare before 1996? The primary reason, as discussed in more detail in Chapter Six, was the scope and role of the pre-1992 pilots. Before 1992, the waiver programs were numerically small and often tested minor reforms. Between 1987 and 1991, there were an average of 1.6 waiver requests from the states per year.[32] Between 1992 and 1996, the average number of requests per year exploded to eighteen. In total, the states submitted seventy-two waivers between 1992 and 1996. Many of the later requests were for large, multiyear programs that fundamentally restructured public assistance through work requirements, sanctions (the withholding of cash benefits), and time limits. By 1996, Clinton estimated that 75 percent of all AFDC participants were involved in waiver-authorized pilot programs.[33] This constituted a revolution in welfare before there was official reform. The existence of pilot programs alone was not enough to topple AFDC. Rather, it was the use of the waiver programs as an institutional channel through which the welfare bureaucracy was restructured and the meaning of welfare reform defined that ultimately resulted in the demise of AFDC.

A look at media coverage reinforces the difference between the waivers granted before and after 1992. There were fifty-two articles on welfare reform efforts from 1986 to 1991 in the *New York Times* and the *Washington Post*.[34] In contrast, between 1992 and 1995, there were 327 articles.[35] The post-1992 waiver programs were different from their predecessors in both quantity and quality. For these reasons, welfare experiments that were implemented prior to 1992 did not have the same impact on public policy as those that came after 1992. The waiver experiments that had an impact prior to 1992 influenced policymakers and experts through the strength of their empirical findings. For example, experiments in the 1980s showed that welfare-to-work programs increased the earnings of participants.[36] The pilots in 1992 and before, particularly in the 1980s, created an intellectual momentum for welfare-to-work programs among elites; the post-1992 pilots, in contrast, created broad-based political momentum for reform.

The Waiver Programs

The state pilot programs altered the welfare system from the ground up. The experimental programs weakened the policy legacy of AFDC by dismantling parts of the state structure (the AFDC bureaucracy) and setting up new structures under the guise of "temporary" reform programs. Because the strategy of the pilot programs was always to gain political support for welfare reform, state administrators understood their mandate as "making welfare reform work"—producing statistical evidence of success in their programs.

The first time-limit welfare program in the country was Florida's Family Transition Program (FTP). When the FTP began in 1994, "work-trigger" and "benefit-termination" model time limits were competing for dominance in the welfare reform debate. Work-trigger time limits, initially advocated by Clinton, essentially created a public works program. The policy would have encouraged welfare recipients to find jobs within a particular time frame and provided public jobs to those who failed. The Clinton plan assumed that everyone should work, but that not all welfare recipients would be able to find unsubsidized jobs. The plan advocated by congressional Republicans had a firm time limit. Under this plan, welfare recipients who did not find a job within the time frame allotted would lose their benefits entirely. There would be no public jobs. The debates over these two plans were both ideological and practical. The ideological question was whether the government had an obligation to poor families who could not find work despite good faith efforts. The practical question was how many of these families there would be.

Florida's experimental welfare reform program was set up in part to answer the second question. It had a two-year (and under some circumstances three-year) time limit. The program took welfare recipients and provided them with job training, education, child care, and other services to help them find work. After two years, each participant was expected to have found a job and to be self-sufficient. Every part of the program was devoted to getting former welfare recipients placed in jobs. But there was a safety net. Participants who made a good faith effort to find a job and absolutely could not find one were to be given a public job. How many people would need public jobs, and why, would be a critical test of the assumptions underlying the Clinton and Republican plans. If this small, well-funded program could not make welfare recipients employable, it would heighten fears about too many families being left without support by the Republican plan. If participants were able to get jobs easily, Clinton's work program risked looking like an unnecessary and potentially costly new government program.

On paper, the time limit in Florida's FTP looked very flexible. According to the state law and the federal waivers, participants in the FTP who were "compliant" were guaranteed a job. The time limit could be modified or even voided altogether for clients who did not receive appropriate services from the state. Notably, by law a substantial portion of this discretionary power lay outside the welfare agency in the hands of a volunteer Citizen Review Panel. The Citizen Review Panel was instituted to provide objective oversight of benefit terminations and extensions within the program. In an era marked by a deep distrust of government bureaucracy, the Citizen Review Panel appeared to provide a nongovernmental, nonbureaucratic means for making potentially controversial decisions.

The Citizen Review Panel, which seemed to be granted such a startling amount of power, was in practice powerless. The administrative mechanisms for eliminating the panel's power are discussed in Chapters Four and Five. Central to this shift in power was the definition of the panel's role and of the participants' and program's obligations, all of which were defined by the welfare agency. The FTP administrators perceived that a participant who was compliant and unemployed would reflect badly on the program. As a result, they set up a series of procedures that made it impossible for anyone to qualify for a public job. In a bit of administrative circularity, part of being "compliant" was being employed by the time limit. Anyone not employed by the time limit was *by definition* ineligible for a public job.

The media, however, simply reported that no one who had complied with the FTP needed a job at the time limit; everyone who was compliant with the program had found a job. This obscured the role of administrative procedures in ensuring that everyone who was at risk of being unemployed at the end of the two years was labeled "noncompliant." As it was covered in the press, the FTP appeared to provide support for the idea that welfare recipients who "played by the rules" would find employment under a time-limited system. The Clinton public jobs program thus seemed to address a problem that did not exist.

The media monitored the experimental welfare programs as if they were clinical experiments rather than aspects of a political strategy; they looked for and reported numbers that evidenced the success or failure of welfare reform. The administrators, quite self-consciously, provided numbers that looked like evidence of success. The failure of the media to interrogate the pilot program's claims of success is striking. Arguably, journalists accepted the administrative numbers with less skepticism than usual because so many of the programs were involved in formal evaluations conducted by respected research firms. The respectability of the numbers provided by the evaluation companies may have rubbed off on the administrative numbers the press reported on the same programs.

As time-limited welfare programs appeared to show great success and the street-level structures of welfare were changed to accommodate the waiver programs, two major hurdles of welfare reform were cleared—the idea of firm time limits was accepted as viable policy and the bureaucratic structure of AFDC was weakened. The Florida case shows the mechanisms through which political debate, media attention, and bureaucratic structures interacted with each other and played a role in policymaking by defining what "objectively" worked in welfare reform. As Chapter Six details, the experience of Florida was replicated throughout the country, albeit with important variations. Why did waivers in one place cause change in other places? Once approved, a waiver reduced the uncertainty and information costs of adopting the policy for other states. This created a path dependency toward those ideas that were tested by entrepreneurial states such as Florida and Wisconsin. As reform programs were tested, many appeared to be successful. This boosted the legitimacy of these policy ideas and decreased the political costs of adopting similar waivers and advocating the policy ideas nationally. Politicians pointed to the programs serving their communities as being on the forefront of reform, strengthening families, encouraging work, and saving taxpayer dollars. Before it ever became law, welfare reform was ubiquitous. Time-limited welfare was an idea that many states claimed as their own; by 1996, it was the social policy next door.

CHAPTER 2

Hope and an Experimental Design

[Americans consider] politics to be a constraint on good policy making.

Aaron Wildavsky, 2002[1]

In 1995, a group of new congressional fellows was briefed on the ways of Capitol Hill.[2] A woman wrote two words in large block letters on the black board: POLITICS and POLICY. Politics, she explained, is the fight over values. She acknowledged that politics encompasses complex strategies and grabs for power; no one trying to prepare academics for Capitol Hill would downplay the roles of power in politics. The key point conveyed in that late summer briefing in Washington, D.C., however, was that politics is the fight over whose values dominate. In the day-to-day struggle on Capitol Hill, it is Republican values versus Democratic values. Within the parties, there are political battles over whose values, whose vision of society prevails and goes forward to do battle with the opposition. Do the socially conservative values, which hold abortion as murder, prevail within the Republican Party? Or do fiscally conservative but socially moderate forces, which often view abortion as outside the government's jurisdiction, prevail? For those who are skeptical of viewing politics as a battle over values, it may be useful to think of politics as being about the ends to which the government is working.

POLICY, the woman wrote on the blackboard, is about MEANS. Once there is sufficient political agreement—or arm-twisting—that an end, or social goal, has been agreed upon, policy becomes relevant. Policy questions, she emphasized, are technical questions. Once politicians agree on an end, then policy experts focus on assessing the best means to achieve the goal. In this formulation, policy experts are akin to doctors. They know ways to treat particular problems. There may be, for example, a movement to reduce teenage pregnancy. That is a political goal. A group defines teenage pregnancy as being undesirable, and its reduction as an appropriate goal for the state. The policy question that follows is: What is the most efficient and effective way to reduce teen pregnancies?

The association of politics with ends and of policy with means outlined on the blackboard that hot summer day is appealing. It is a simple and clean split; the messy world of politics, values, desired social ends are lumped together whereas the cool, pristine world of policy, technical knowledge, efficient means sits on the opposite end of the spectrum. Yet the difficulty of separating politics and policy leaps out immediately. In the case of teenage pregnancy, for example, one policy expert may identify contraceptive education and availability as the best way to reduce pregnancies. In this case, contraceptive education and availability are means to an end. Contraception education and availability, however, may also be viewed as ends in themselves. The Catholic Church views contraception as a sin, therefore undesirable in itself. The Catholic Church could not endorse a teenage pregnancy prevention program that emphasizes birth control even if it was 100 percent effective. That is because, for the Catholic Church, birth control is not only a means to prevent teenage pregnancy—a goal that the Church might support. It is also an end, the prevention of conception, which the Church does not support. Thus, the existence of contraceptive programs may be a value—or end—that is opposed politically. This is true even if it is an effective means to achieve another politically desirable goal—the reduction of teenage pregnancy.

Every policy contains within it provisions that are clearly political. A policy to reduce the number of shooting deaths in the United States could contain provisions to reduce the availability of guns in the United States. The broad goal of reducing gun related homicides might be widely shared. Yet many Americans would still view gun ownership as a right protected by the Second Amendment and might oppose the restriction of gun ownership in the United States, even if it were a technically efficient way of reducing the homicide rate. "The end doesn't justify the means" is a phrase commonly used when means to desirable ends violate other ends, other values.

The distinction between politics and policy made on the blackboard during the congressional fellows orientation is a useful fiction. It highlighted two aspects of day-to-day political work. It also reflects a wish to divide what we want from what we know. What we want, our political choices, necessarily involves conflicting values and ideologies. Americans are uncomfortable with ideological politics, which we often associate with fascism, communism, and totalitarian atrocities. As a country, we are much more comfortable with pragmatic issues of what works. American academics and intellectuals have also been enamored of an apolitical and empirical approach to policymaking. Scientific pragmatism is a strand of American pragmatism. Particularly after the Great Society programs failed, academics, many of whom had been involved in designing the programs, wanted to bring their expert, objective knowledge to social policy. This impulse to bring scientific methods to policy questions ultimately led to the development of randomized experimentation and testing new policy ideas in pilot programs. But is there a realm in which questions of policy truly can be removed from politics? Do experimental pilot programs create that realm?

In this chapter, I trace the history of social science and its relationship to public policy in the United States from the advocacy research of the Progressive Era through the randomized welfare experiments of the 1990s. By the late 1990s, the legitimacy of social science research in public policy implicitly rested on the—I argue fictitious—abstraction of public policy from its political context. The attempt to remove policy from politics has made evaluation research less objective because it places key empirical facts outside the purview of research.

The idea that policy research can and should black out the political context of policy adoption and implementation rests on a fundamental error—the idea that we can understand causal relationships and predict how social policies will work in the future without drawing on our values and our politics. Our values and our politics are inextricably woven together, and they create the frameworks through which we interpret the "data" all around us. We cannot understand cause and effect without such frameworks. For example, the drop in the welfare rolls that occurred in the late 1990s would have been a meaningless statistic without the implicit understanding that welfare use contributed to social ills and that its decline in itself was good. Equally, the assumptions that a drop in the welfare rolls was bad or neutral also would have rested on causal assumptions about the relationship of welfare use to other social phenomena. Normative judgments are essential for thought and action. Some judgments may be based on a more solid foundation of accepted ethics and more reliable information than other judgments. Nonetheless, all rest on some set of unproven—and in fact often unprovable—assumptions about how the world works. Few relationships in the social world are so direct that they can be scientifically proven to exist independent of any ontological assumptions. Even the predictability of events with a one-to-one correlation is absolute only to those who accept a scientific rather than a theistic framework. Values, politics, and our assumptions about how the world works, therefore, necessarily intertwine and shape the questions that we ask in our research, the data that we gather, and the interpretations that we give to that which we have learned. What we discover may be real, but it is equally a child of our own creation and time.

Ironically, the evaluation community's attempt to remove policy from its political context, although effective in minimizing the overt manipulation of evaluation findings, opened the door to the political use of policy experiments themselves. By defining pilot programs as addressing technical issues, policy evaluators contributed, however unwittingly, to concealing the experiments' normative and legitimating functions. In this book, I take the position that this development degraded both the research community and the political process. This reflects my own normative assumption about how the world works and how it should work. Readers who disagree with my assessment, I hope, will still find interesting the story of how the dramatic restructuring of welfare reform in 1996 came to be. The truly Machiavellian reader may even consider the following chapters as a how-to guide for policy advocates who wish to further an idea beyond where official political channels might otherwise take it. Following my view of the appropriate role of social science in public policy, I will simply present the facts and explicate the politics, including my own, that shape the story and its telling.

Can Policy Research Be Removed from Politics?

Administrators, Herbert Simon famously argued, cannot simply discern one technically correct way of reaching a specified policy goal; they cannot separate the ends from the means. There might be many ways to attain a goal. For that matter, a policy might have ambiguous or conflicting goals. Moreover, administrators do not make decisions with total knowledge of all possible actions and a certainty of the resultant outcomes—the necessary prerequisite for a rational choice among various technical solutions. Administrators make each decision within "an environment of 'givens'—premises that are accepted by the subject as bases for his choices."[3] The "environment of givens" is the cultural, organizational, and political context of administration. Within this context, some actions are perceived as legitimate and others are not, regardless of their technical merit—their efficacy in attaining a goal.

To illustrate Simon's point in the context of a contemporary debate, in the United States there is widespread concern about women addicted to drugs and alcohol exposing fetuses to harmful substances. One technically efficient means of addressing this concern is to sterilize all women who have drug or alcohol addictions. Many people in the United States, however, would view this technically efficient solution as politically and morally abhorrent. This example can be taken to an even greater extreme; the state could sterilize all daughters of drug and alcohol addicts in childhood. Since we know that there is a strong genetic component to addiction, this would be an efficient means of reducing prenatal exposure to drugs and alcohol in the population overall. This solution, however, is politically unthinkable in the United States. It violates our assumptions about the rights of the individual and our reluctance to venture too far in the direction of eugenics. This example, however, is not so far from the forced abortions that come from China's one child policy. Politics determines the range of policy options. The political environment makes up a key component of the "environment of givens" in which administrators and policymakers operate.

Simon's observations cast doubt on the idea that bureaucracies can function apart from the larger political and cultural context. If this is true, then is it possible or wise to study the outcomes generated by an experimental policy program without taking into consideration the political and cultural context in which it operates? The very survival of particular programs and policy ideas may depend on the public's perception that they are legitimate. Perhaps the only "rational" action administrators can take at times, as we will see in Chapter Five, is to conform to public expectations. Can policy research be removed from politics when its subject is not? To address this question, it is useful to briefly review the history of social science research and policymaking in America. The connection between social knowledge and public policy is deep-rooted, but the contemporary vision of an almost clinical form of policy evaluation is fairly new, emerging in the 1970s.

Objectivity, Research, and Policymaking

As early as the Progressive Era, there was a strong interest in *learning* about social problems and even social experimentation. Yet, the Progressive Era's semiscientific approach to the social world was really quite different from contemporary attempts to develop scientifically based public policy through evaluation. Although much early social research lacked the rigor of true social science, the scientific impulse of the time did focus on identifying and classifying social patterns. For many involved with the Settlement House movement, for example, the aim of research was to provide documentation of social horrors in order to influence policymakers. Florence Kelley and Josephine Goldmark compiled research on women and excessive work hours that led to the establishment of labor protections for women and, in time, the establishment of the eight-hour work day.[4] Similarly, the National Child Labor Committee, which included such leading Settlement House figures as Jane Addams from Hull House and Lillian Ward, founder of the Henry Street Settlement House, used social research to construct a vivid case against child labor.

The Charity Organization Society, which, along with the Settlement House movement, formed the core of Progressive Era social reform, spearheaded a survey of social conditions in the Pittsburgh area in 1907–1908. The Pittsburgh Survey was one of the first large-scale, high-profile investigations into social conditions in the United States. Funded by the Russell Sage Foundation and other organizations, the Pittsburgh Survey assessed a variety of social issues including prevailing wage rates, education, and the health of people within the Pittsburgh area. The survey results were widely distributed in the popular and professional presses. The social science research methods used in the Pittsburgh Survey were rigorous for their time; it was produced and administered by a team of social scientists and social workers. The survey painted a dire picture of social conditions in areas as diverse as child health and local police protection. It became a critical piece of evidence and propaganda for broad-based social reforms.[5]

Progressive Era social research tried to generate pictures of social conditions, snapshots of poverty and hardship. Reformers thought that if they could accurately determine and depict the scope and nature of social problems in the United States, then there would be the political and social will to ameliorate at least the very worst conditions. The ideology of municipal housekeeping promoted by female reformers of the time clearly underlies this approach. "Soft" feminine concerns such as child well-being and maternal health were translated into factual, objective reports that would generate public outcries and spur men to action.

It was, of course, not only progressive women or those involved in the Settlement House Movement or Charity Organization Societies who were deeply involved in social research. Upton Sinclair famously wrote about social issues of the day. Academics, who at the time were overwhelmingly male, were also deeply involved in social research. In the 1920s, sociologists of the Chicago School, such as Robert Park, began to investigate the nature of the cities using ethnographic methodologies, which involve direct observation of social life and copious notes of the details observed. Through ethnographic observation, academic researchers hoped to identify patterns of social life and learn more about the fundamental structure of social interactions. In much the same way that a biologist might take detailed notes about the eating, sleeping, and migratory habits of an iguana, social scientists used ethnographic methods to document the cultural habits and patterns of people.[6]

Inhabitants of cities provoked particular interest, as they often do. Cities formed the core study site of the Chicago School for several reasons. Based at the University of Chicago, Chicago School researchers had access to a city with a rich history and deeply rooted ethnic neighborhoods and traditions. The interest of the Chicago School sociologists also sprang from the early twentieth century's concern with cities as places of ill health, immorality, and general denigration. Concerns about industrialization and urbanization permeated social and academic discourses at the time. In the early 1900s, there were appalling death rates in working class slums. Infants and small children were particularly vulnerable to diseases. Overcrowding, unclean, and often inadequate water and food sources and a steady flow of immigrants created a lethal mix of easy contagion and poor resistance. Virtually every family could expect to lose at least one child.[7] Crowded and sometimes violent tenements gained public attention both for their raw horror and because many elites feared their existence could jeopardize the health and well-being of America as a nation. The desire to contain and tame the cities, the tenement dwellers, and their unfamiliar habits, foods, and religious practices was woven through more generous impulses to improve housing and health. Science and research were vital tools for the Progressive movement. Yet the "science" was highly popularized and loose, bearing a greater resemblance to investigative reporting than to contemporary social science research.

The Charity Organization Societies and the Settlement House movement dominated Progressive Era reform and grew out of the Scientific Charity movement that emerged around 1870.[8] Scientific Charity assumed a sharp divide between the worthy and the unworthy poor. The worthy poor were people who had simply fallen on hard times: a hardworking woman suddenly widowed by an industrial accident and left with five young children; a man out of work after a factory burned down; an orphaned child. These people, according to the tenets of Scientific Charity, were *potentially*, but not necessarily, the appropriate targets of assistance. Proponents of Scientific Charity feared that assistance, particularly cash assistance, could easily corrupt a good person who had fallen on hard times. In contrast to the worthy poor were the unworthy poor, men and women who lacked the work ethic, temperance, or some other moral attribute and were *for that reason* poor. Their material poverty, proponents of Scientific Charity argued, reflected a spiritual poverty that no amount of public assistance could change; assistance given to such a person would only further degrade their morality.[9] Proponents of Scientific Charity viewed cash assistance as a strong medicine. Administered in just the right dose, it could save lives. Administered indiscriminately to those for whom it was not appropriate, it could be deadly. One "scientific" aspect of Scientific Charity was assessing the appropriate dose for everyone who sought aid. Most often the best dose was determined to be none at all. Reaching back to the early 1800s, poverty had been even more closely associated with personal vice. One minister of the time made the point with searing clarity, "Let me repeat it, the causes of poverty are to be looked for, and found in him or her who suffers it."[10] The popular perception that poverty reflected a moral flaw was later bolstered by the Social Darwinist ideas. These ideas emphasized the "survival of the fittest" in society, and the inherent unfitness of those at the bottom of it.

Science and research have a long history in the politics and provision of social welfare in America, which is well documented in Alice O'Connor's *Poverty Knowledge*. The issues of what constitutes "science" and whether research focuses on social problems or the government programs that address them, however, have shifted considerably. In the

Progressive Era, research was a tool used to determine the nature of the problem. Despite the great faith in science and enthusiasm for research, progressive reformers did not conduct research on programs aimed at solving social problems, as contemporary evaluators do. Research was a diagnostic tool. Once a specific problem had been defined, progressive reformers seem to have accepted that competent administration could address the problem. Social science defined problems; morality and reason solved them.

Researching Social Programs as Well as Social Problems

In his book *Speaking Truth to Power*, Aaron Wildavsky presents an interesting theory on when and why research focuses on programs and policies themselves, as opposed to the identification of social problems. Policy evaluation, according to Wildavsky, is unnecessary when there is general agreement that the experts who are officially charged with making policy decisions are capable of doing so based on their own wisdom and experience.[11] One does not ask a wise man what calculations he uses to come to his decision. One might bring the wise man a detailed assessment of the facts related to a problem, so that he might fully grasp its scope and nature, but that is where the emphasis on facts ends. Wisdom and authority then take over in the determination of the appropriate response. To take the point to a more extreme level, one would not attempt to measure the "gain" of following Buddha, the "gain" of following Muhammad, and the "gain" of following Jesus in order to determine which religious code was best. If there is faith in higher authority, facts become less relevant.

Policy analysis and evaluation, Wildavsky argues, is a kind of democratization and decentralization of policy ideas that comes about when people lose faith in the wisdom of policymakers. It also comes out of a particular social order in which the loss of faith cannot be addressed through the political system. In most of Europe, Wildavsky notes, a loss of faith in civil servants and policymakers often results in the election of the opposition party to power. The fundamental restructuring of the government thus provides a way for the loss of faith in decision makers to be, if not restored, then at least refocused on the larger, more ideological political questions. In traditional societies, Wildavsky argues, such as Japan, there is a stronger familial loyalty to those in power. Therefore, there is not a strong cultural impulse to question the fundamental ability of policymakers to base their judgments on wisdom rather than objective—thus democratically accessible—fact, even when faith is shaken in the current policy actors. The United States, with its highly centrist two-party system and the continuity and stability brought about by the balance of judicial, congressional, and executive powers, does not either inspire the loyalty of the Japanese system or contain the pressure valve of the more volatile European systems. It is not surprising, therefore, that policy evaluation in the United States began sooner, became more powerful, and was separated from party politics more explicitly than anywhere else in the world.[12]

Wildavsky's cross-national claims, though beyond the scope of this book, highlight a probable reason for the lack of attention to program evaluation in the Progressive Era despite its focus on research; Progressive Era reformers were confident in their own wisdom and judgment. The leaders of reform movements were often socially prominent and connected to political and business leaders. There was great confidence that once problems were accurately identified and systematically thought through, then they could be addressed, bettered, or even fixed. The zeal for reform had not yet been tempered by failure. It was axiomatic that municipal housekeeping could improve society as much as a mother's presence benefited her family. Beneath the scientific rhetoric and trappings of research, the Progressive movement clung to the ideal of government as a patriarchal family headed by men with wisdom, judgment, and benevolence. Evaluating the programs and policies aimed at the poor, rather than the poor themselves, would have seemed like a strange endeavor.

During the Depression, there was a vast expansion of social programs, but little growth in policy-oriented research and evaluation. Social research was conducted in the Work Projects Administration (WPA), but it was more descriptive than analytic. For example, the Federal Writers' Project and the Folklore Project collected oral histories of American life. The WPA research did not focus on identifying and ameliorating social problems. The major policy initiatives of the era, similarly, did not focus on research. The Social Security Act of 1935 did not contain evaluation requirements for any of its programs.[13] It is not hard to imagine why in the depth of the Great Depression there was little attention and money given to policy research. The problems facing the United States were easy to define. A massive economic breakdown had left Americans devastated. People needed work, food, and shelter.

There was some expansion in social policies in the 1940s and 1950s. In 1946, the National School Lunch Program was enacted. In 1954, a Milk Program followed. Disability was added to the social insurance programs in 1956. During this time, the United States was more focused on the perceived external threats, first of fascism and then of communism, than it was on domestic social policy. Even by the late 1950s, when the harsh anticommunist attacks of Senator Joseph McCarthy were receding from the political stage, foreign politics still shaped domestic policy. Americans were growing hostile to public welfare programs that many viewed to be un-American and an encroachment of socialism.[14]

It is important to note that the sharpest criticisms of social welfare programs during the late 1950s were not that they did not work, but rather that they were in opposition to the American way of life. It was a question of values. There was no need to study the minute details and impacts of particular policies because the political debate was not about which program made a marginal improvement in the condition that it targeted. The discussions were broad based and fundamentally political. What is the nature of the American way of life? What is socialistic? What is good? What is bad? Cynics might rightly add that more routine political questions—such as what will help our dairy industry—were also dominant. What was lacking was a sense that research could guide policymaking.

The Great Society

> The fact of the matter is that most of the problems, or at least many of them, that we now face are technical problems, are administrative problems. They are very sophisticated judgments which do not lend themselves to the great sort of "passionate movements" that have stirred this country so often in the past.
>
> President John F. Kennedy, 1962[15]

It was in the 1960s that evaluation research, as we know it today, began to develop.[16] As in the Progressive Era, policy research in the 1960s grew out of optimism and a reform movement. Academic and popular books and articles documented social problems and served as calls to arms. In *The Other America: Poverty in the United States*, Michael Harrington described life for poor Americans, black and white, rural and urban, with keen attention to the brutality and tediousness that so often define poverty. *The Other America* brought attention to the fact that nearly one in four Americans was poor even as the nation celebrated its affluence. Harrington wrote, "This book is a description of the world in which these people live; it is about the other America. Here are the unskilled workers, the migrant farm workers, the aged, the minorities and the others who live in the economic underworld of American life."[17] *The Other America* is similar in tone and function to Progressive Era research. A slim and simple volume, it was accessible to nearly any reader, and appealed to popular, academic, and policy-making audiences. With it, Harrington helped to ignite, or at the very least to popularize, the War on Poverty and the Great Society.

In 1961, Abraham Ribicoff, Kennedy's secretary of Health, Education, and Welfare (HEW), appointed an ad hoc committee to review public assistance and identify new directions and goals. The committee recommended that the role of professionally trained social workers be expanded and that the program aim to reinforce the "capacities of persons to meet their problems and behave responsibly."[18] In 1962, Kennedy sent a message to Congress. It was the first presidential message to focus exclusively on welfare. In it, Kennedy argued for an expanded role for social work experts in public welfare: "Meekly responding with a relief check to complicated social or personal problems . . . is not likely to provide a lasting solution. Such a check must be supplemented, or in some cases made unnecessary, by positive services and solutions, offering the total resources of the community to meet the total needs of the family to help our less fortunate citizens help themselves."[19]

Kennedy's call to action reformulated the problem of welfare in America. Now the problem was that people were not being shown how to help themselves properly. The emphasis subtly turned from the poor themselves to a question of the *quality* of social welfare programs. The *programs* themselves could be improved. On July 25, 1962, Kennedy signed the Public Welfare Amendments to the Social Security Act. The overwhelming message of reform was that with proper support services, the poor would be able to transform their lives. Perhaps not all would leave poverty, but their lives would be better and their families would be stronger.

The 1962 Social Security amendment laid a foundation for the emergence of contemporary policy evaluation. Kennedy began a movement to address America's social problems comprehensively and with expert guidance. After Kennedy's assassination, Lyndon Johnson furthered

Kennedy's efforts in the War on Poverty and Great Society programs. Ironically, the movement toward contemporary research methods resulted as much from the failures of the Great Society as from its successes.

The antipoverty programs of the 1960s were far more complex than those of the New Deal. They aimed to change the fabric of society and in some cases, such as the community empowerment initiatives, to reorder social relations. They were ambitious. New Deal programs largely depended on the very straightforward assumption—and therefore a short causal chain—that material hardship and a lack of jobs could be eased with material resources and the provision of jobs. In contrast, Great Society programs were more ambitious and complex. They were premised on long causal chains; the problems of the poor would be solved through strengthening communities, increasing job opportunities and education for the young, and empowering the disenfranchised. Each link in this chain is subject to contention. Progress on such holistic approaches to poverty is also hard to measure. For example, what if an empowerment program brings increased political participation but not decreased poverty? Is the program successful or not?

What ended up being one of the most significant parts of the 1962 amendments was hardly noticed at the time. In the Public Welfare Amendments, there was a provision for "waivers" from the federal rules for Aid to Families with Dependent Children (AFDC), formerly known as Aid to Dependent Children (ADC). The waivers gave the states the right to apply for permission to run small demonstration, or pilot, programs in order to test new ideas in welfare policy. Under AFDC, the states had some freedom in how they ran their welfare programs, but they were required to follow federal guidelines. Court decisions in the late 1960s and early 1970s, discussed in greater detail in Chapter Three, would make these federal requirements far more stringent and limit state authority.[20] The early waivers were used to test new, often minor, changes to the welfare law. It was not until the 1980s that waivers began to be used by the states as a tool for state-led policy innovations, and it was not until the 1990s that they were used to bypass federal law altogether.

The idea embodied in the waivers was simple and very much in line with Kennedy's vision of improved welfare services dominated by experts. If a state wanted to change the rules of welfare in order to better meet the goals of the 1962 welfare amendments, then it would be permitted to try out the idea on a small group of welfare recipients for a limited period. The primary constraints were (1) that the experiments had to be cost neutral to the federal government (they could not be more expensive than the traditional AFDC program would have been), (2) that there could not be more than one statewide experiment, (3) that health and safety standards had to be observed, (4) that employed workers could not be displaced by the program, (5) that work was to be compensated at the prevailing wage and participants were to be eligible for workman's compensation, and (6) participation in the waiver programs had to be voluntary.

As Steven M. Teles writes in *Whose Welfare? AFDC and Elite Politics*, virtually all of these provisions were ignored in the 1990s—cost neutrality being the notable exception.[21] In 1962, however, the waivers were a small provision in a law that anticipated great shifts in the American welfare system through professionalization and social services. Like so many attempts to reform welfare, the 1962 amendments to Social Security failed to produce the expected results. In fact, they appear to have done the opposite. The number of families on the welfare rolls increased, federal spending increased, and faith in a purely social service approach to ending poverty quickly evaporated. A little over a year after the amendments passed, Kennedy called for a much broader attack on poverty and its underlying causes.[22]

Kennedy rapidly shifted his focus from individual people and well-trained social work professionals to a structural view of poverty that emphasized why people were poor and the interaction among social problems such as poverty, crime, and low education levels. After Kennedy's assassination, Lyndon Johnson took the new approach to poverty to its apex, with mixed results.

Research had played a significant role in motivating the War on Poverty. Michael Harrington and John Kenneth Galbraith, whose 1958 book, *The Affluent Society*, had made the case that America could provide better social services, were two of the most visible and popular scholars of poverty. But many other scholars, often with deep roots in the academic world, played critical roles. Economist Robert Lampman provided evidence that economic growth was no longer affecting poverty as it once had. This seemed to suggest that the poor were becoming detached from the larger American society, set apart in some way they had not been previously. Leonard Cottrell, who had been a part of the Chicago School of sociology in the 1930s, brought research on the ecology of neighborhoods to the discussions of community development as a solution to poverty. Lloyd Ohlin and Richard Cloward developed sophisticated structural models to explain poverty and delinquency and to identify target areas for government reform.[23] Before this awakening of interest in poverty, there had been remarkably little government or academic research on poverty since the Progressive Era. In the early 1960s, a comprehensive bibliography on poverty did not fill two typewritten pages. The first official statistics on poverty in America would not be released until 1965.[24]

Academics and intellectuals, therefore, played a major role in constructing the Great Society programs, and unlike those of the New Deal, Great Society programs did contain evaluation requirements.[25] The Great Society took place during a time of affluence, when attention and resources could be put toward understanding the effects of particular social programs. Research attention moved beyond social problems to the programs themselves. Evaluation research slowly moved toward the randomized experimental model that was dominant by the middle 1990s.

Two competing theories of poverty emerged in the early 1960s, both of which were fundamentally sociological. One explanation was cultural and the other structural. These were marked departures from the highly individualistic, psychologically and morally based views of poverty that characterized the little attention given to poverty between the New Deal and the Kennedy administration. In both the cultural and structural theories, poverty was seen as growing out of the social context rather than being a manifestation of individual failings or weakness. Harrington, a leading advocate of cultural theories of poverty, stressed the social context of culture. He wrote, "Take the gangs. They are violent, and by middle class standards they are anti-social and disturbed. But within a slum, violence and disturbance are often norms, everyday facts of life. From the inside of the other America, joining a 'bopping' gang may well not seem like deviant behavior. It could be necessary for dealing with a hostile world."[26]

Culture of poverty arguments were criticized for "blaming the victim," yet they did focus on external causes of poverty. In contrast, the Social Darwinist perspectives of the Progressive Era held that poverty was a manifestation of the individual's fundamental unfitness. Thus, the movement toward a cultural explanation of poverty did go beyond individualistic interpretations of poverty and toward a sociological explanation. The culture of poverty argument retained the idea that poverty is more than a lack of money or a disadvantaged social position. It kept the idea that the poor are fundamentally different from other Americans. The structural view of poverty—also known as the environmental view—took a far more radical and sociological view of poverty. Building on economists' views of rational decision making within environmental opportunities, the structural view of poverty held that virtually all aspects of poverty were direct results of structural opportunities.

The aptly named Opportunity Theory is one prominent example of a structural view of poverty. In 1960, Richard Cloward and Lloyd Ohlin proposed their Opportunity Theory to explain why young people who were poor were more likely to engage in crime.[27] Cloward and Ohlin, building on Robert Merton's Social Strain theory, argue that young people in poor neighborhoods simply take advantage of the opportunities that are available to them. With few legitimate opportunities available, and very limited prospects for advancement within those that are available, young people seek out advancement through illegitimate means. Build opportunity structures in poor neighborhoods comparable to those available for middle-class children, Cloward and Ohlin argued, and poor children will take advantage of them.

The Clinton welfare plan in the early 1990s took a modified structural view of poverty. The plan assumed that some people on welfare will "play by the rules" and still not find jobs. The idea that welfare recipients could do everything right and still not be employed is a structural view of poverty. It assumes that jobs may not be available even to those who are willing to work. The structural assumptions about poverty that gained prominence in the 1960s, however, were contested during the welfare reform debate of the 1990s. The Republican plans were based on a more individualized view of the causes of poverty. They were based on the assumption that personal choices, not structural barriers, lay at the heart of poverty.

Not since the Progressive Era had research played such an important role in welfare policy. In the 1960s, researchers identified differences between the rich and the poor that went beyond simply money. They theorized about the relationships between social structures and undesirable outcomes, such as delinquency and chronic poverty. Congress enacted massive new social policies in health, poverty, job training, and educational opportunities for the poor. Many of these programs had mandated evaluations attached to them. There was an extraordinary optimism that social problems could be solved by paying sufficient attention to the technical problems involved in designing appropriate policy.

By 1964, psychology and social work still played a role in antipoverty policy, but they were contained within sociological and economic frameworks. The focus was no longer the individual and the caseworker isolated from the rest of the society; it was on the social structures and contexts. In 1964, the Office of Economic Opportunity (OEO) was created as a centerpiece of the War on Poverty.[28] Opportunity was seen as the road to social improvement. Research would help to identify the best ways of maximizing economic opportunities and social empowerment.

The focus on research and social science was not limited to the War on Poverty. It also played a prominent role in national defense. Robert McNamara's introduction of policy analysts to the Department of Defense in the 1960s was another critical turning point in policy research.[29] Using economic models, Defense Department analysts calculated cost-benefit analyses to weigh the relative advantage of different weapons systems. Although these policy analysts were not assessing the effects of a policy to improve it, they were beginning to use rational, objective calculations to provide a foundation for policy choices. This was an important step toward creating an apolitical role for policy evaluation. More expressly political uses of evaluation were also blooming. Senator Robert Kennedy made sure that the Elementary and Secondary Education Act of 1965, which targeted disadvantaged children, included an evaluation requirement. Kennedy hoped that an evaluation would provide useful information on the effects of the policy. As the politically astute senator realized, however, there was an added bonus to an evaluation requirement. Evaluating the program would also ensure that reform was truly implemented and that it did not get lost in the educational bureaucracy.[30]

By 1968, many of the War on Poverty's main programs had become controversial. The race riots of the summer of 1967 made many Americans less open to the argument that poor communities needed empowerment. Poverty had become caught up in the battle over civil rights. The ambitious programs of the War on Poverty were failing. Even evaluators and policymakers were questioning the programs.[31] From its optimistic start in 1964, the War on Poverty had crumbled into frustration and disappointment. Cities were not revitalized; they were burned during race riots. Americans in 1964 wondered why anyone was left out of the nation's economic prosperity. By the late 1960s, the same nation was struggling not to pull apart at the seams.

Ironically, it was not the hopes and ambitions of the Great Society that created contemporary evaluation, but these failures. Starting with the 1962 Public Welfare Amendments to the Social Security Act, the Kennedy administration had begun to privilege expert knowledge—early on in the form of social workers—as critical to changing welfare. The waiver provisions, although minor at the time, also contained within them the idea that public policy could be experimented with and learned about. Public policy itself, not merely social problems, could be the object of study.

The 1964 shift toward structural approaches to poverty generally, rather than public assistance specifically, brought academics and intellectuals into the heart of policy debates and gave them unprecedented power. Many of the Great Society programs contained evaluation requirements. The evaluations, however, were often unsystematic and subjective, and it was difficult to measure "outcomes" such as community empowerment. When the programs failed to live up to expectations, many of those involved brought a researcher's perspective to the issue and asked: Why did they fail? What can we learn from them? Were parts of the programs successful? The failure of the Great Society programs to change social conditions shifted attention to evaluating the programs themselves.

The Professionalization of Policy Evaluation

Aaron Wildavsky traces the development of public policy schools directly to the failures of the Great Society.

> For whatever reason by 1968 serious doubts were being expressed by evaluators (stipulated objectives were not being met) and by politicians. On the political right, social programs were being damned for increasing dependency (and at a high cost), on the left for buying off protest too cheaply while actually perpetuating institutions that oppressed the poor. Analyzing public policies to see what went wrong, to learn how to do better and to teach this understanding was the major motivator for establishing graduate schools devoted to the analyses of public policies.[32]

The failures of the Great Society compelled researchers to turn their attention to programs and policies themselves and to create a body of knowledge from which policymakers and administrators could draw. Harvard's Graduate School of Public Administration shifted away from classic public administration and toward a curriculum based on policy analysis. By 1978, the school was renamed the John F. Kennedy School of Government and explicitly aimed to bridge the academic world of policy-relevant research and the practical political concerns of government.

The idea of testing and evaluating small programs before implementing them quickly gained prominence in the 1970s. Chastened by the visible public failure of the War on Poverty, policymakers wanted to take smaller, more incremental steps. A policy evaluation industry began to emerge to evaluate programs and provide feedback to policymakers. In the early 1970s, the nonprofit policy evaluation corporation Manpower Demonstration Research Corporation (MDRC) was formed. As the president of MDRC, Judith Gueron, explains, MDRC "began applying the tools of classical, random assignment field experiments to the key policy questions about these [welfare] initiatives. Would they work? Could they reduce the welfare rolls? Would they save money? Would they cause people to get good jobs and move out of poverty?"[33]

The transformation of dowdy schools of public administration into slick new schools of public policy gave evaluation its academic credentials. Research corporations such as MDRC provided a key sector of employment and the government with an unofficial nonpartisan arm that was clearly separated from the universities, which are often viewed by policy actors as biased to the political left.[34] The professionalization of policy evaluation was completed by 1979 with the establishment of the Association for Public Policy Analysis and Management (APPAM), which two years later launched the influential *Journal of Policy Analysis and Management (JPAM)*.

Experimental Design

> Evaluators often long for a world where rationality holds sway and decisions are made on the basis of evidence, not politics.
>
> Carol H. Weiss, 1998[35]

Contemporary policy evaluation grew out of a desire to bring reason, rationality, and the scientific method to social policy. There is a peculiarly American feel to the idea that proper social policy can be determined objectively, pragmatically and without politics. It would be an overstatement to say that the evaluation movement was completely apolitical. Many evaluation scholars were—and are—deeply committed to political ideals. Schools of public policy recognized the inextricable connections between politics and social policy. Yet the idea of policy evaluation rests on the assumption that some part of social policy can be taken out of politics—that we can extract some core technical questions and analyze them under a microscope.

The promise of policy evaluation was that it would bring science to public policy and permit us to separate what works from what does not work, all politics aside. The ascendance of policy evaluation in the 1960s and 1970s appeared to create a channel for taking some ideas out of the political domain. One type of policy evaluation in particular seemed to be the most promising—randomized policy experiments. Without randomization, it is remarkably difficult to gauge how well a policy works, even with skilled evaluation researchers. To illustrate the point, I will consider two examples of nonrandomized evaluations and their limitations.

First, let us imagine that a new public school has been set up in a school district that has very low student test scores. The school has a new curricular model designed to help disadvantaged children succeed academically. Any child from the district can apply and, space permitting, will be admitted. The teachers are all drawn from the same district. Test scores in the school are dramatically higher than in other schools in the district. An evaluation team wants to find out whether implementing the curricular innovation districtwide would significantly raise test scores.

This superficially simple question is remarkably complex. The seemingly obvious solution is to compare the new school's test score to the scores in the rest of the district. If they are markedly higher, then the new curriculum should be implemented. This approach, however, is deeply flawed. It could result in the district spending scarce resources on an innovation that will not help the district students at all. How is this possible? The higher test scores from the new school may not be the result of the new curriculum. Why? First, the student body is not randomly selected. Admission to the school may be open to all families, but that does not mean that each child in the district has an equal chance of going. Since the child or the child's parents must be motivated to apply to get into the school, it is likely that the children in the school will be different in some critical way from most children in the district. It may be that more educated parents are likely to seek out information about new schools. If most of the information on the school is in writing, then illiterate parents may not have access to it. Since we know that parents' education level is correlated with children's educational attainment, the parents' education alone might account for the difference between school test scores. Or perhaps, education aside, only the most motivated and involved parents apply. Similarly, parent involvement is also related to children's educational success. Even if the children in the new school are demographically identical to their peers in the district—something that is very unlikely actually to occur—there is still the great possibility that an unmeasured difference in child or parent motivation accounts for at least a portion of the difference in test scores. The teachers, too, may be more gifted, and therefore are recruited by the new principal, or they may be more motivated, and therefore apply for the teaching position. Then there is the fact that the program is new. It is common for college freshmen to do better in their first semester than they do in their second. A new school can motivate students and teachers to work harder. That extra work may produce real gains within the school, but these gains may not be replicated over time if the curriculum is implemented districtwide. It is possible that the new curriculum creates an immediate improvement in students' test scores but that over time the scores return to the expected level. In such a case, the district would not want to spend the time or money to switch to the new curriculum. There are numerous obstacles in trying to tease out the effect of the new curriculum in such a scenario.

The problems of testing a new policy in a voluntary demonstration program, such as the fictitious school reform mentioned above, are clear. There is no comparison group. You do not know how much of the "change" is really just selection bias or some other factor unrelated to the effect of the policy. To avoid this problem, a researcher may opt to compare the same population before and after a policy is implemented. This "before and after" approach is appealing because it looks at roughly the same population and thus seems to isolate the effect of the policy. However, serious issues emerge with this approach as well.

The welfare reform of 1996 provides a good example of the problems with a "before and after" design in research. In the late 1990s, there was a dramatic increase in poor, single women's work hours. At first glance, the soaring rates of labor force participation by single mothers, which began in 1996, might seem like it could only be attributed to welfare reform. It occurred simultaneously with reform and it was one of the stated objectives of reform. Welfare reform, however, did not occur in isolation. Other critical factors, such as the strong economy and changes in the Earned Income Tax Credit (EITC) occurred at the same time and very likely affected women's labor force participation. Poor women overall, not simply those with welfare histories, were working more during this time.

Determining the specific effects of welfare reform is exceedingly difficult. The best estimate from state panel studies on caseload decline from 1996 to 1998 is that about one-third of the caseload decline was due to policy changes.[36] Even if we take the tentative estimate of one-third as definitive, we still know very little about the impact of welfare reform on women's labor force participation because that estimate fails to capture what aspects of the policy changes caused the increase. Was it the specter of time limits? The encouragement to work? Benefit sanctions for nonwork? The improved availability of affordable child care? When looking at programs that are implemented broadly, it is very hard to know what is an effect of the program, what is simple historical change, and what is an historically contingent effect of the program— an interaction of the policy design within a particular historical context. Employment rates change over time. Women's labor force participation changes over time. An historical change is one that would have occurred without the policy. An historically contingent change can be understood as a "favorable condition" change; a work program may show a stronger effect during a good economy than in a recession. How can we precisely measure the effects of the policy?

Randomized experimental design provides the greatest ability to isolate the effects of a policy. This approach takes the treatment and control of research design from clinical science and applies it to public policy. Ethical issues are raised by this approach, but in terms of pure empirical methodology, randomized design is the gold standard.[37] Research corporations such as the MDRC conduct these evaluations and often provide technical assistance to the states in setting them up. In a randomized experiment, every client who comes into the experimental program has an equal chance of being selected for the treatment group or the control group. The treatment group participates in the new program. Participating in the experimental program is akin to being given a therapeutic drug in a pharmaceutical experiment. The control group is either given no services or participates in the current, not the experimental, program. This is comparable to the control groups that receive a placebo pill in pharmaceutical experiments. In the case of the welfare reform experiments, clients either applying or reapplying for welfare benefits were randomly assigned to the treatment groups, which received benefits under new rules, or the control groups, which received benefits under the old AFDC rules. Evaluators then tracked information such as the work rates, wages, marital status, and fertility of the two groups. In experiments like these, statistically significant differences between the treatment and control groups are viewed as the effects of the treatment. Randomized experiments are the core of contemporary policy evaluation, particularly of evaluations mandated by the federal government.

Randomized experiments bring with them true methodological advantages. They also bring a language of clinical experimentation into the world of public policy. With the language of clinical experimentation come, almost inevitably, scientific imagery and clinical metaphors, such as viewing the states as "laboratories of democracy." Ironically, it was the linguistic removal of policy experiments from the political realm that made pilot programs an effective political tool. By talking about welfare experiments as if they were scientific experiments, the media and political actors obscured the political origins and objectives of the pilots.

Framing the waiver programs in research terms made them difficult to attack politically. Implicit in the experimental frame is the idea that these programs were nothing more than tests of policy ideas. If they did not work out, the policy idea could be abandoned with little to no harm done to the social safety net. Arguably, the experimental frame also encouraged liberal political actors who might otherwise have opposed the programs to accept them as temporary research efforts; what is there to oppose in research?

The political consequence of framing the waiver programs as pilot programs did not depend on all of the relevant actors accepting this definition as literally true. Mary Jo Bane and David T. Ellwood of HHS were clearly aware of the political dynamics that surrounded the waiver programs. Nonetheless, the framing of waiver programs as experiments, which was clearly done by both the Clinton administration and the media, affected the discourse around the pilot programs even if it was viewed as only a partial truth by many of those directly involved. The experimental language that surrounded the waiver programs may have been nothing more than a politically useful fiction, but it had real consequences.

Both Presidents George H. W. Bush and Bill Clinton had turned to waiver of authorized randomized experiments as a political tool for claiming movement in welfare reform in the early 1990s, when there was not sufficient political support to make legislative changes at the federal level. In essence, randomized experiments provided an opportunity for political actors to assure the public that experts were hard at work in their laboratories designing solutions for American problems. The clinical language of experimental evaluation is an expert language that few people speak. The process is not open to public debate. Once the results are released, they become public facts and arguably can be used to democratize public policymaking. Yet even those "facts" that the public receives are filtered through media reporting. Thus, for the period of evaluation, randomized experimentation can remove a policy idea from public debate.

The Political Role of Policy Experimentation

The political role of policy experiments as an institution—the focus of this book—is complex, and it is useful to specify two dimensions of evaluations. It is crucial to distinguish between the political role of evaluation *results* and the political role of pilot programs as an institution. The two are often spoken of as if they were the same. The political role of the *results* of evaluation research on pilot programs is limited to the impact that the findings from research conducted on a policy experiment have on the policy-making process. Not surprisingly, this is often quite small. The political role of pilot programs *as an institution* is much broader and largely unexplored.

The 1988 Family Support Act (FSA) is arguably the high mark of the political influence of evaluation *results*. The MDRC had conducted rigorous research on welfare-to-work programs that suggested that welfare reform could increase employment and incomes among the poor. After the numerous disappointments of the Great Society, this rigorously documented evidence of success was viewed as a triumph. At the same time, conservative political theorists were articulating a vision of work as a primary goal of welfare reform. Articulating the causal logic that supported a work-based welfare reform, political scientist Lawrence Mead made the compelling and controversial argument that work is a prerequisite to social citizenship in the United States and that public assistance should carry with it reciprocal obligations of work and adherence to behavioral standards.[38]

Political attacks on welfare and welfare recipients had become common. Throughout the 1980s, President Ronald Reagan had disparaged welfare and helped to cast the program as a public problem greater than poverty itself. When the rigorous, empirical research of MDRC showed that public policy could increase work among the poor, the findings had tremendous political resonance. Improvements in social science research made the findings more reliable, which contributed to their political impact. MDRC had also staked out an apolitical position that made their results trusted by both the political right and the political left, a marked departure from much of the preceding social science research rooted in social advocacy.[39]

The FSA seemed to build directly on social science research. It contained policies similar to those tested by MDRC. Yet, it is unclear whether social science research helped to create a political momentum or simply happened to bolster an idea that already had sufficient political force to become law. Several years before the FSA, Henry J. Aaron had noted that social science often gains prominence because it happens to correspond to a political current rather than shifting the political current through the force of its evidence. "[A]n idea of a social scientist is seized by laypersons because it accords with views they independently hold. With the passage of time, academic criticism undercuts the analysis and external events move on, leaving the idea, like last year's clothes, a little shabby and unfashionable."[40]

The idea that American social policy should encourage work is too deeply rooted in American politics to be dismissed as a passing fashion. And the MDRC findings did produce technical knowledge that helped welfare-to-work programs learn from the successes and failures of their predecessors. Yet the modest success of welfare-to-work pilot programs did not by itself create the political will to reform welfare. Nor was every empirical finding directly transformed into a new social policy; politics still mattered. The new empirical knowledge was important, but it did not transform policymaking.

R. Kent Weaver, in his excellent book *Ending Welfare as We Know It*, argues that the role of empirical research in the early 1990s was far weaker than it had been in the late 1980s. In part, Weaver attributes this to researchers' inability to document politically resonant successes. Many of the evaluations that were in place when Clinton came into office focused on reducing teen pregnancies.[41] Government programs have been notoriously ineffective in reducing teen pregnancies and encouraging marriage. Even strong supporters of "family values" conservatism recognize the consistent failure of government programs that target marriage and fertility among the American poor.[42] As Weaver notes, "The results [of these evaluations] were almost universally discouraging: Few programs had substantial effects on reducing teenage pregnancies, and some even increased them."[43]

The failure of research to identify successful policy strategies did not deter policymakers from moving forward with welfare reform in the mid-1990s, some versions of which explicitly targeted out-of-wedlock childbirth. The political will to reform welfare and the unique opportunity afforded by the Republican majority of the 104th Congress combined to create a rapid welfare reform movement that outpaced methodical evaluation research. Weaver also notes that policymakers did not wait for the final results from evaluations of the numerous pilot programs testing welfare time limits, work requirements, and other initiatives central to reform that began between 1993 to 1996.[44] Congress passed the Personal Responsibility and Work Opportunity Reconciliation Act (PRWORA)—welfare reform—in 1996 when there was virtually no hard evidence from any of the pilot programs. The empirical *results* of these evaluations were not important politically.

Evaluators would love to see evaluation results play a large political role. If *only* the numbers mattered! Because the empirical results of policy evaluations have played an extraordinarily small role in policymaking, many evaluation experts and political scholars have concluded that policy experiments have only a slight political role.[45] Narrowly defined, it is true that evaluation *results* have had little political impact. Up to this point, that fact has served to stifle the discussion of the political role of pilot programs. If experimental *results* are not important, then how can policy experiments play a political role? If no one cared enough to hold off on passing welfare reform until the findings from the experimental pilot programs were complete, then how could the pilot programs of the early 1990s have been critical to the passage of PRWORA?

Shadow Institutions

To understand the political role of the pilot programs, we must shift our thinking about experimental pilot programs away from the empirical and toward the institutional. The empirical findings from pilot programs had a negligible role in welfare politics, particularly in the mid-1990s. The *existence* of the programs as an institutional channel defining welfare reform, however, was critically important to the fundamental restructuring of the American welfare state that took place in 1996. By the time PRWORA passed, 75 percent of welfare recipients were involved in a pilot program rather than the old AFDC program.[46] As we will see in Chapter Six, there was an explosion in state applications for waivers. Newspapers such as the *New York Times* and the *Washington Post* ran hundreds of stories on the pilot programs. Political actors referred to the successes of these programs well before any had been documented. The pilot programs did play an important political role, just not the one that was expected.

In "Experimenting with Welfare Reform: the Political Boundaries of Policy Analysis," Evelyn Brodkin and Alexander Kaufman distinguish between the manifest function of policy evaluation and its latent functions.[47] The manifest function of policy experiments is to produce academically rigorous tests of policy ideas—to find out what works. This manifest function is fundamentally apolitical. The numbers simply state the facts. The manifest political role of policy experiments, therefore, is limited to the political impact of the results of policy experiments. This role is very small. However, reviewing the history of controlled analysis in welfare policymaking, Brodkin and Kaufman identify three latent functions of controlled analysis: (1) legitimating ideas, (2) articulating and interpreting social concerns, and (3) diverting or incubating policy ideas. It was these latent functions of pilot programs that were politically important in the 1996 welfare reform.

Pilot programs are, to use Brodkin and Kaufman's phrase, "shadow institutions." They lack the endurance and weight of the institutions we typically associate with policymaking, such as the United States Congress or the courts; they can be built and dismantled with relative ease. Yet, once in place, pilots provide an alternative policy-making channel. The removal of a policy question from normal political channels changes the political dynamics of the debate that surrounds it, which is exactly why political actors make use of this strategy. In the case of welfare reform, the two key moments of expansion in the pilot programs directly resulted from political strategies by George H. W. Bush and Clinton to shift the welfare debate in politically advantageous ways. Both presidents, as I discuss in more detail in Chapter Three, used the experimental pilot programs to claim movement toward reforming welfare when they did not have the political ability to reform it at the national level. They employed the waiver provisions to change the political debate, and, to a degree, to deflect attention from their immediate inaction on the subject. Clinton/Gore 1996 campaign materials noted, "President Clinton's 61 waivers represent a quiet revolution in welfare policy—and it's working."[48] The waivers were a revolution in welfare policy, not because of their results or empirical findings, but because they provided an institutional channel for restructuring the American welfare system from below and legitimating the idea of time-limited welfare. They undermined bureaucratic structures supporting old policy models and made it easier to shift to a new policy. The pilots were involved in rigorous empirical evaluations, and our political leaders claimed that the new policies were working. They did not need the evaluation results to claim success; they only needed the existence of pilot programs "testing" new ideas. The political neutrality of evaluation took the pilot programs out of the realm of public political debate and, as a direct result, imbued them with an unprecedented power to legitimate and facilitate policy ideas that otherwise might have been politically untenable.

CHAPTER 3

The History of AFDC

Everyone hates welfare.

David T. Ellwood, 1986[1]

There has never been a federal program called "welfare." "Welfare" is a term used to describe programs for the poor. In the popular debate, "welfare" often means "unearned" public assistance and, not surprisingly, is politically unpopular. In contrast, social insurance programs, such as Social Security and Unemployment Insurance, are tied to labor force participation and enjoy much broader public support. This distinction has its roots in the history of the American welfare state. As Linda Gordon writes, "The Social Security Act created the contemporary meaning of 'welfare' by setting up a stratified system of provision in which social insurance programs were superior in both payments and in reputation, while public assistance was inferior—not just comparatively second-rate, but deeply stigmatized."[2]

Although the term "welfare" is often used to label anything thought to be undeserved, the phrase "welfare mother" pointedly referred to women who received Aid to Families with Dependent Children (AFDC), the primary targets of welfare reform.[3]

The first half of this chapter outlines the history of AFDC. In order to understand the politics of welfare reform in the 1990s, it is important to understand how AFDC came to be an almost universally hated program. The history of "welfare" reveals fundamental tensions within American social policy. Particularly, AFDC and its predecessors were shaped by cultural understandings of what should be expected of different segments of the American population. Social expectations surrounding what is desirable for women and men and for blacks and whites have shaped both the design of welfare policy and its implementation in various ways over time. In fact, the social norms embedded in welfare policy at one point have often become key points of contention as social relations and expectations have shifted. In addition, the goals of individualized treatment versus equal treatment by social welfare agencies have remained in constant competition for dominance, with equality dominating in the 1970s and 1980s and then receding as individualized treatment and local control assumed dominance in the 1990s.

Readers familiar with the history of welfare in America may wish to skip ahead to the second half of the chapter, which focuses on the politics of welfare that directly preceded the 1996 welfare reform. For those readers who are less familiar with the history of welfare reform, I suggest reading the first half of this chapter. Although the history of welfare presented here is far from comprehensive, it is useful to highlight recurrent themes in the American welfare debate.[4] Many of these themes—Who deserves what? What is the proper role of the state? Should mothers be expected to work? Is treating everyone the same a desirable goal?—reemerged in the welfare debate of the 1990s and, interestingly, even in the street-level implementation of Florida's Family Transition Plan (FTP). In welfare, as in all social policy, the past explains much of the present and therefore it is a useful place to start.

Aid to Families with Dependent Children

Established in the 1935 Social Security Act, Aid to Dependent Children (ADC), renamed Aid to Families with Dependent Children (AFDC) in 1962, was a modest program to aid the children of poor, single mothers, primarily widows. An outgrowth of the "mothers' pensions," also known as "widows' pensions," which began in 1911, ADC was a locally oriented, highly discretionary program aimed at keeping poor children out of orphanages and enabling poor mothers and their children to limit their paid labor.[5] Funded in partnership with the federal government, state programs could impose a number of eligibility requirements in addition to those established nationally, including stipulations regarding the suitability of the home or the moral fitness of the mother.

Cultural expectations about proper behavior, largely defined by class, race, and gender, were central to the provision of public assistance in the early part of the twentieth century. Gwendolyn Mink notes that mothers' pensions stemmed from a desire to insure that children, particularly immigrant children, were raised to be good Americans. In the midst of a panic about immigrants threatening the quality of the "republican stock," social welfare programs were designed to improve the quality of women's child rearing, particularly among Eastern and Southern European women.[6] "The early American welfare state targeted women rather than workers in policies devised to uplift democratic character. . . . Middle class politics linked the problem of racial order to the material and cultural quality of motherhood. Motherhood, in this view, held the key to vigor in the citizenry. But the only way mothers from a new race could produce ideal American democrats would be through reform and reward of maternal practices."[7] Mothers' pensions were premised on the idea that women who had been widowed or abandoned should be provided with the cash assistance and moral guidance that would help them to raise their children according to middle-class standards.

In essence, the state would take over the role of the absent husband. It was argued that this would create a stronger nation by improving the quality of poor women's offspring.[8] Assistance was given only to women who were thought to be capable of raising good children. Many southern states explicitly denied assistance to black women; other states did so in practice though not in policy.[9] Mothers' pension benefits were very firmly tied to the "moral fitness" of the mother, which was defined primarily in terms of a woman's adherence to cultural expectations of motherhood, such as keeping the house clean, supervising the children according to local standards, and even cooking American food rather than traditional ethnic dishes.

Mimi Abramovitz has argued that welfare preserved the family ethic by distinguishing between "deserving" women and "undeserving" women on the basis of their relationships to men. The family ethic, as Abramovitz uses the concept, places women under the supervision of men either in the private sphere, through marriage and legal restrictions on married women that were once common, or in the public sphere through the supervision of male-dominated government agencies. Abramovitz argues that the welfare system has served the function of structurally reinforcing women's inferior social position within the patriarchal society. Mothers' pensions and subsequent welfare programs ensured that most women were supervised either by fathers, husbands, or the state. This was particularly true early on when they were coupled with "protective" labor regulations for women and low wages for female workers.[10]

Abramovitz's argument is broad, and perhaps overemphasizes gender domination while underemphasizing the effect that cultural understandings of gender had on the development of the American welfare state. Able-bodied men, for example, have often been the least able to receive public assistance.[11] This may be explained by the cultural assumption that able-bodied men can and should work, but it seems hard to explain in terms of pure gender domination. Nonetheless, it is true that welfare was initially a discretionary system that supported "good" women and enforced socially desired behaviors.

In the 1960s, federal court decisions diminished state discretion in administering the program and edged toward establishing welfare as a "right."[12] Federally mandated changes in AFDC administration also altered the character of the state-run programs. In 1967, Wilbur J. Cohen, outgoing secretary of the Department of Health, Education, and Welfare (HEW), issued an order to separate social services from income maintenance benefits. The separation of benefits from social services, which was fully implemented several years after Cohen's order, strengthened the rights-based income-maintenance orientation of welfare and removed some of the "therapeutic" justifications for welfare payments.[13] Caseworkers were no longer supposed to help welfare recipients reorder their lives (and kitchens); they were now asked to determine eligibility and hand out checks. Little illusion remained that welfare did anything but subsidize impoverished lives.

The number of people on the welfare rolls skyrocketed between 1967 and 1972, with an annual average growth of 16.9 percent.[14] This welfare expansion is often attributed to changes in the eligibility requirements of AFDC, coupled with a National Welfare Rights Organization campaign to enroll as many of the poor in AFDC as possible.[15] The rapid expansion of the welfare rolls created a political and fiscal crisis, focusing public attention and criticism on the program. The increasing association of welfare with black, never-married mothers rather than with white widows that followed the expansion of welfare benefits also undermined support for the program.[16] At the same time that the welfare rolls were exploding and the client population was shifting, the consensus that mothers should, if at all possible, not work outside of the home disintegrated, and with it went the cultural foundation of AFDC.[17]

Discouraging paid work outside of the home had once been viewed as a benefit of public assistance for single mothers, but as more and more women worked outside of the home, direct payments to poor, nonworking mothers became undesirable. By providing welfare benefits without reciprocal obligations on the part of recipients, Lawrence Mead argues, AFDC pushed recipients to the margins of society and impaired their ability to function.[18] In "A Genealogy of Dependency: Tracing a Key Word of the U.S. Welfare State," Nancy Fraser and Linda Gordon make a similar point from a philosophical and historical perspective. They note that once the almost universally held belief that women are by nature dependent became contested, the already tenuous public support for welfare programs deeply eroded. Other feminist scholars of the welfare state, notably Jane Jenson, Gwendolyn Mink, Barbara Nelson, and Diana Pearce, have also stressed the relationship between social expectations for women and the provision of public assistance.[19] Although the philosophical orientations and policy prescriptions of these feminist welfare state theorists radically differ from those of Lawrence Mead, there does seem to be a consensus that support for AFDC was dramatically eroded with the change in both the client population and cultural expectations surrounding women and work.

Who deserves welfare is tightly bound with the question of who should work and under what conditions. But who should work is not always a clear-cut question. Although showing little support for AFDC, Americans in the 1990s were ambivalent over whether mothers with young children should be expected to work. A 1995 survey found that 42 percent of Americans believed that it is important for a mother with young children to stay home even if it means having to provide her with welfare. The same survey, however, found that 68 percent of respondents favored ending welfare payments to able-bodied welfare recipients, including women with preschool children, and requiring them to take a job.[20]

Expectations around work and public assistance are often based on race and gender. Men in America are defined as "deserving" or "undeserving" primarily based on their relationship to the labor force. Michael B. Katz has argued that able-bodied men are particularly likely to be categorized as undeserving in America if they fall into poverty, providing a powerful incentive for men to work at any wage.[21] Piven and Cloward similarly have argued that a primary function of welfare is to regulate and stabilize the labor market.[22]

As Piven and Cloward, Theda Skocpol, and Jill Quadagno have documented, welfare was often withheld from black women in the South when field laborers were needed, and the federal government intentionally crafted welfare policies in which this exclusion would be permissible.[23] Skocpol further argues that "blacks were only marginally included in the social security programs launched by the New Deal," with agricultural and domestic occupations (those most open to blacks at the time) not covered by social insurance programs.[24] Skocpol also points out that discretion in welfare policy enabled southern states to provide assistance differentially to blacks and whites. She writes that the Social Security Act "gave free rein to state and local officials to exercise administrative discretion. This meant that blacks in the South could be deprived of adequate welfare assistance."[25] Similarly, Jill Quadagno has documented the significant role that race has played in American welfare policy, noting in particular that "No program better exemplifies the racially divisive character of the American welfare state than Aid to Families with Dependent Children (AFDC)."[26]

Slight pressure to equalize treatment in welfare came after 1948, when the first statistics on the racial composition of the welfare rolls were compiled. In seven southern states, African Americans comprised less than one-third of the rolls, far less than would be expected on the basis of need.[27] In response, the federal government tentatively stepped in.

[T]he federal government exerted some pressure for a relaxation of discriminatory practices—for example by requiring the establishment of a formal application process, thus making it somewhat more difficult for welfare officials to brush off applicants by treating their requests as mere casual inquiries. Between 1948 and 1953 (when the next census of the relief rolls was taken), the proportion of blacks on the rolls rose by at least 25 percent in eleven of the seventeen southern states.[28]

In the 1950s, African Americans increased their representation in welfare, but still faced inequitable treatment. The centrality of local discretion in American public assistance programs up until the late 1960s can be viewed as a result of America's unwillingness to provide welfare equally to all racial and ethnic groups. For example, in 1960, when Louisiana instituted a more stringent "suitable home" law, 95 percent of the children dropped from the rolls were black.[29] The fact that the "suitable home" rules in southern states were used almost exclusively against black recipients is further evidence that public assistance was not always administered in a race-neutral way.

Limiting Discretion: The Late 1960s
to Early 1970s

In the late 1960s and early 1970s, the Supreme Court ruled on a number of cases regarding public assistance and severely limited states' discretionary powers. In *King v. Smith* (1968), perhaps the most famous of these cases, the Supreme Court struck down Alabama's "substitute father" regulation, popularly known as the "man in the house" rule. These regulations stipulated that if a mother "cohabited" with a man, she and her children were ineligible for assistance from the state.[30] More than 90 percent of the children who lost their benefits under this rule were black.[31] In arguing *King v. Smith*, the plaintiff's attorney, Martin Garbus, asked the court to "give us a decision interpreting the Social Security Act as having rejected the concept of the worthy and unworthy poor."[32] The Supreme Court's unanimous decision against the state of Alabama in *King v. Smith* sent that message clearly, though later rulings would be more ambiguous.

Other cases also limited states' discretionary powers. In *Shapiro v. Thomson* (1969), the Supreme Court ruled that Connecticut's prohibition of welfare benefits to residents of less than a year was a violation of equal protection under the law. *Goldberg v. Kelly* (1970) held that New York City's termination procedures were constitutionally inadequate because they failed to allow the recipient to appear with or without counsel to present evidence or examine witnesses. Between 1969 and 1975, the Supreme Court decided eighteen cases regarding AFDC.[33] These rulings radically limited the discretionary authority of local agencies and strengthened the fair hearing rights of recipients. The lower courts were even more active in reviewing AFDC cases and strengthening the "entitlement" to welfare benefits. The Supreme Court and lower federal court rulings of the late 1960s and early 1970s never went so far as to establish welfare as a legal right, but they greatly decreased state barriers to eligibility and made the termination of welfare benefits subject to due process.[34]

In this period, the casework-oriented approach to welfare was criticized by both the political left, which was critical of the abuses of discretion and the intrusions into recipients' daily lives, and by the political right, which was critical of the number of technically ineligible people receiving benefits. Home visits, in particular, had created conflicting roles for caseworkers. Caseworkers were supposed to be involved with families with whom they worked, but they were also supposed to determine whether these families were eligible for benefits. Because of the personal relationships between caseworkers and clients, caseworkers often overlooked eligibility infractions. As a result, a high proportion of payments to AFDC clients were in error.

As late as 1973, 16 percent of welfare payments were overpayments or payments made to ineligible families.[35] Welfare rights advocates argued that caseworkers also abused their discretionary powers, particularly by discriminating against minority recipients. By the early 1970s, the HEW order to separate income maintenance from social services, the Supreme Court decisions restricting state eligibility requirements, the federal quality control drive to reduce payment errors, and increasing concerns about discrimination combined to limit caseworker discretion and shift the administration of welfare toward a more bureaucratic model that emphasized adherence to rules and procedures. In *Welfare Realities: From Rhetoric to Reform*, Mary Jo Bane and David T. Ellwood quote a Department of Public Welfare director of labor relations as saying "We've been trying to get the people who think like social workers out and the people who think like bank tellers in."[36]

The Bureaucratic Model: Middle 1970s to Late 1980s

After 1972, bureaucratization and eligibility determination became the defining characteristics of welfare administration. During this period, welfare administration focused on determining eligibility, and the error rates dropped substantially—from 16.5 percent to 7.8 percent between 1973 and 1980. Invasion of client privacy and the discretionary power of caseworkers also declined.[37] The bureaucratization of welfare, however, also created problems. The new bureaucratic system, although more efficient and equitable, did not provide the individualized treatment that was characteristic of the old casework-oriented system. This led to concerns that welfare no longer helped individuals with their specific problems, but simply handed them a check without additional guidance. Bane and Ellwood describe this shift and the resulting tensions: "The casework model had held out the promise that with welfare would come social service intervention that would help recipients to correct the problems that led them to welfare in the first place. With the collapse of this model many came to see welfare as a dependency trap, in which clients received income maintenance for long periods with little hope of moving off welfare."[38]

Thus, while increasing the perception, and perhaps reality, that welfare recipients were being treated more equitably, the bureaucratization of welfare also increased public concern that people who did not deserve or misused their benefits were receiving public assistance indefinitely.

Some scholars have argued that the increase in public concern over AFDC that began in the late 1960s had more to do with the changing characteristics of recipients than the shift in administrative philosophies:

> The federal courts and welfare rights activists forced open the ADC gates. Welfare became a "right," and it streamlined the previously excluded—women of color, divorced, separated, deserted, and, increasingly, never-married. Were these previously excluded, morally problematic recipients now to be treated as the deserving poor and excused from work? Not so. Welfare was now in "crisis."[39]

> AFDC was at the outset the most broadly acceptable of the New Deal innovations in social welfare. From this innocuous beginning AFDC evolved into the bête noire of the social welfare system. By the fifties it had become embarrassingly, outrageously clear that most of these women were not widows. Many of them had not even been married. Worst of all, they did not stop having babies after the first lapse. They kept having more. This had not been part of the plan. The most flagrantly unrepentant seemed to be mostly black, too.[40]

Historical work casts some doubt on the accuracy of such benign pictures of pre-1950s attitudes toward welfare recipients.[41] Nonetheless, there was undoubtedly a shift in the public perception of welfare between the 1950s and the early 1970s.

In 1988, Congress attempted to address public concerns about welfare by passing bipartisan legislation, the Family Support Act (FSA), aimed at moving welfare recipients into the workforce.[42] The FSA passed by an overwhelming margin of 96–1 in the Senate and 347–53 in the House.[43] This bill changed the AFDC program by expanding work requirements and opportunities through the Job Opportunity and Basic Skills (JOBS) program. JOBS required that welfare recipients, excluding those with young children, participate in education, job training, or some other work-related activity. It also made two-parent families universally eligible for AFDC, although still under more stringent criteria than single-parent families. Before the FSA, states had the option of permitting two-parent-family eligibility but were not required to do so.

In practice, the FSA had little impact on AFDC. The JOBS program reached only about 13 percent of mothers on welfare in 1992, and 60 percent were fully exempted from the program.[44] Critics argued that the JOBS program failed to produce the revolutionary changes in the structure and incentives of the welfare system necessary to increase work or reduce welfare rolls.[45] Although individual JOBS programs did have some success in increasing welfare recipients' work hours and wages, the FSA ultimately did not produce the sweeping, dramatic changes necessary to restore public faith in AFDC.

By the 1990s, welfare had become a deeply unpopular program. Since the late 1960s, AFDC had operated as an entitlement program; anyone who met the eligibility requirements—generally being a poor, single parent or guardian of a minor child—received a check for as long as he or she met those requirements. Although federal welfare reforms in 1967 and 1988 sought to increase work for welfare recipients, they had little effect on most recipients.[46] The public perception that welfare was "something for nothing" remained. By 1994, 79 percent of Americans thought that the welfare system was not working well, and fewer than 20 percent believed that most welfare recipients deserved to receive benefits.[47]

Moral Worthiness and Decentralization

> Resources are finite. Neither the state nor private charity can distribute them in unlimited quantities to all who might claim need. On what principles, then, should assistance be based? Who should—and the more difficult question, who should not—receive help?
>
> —Michael B. Katz, 1986[48]

In welfare, the questions of who deserves assistance, in what form, and for what duration are as much questions of the proper role of government as they are more abstract questions of moral worthiness. From the perspective of a proponent of small government, an individual might be abstractly deserving of assistance on moral grounds, but not deserving of assistance from the government any more than he or she is deserving of assistance from a corporation or a stranger on the street. Equally, from the perspective of a socialist, an individual might not be morally deserving of assistance at all and still be deserving of assistance from the government as a right of citizenship. These philosophical extremes are more moderate in practice; human need constrains the first whereas limited resources constrain the second. In practice, the policy question is, what will the government provide, to whom, and under what conditions?

At the federal level, decisions about who should receive what from the government are made about categories of recipients, not about individuals. Legislators decide whether an assistance program should be created for a particular group, such as single mothers or workers. Legislators also decide what form the program should take—will people who are eligible have a legal right to the benefits or will they only receive them if there are sufficient funds? In other words, will they be entitlements or discretionary programs? The terms "entitlement" and "discretionary" have strict meanings in the budgetary process, distinguishing between those programs that are not subject to annual appropriations (entitlements) and those that are (discretionary), but they also have broader meanings. Comparative welfare state scholars often use the term "entitlement" to refer to programs that are available to virtually all citizens as a right of citizenship. Under this definition, AFDC was never an entitlement. In the American debate, however, "entitlement" has come to mean benefits that one is entitled to receive as long as programmatic eligibility can be proven.[49] Conversely, "discretionary" has come to mean a benefit to which one does not have a legal right. Battles over welfare reform have often hinged on what the state must provide and what it may give as a gift to those it finds deserving or for only as long as there are available funds. These are the definitions of "entitlement" and "discretionary" used in this book.

In an entitlement program, the government designates a group as being categorically deserving of assistance. The moral worthiness of individual recipients is, at least theoretically, irrelevant. If the government designates a group as being categorically undeserving of assistance, the merits of individual cases are also unimportant—there are no federal programs designed for the categorically undeserving.[50] Arguably, General Assistance (GA), which serves able-bodied adults without children, often men, is a program for the "undeserving." However, GA is not a federal program, and in the states that provide it, the benefits are extremely meager. It is not comparable to federal programs such as AFDC or Social Security Insurance (SSI). When the government is divided over or uncertain about a category of recipients, it may create discretionary and decentralized assistance programs in which the merit of individual cases becomes important.[51]

The perception that the worthiness of individual cases is not a very important factor in the administration of entitlement programs ultimately creates political tension that can undermine support for these programs. In *The "Deserving Poor,"* Joel F. Handler and Ellen Hollingsworth argue that discretionary relief programs enable federal and state legislators to avoid engaging the politically difficult task of sorting out which of the poor are deserving of aid and which are not. "Relief for the morally blameworthy poor—in an older day the "undeserving poor"—has always created severe conflict in our society. The top-level decision makers delegate authority as the principal technique for avoiding the political risk of resolving these conflicts. With rare exceptions, the major policy questions of the AFDC program have been decided at the local level."[52] Decentralization in poverty relief programs mitigates the tensions created by the politically volatile question of who is deserving of what. Handler and Hollingsworth were writing at a time when American welfare programs were undergoing a transformation from extremely decentralized, local programs to a more centralized system. The transformation to a centralized system was forced by the courts and the Department of Health, Education, and Welfare (now the Department of Health and Human Services) and not by the Congress. This lends support to Handler and Hollingsworth's argument that legislators are disinclined to centralize poverty relief for controversial categories of recipients, such as single mothers.

Michael Lipsky used the term "street-level bureaucrats" to refer to people within bureaucracies who work directly with the public, such as police, teachers, and social workers. He argued that the policies of bureaucracies are mediated, and in some ways created, in the interactions of street-level bureaucrats with the public. As Lipsky writes, "Street-level bureaucrats make policy in two related respects. They exercise wide discretion in decisions about citizens with whom they interact. Then when taken in concert, their individual actions add up to agency behavior."[53] When the behavior of these agencies is then taken in concert, it could further be argued, their individual actions add up to the social policy of a nation.

Although street-level bureaucrats always have power to exercise informal discretion, such as accepting a particular form of documentation or informing clients of options available to them by law, formal discretion greatly increases their power. Therefore as political actors shy away from making categorical decisions about moral worthiness, the power of street-level bureaucrats increases.

In Florida's experimental Family Transition Program, for example, the actions of the Citizen Review Panel helped to define time limits on welfare as benefit termination time limits by finding that no participants who "played by the rules" were unemployed by the time limit. The review panel's actions lent support to critics of structural explanations of poverty who claimed that poverty was a choice, not a result of external factors such as the labor market.[54] The movement away from a centralized, bureaucratic welfare system and toward a decentralized, discretionary system brought with it all of the benefits and perils of welfare before the administrative changes and court decisions of the 1960s and 1970s. It permitted more individualized treatment of cases and provided localities the flexibility to respond to local conditions. It also opened up the possibility of discrimination.

The waiver programs, and ultimately Temporary Assistance for Needy Families (TANF), brought discretion and individualized treatment back into welfare administration. Proponents of the return of discretion argue that the United States no longer has the level of racial discrimination of the 1930s, 1940s, and 1950s. Moreover, there are now civil rights laws that protect individuals from racial discrimination. It is indisputably true that official discrimination, embodied by the Jim Crow laws and other formal norms, is no longer a part of American society. It is equally clear that race still matters in the United States and that redress through the civil rights laws for discrimination in the administration of welfare benefits may be costly and difficult to obtain for poor families.

Despite all of the potential perils, it is not difficult to see why so many reformers in the 1990s wanted to return to a discretionary system. Welfare after the 1960s had been characterized by its rule-bound emphasis on eligibility determination. By the mid-1980s, the AFDC system was nearly as rigid as it could get. Partly in response to the abuses of the early 1960s, states had little flexibility in administering AFDC. Caseworkers verified eligibility and handed out checks. Formal caseworker discretion was largely eliminated, and, with the exception of benefit levels, AFDC programs looked very similar from state to state.

By the 1980s, the bureaucratic model of welfare administration was under attack for handing out checks that helped to subsidize "antisocial" behaviors such as nonwork and out-of-wedlock childbearing. As a

result, there was a movement to make welfare administration more decentralized and discretionary. Returning welfare to the states would allow for more innovative and flexible welfare programs that would, proponents argued, be better suited to addressing the problems of the poor
in each area. The bureaucratic model of welfare administration was an
equitable but unpopular system that seemed like it might stay that way
forever. The failure of the Family Support Act to effect appreciable
changes in welfare reinforced the perception that welfare was immov-
able. Then, as often happens when competing tensions seem to have
produced paralysis, a new channel was found.

State Waivers

In the mid-1980s, Section 1115 in the 1962 Public Welfare Amendments
to the Social Security Act was used to increase state-level experimentation and flexibility in the administration of AFDC. Originally created as
a research tool, Section 1115 permitted states to test welfare reform
ideas that were consistent with the goals of the Social Security Act, such
as reforms to strengthen family life or to help parents become self-supporting. Through Section 1115, states could apply to the federal government to have particular (federal) AFDC rules waived to create experimental welfare programs. President Reagan began using Section
1115 to increase state flexibility, but it was not until 1992 that federal
waivers became a central part of American welfare policy.[55]

In the mid-1980s, the Reagan administration, unable to garner sufficient congressional support to change the structure of welfare, centralized the decision-making process for approving waivers in a White
House working group, the Low-Income Opportunity Advisory Board
(LIOAB). Through this group, the administration began reducing the
barriers that prevented states from seeking waivers to run experimental welfare programs.[56] When President George H. W. Bush came into
office in 1988, welfare reform was no longer an executive priority, and
the waiver program temporarily receded in importance.

In 1992, candidate Bill Clinton harnessed the political power of advocating welfare reform by pledging to "end welfare as we know it" if
elected president. The political resonance of reforming welfare was too
powerful for the Bush administration to ignore, but it had no welfare
reform plan of its own to present. As Steven M. Teles writes, "They
[members of the Bush administration] were playing catch-up, did not

have time to create a full fledged welfare reform proposal, and thus reached out to the easiest and most timely strategy that they could find: granting new authority to the states [through the waivers]."[57] When President Clinton came into office, he eliminated the LIOAB and returned the power to grant waivers to the Department of Health and Human Services (HHS). The number and scope of waiver-authorized demonstration projects grew phenomenally. In 1996, Elisabeth Boehnen and Thomas Corbett noted, "Waivers are no longer being used to learn more things to inform national policy; they are increasingly granted to circumvent national policy."[58]

By the mid-1990s, politicians and academics were arguing that the states were reforming welfare even as federal reform was gridlocked. "In the beginning, waivers were granted sparingly and to add to our stock of knowledge," wrote Elisabeth Boehnen and Thomas Corbett. "Now waivers are routinely granted, and virtually all states are actively pursuing reforms, many of them quite ambitious. Some observers, indeed, question whether a national welfare policy still exists."[59] The strategy of devolution—allowing de facto reform in the states through the use of waivers originally created as a research tool—enabled Clinton to respond to the pressure for welfare reform without having the political consensus necessary to enact federal level reform.[60] Decentralization of welfare was a strategy of last resort for both Bush and Clinton. Bush took up the waiver strategy when the Clinton campaign forced him to articulate a vision of welfare reform that he did not have. Clinton, who had a vision of welfare reform, used the waivers to promote innovation, shift power to the governors, and claim movement toward "ending welfare as we know it" even after his own welfare reform plan stalled.

The waiver program created a tapestry of welfare policies in the United States. Among the provisions tested were increased earning disregards, removal of restrictions on two-parent families, school attendance requirements, family caps, work requirements, and time limits. Of all these provisions, time limits represented the most fundamental change in American welfare policy, reconstructing welfare as a limited-assistance program rather than a guaranteed safety net.

The policy dilemmas that had produced gridlock in welfare reform at the federal level for so long still existed at the state level: being tough with parents without hurting children, allowing for more caseworker discretion without bringing back discrimination, enforcing behavioral standards without encroaching on individual freedom, and demanding that everyone work without adequate day care or a full-employment economy. In fact, although it was at the federal level that these issues were most hotly debated, it was at the local level that they most fundamentally shaped policy. Many of the new welfare reform programs gave considerable power to street-level bureaucrats. In fundamental ways, the actions of caseworkers would define welfare policy as much as the actions of Congress.

The Politics of State and Federal Welfare Reform Initiatives

Perhaps the most treacherous area for politicians who advocated welfare reform in the early and middle 1990s was defending the potentially negative impact of reform initiatives on children. As popular as get-tough welfare reform was, it was still political poison to be perceived as endangering children.[61] The public sharply criticized Speaker of the House Newt Gingrich and other Republicans involved in the Work and Personal Responsibility Act of 1995, also known as H.R. 4, for their plan to build orphanages for children whose parents would not be able to care for them under the new welfare rules. Plans to change the school lunch program as a part of welfare reform were also widely criticized. The charge that H.R. 4 would hurt children was ultimately used by opponents of H.R. 4 to pressure Clinton into vetoing the bill. In November 1995, the Office of Management and Budget released a study, "Potential Poverty and Distributional Effects of Welfare Reform Bills and Balanced Budget Plans," which claimed that H.R. 4 would push between one and two million children into poverty.[62] Advocacy groups used these numbers to paint the Republican party as heartless. Ultimately, this only delayed the passage of H.R. 4-style welfare reform, as the Personal Responsibility and Work Opportunity Reconciliation Act that Clinton signed several months later was very similar to H.R. 4. Nonetheless, public perception of how such a policy would endanger children was a powerful factor in the politics of welfare reform.

There was intense pressure for politicians to be seen as reforming welfare, yet to attempt actual reform was to enter a minefield. This was particularly true for those in federal office, whose actions the national press closely monitored. The press has a keen interest in highlighting colorful controversies, such as those over eliminating school lunches and building orphanages. The benefits of being on the cutting edge of welfare reform were perhaps greatest and the risks lowest for the governors who could implement pilot welfare reform programs and take credit for trying to reform welfare in small, experimental programs without being seen as trying to dismantle the federal safety net. Because they were experimental, the pilot programs could be more radical and yet be viewed as less threatening than federal reform efforts. If they failed, the governors could terminate the programs and the federal safety net would still be intact. If they succeeded, the states could claim credit for solving a problem that had stymied the federal government for decades. By contrast, if the federal safety net were dismantled and the new welfare reform program that took its place failed, the effects would be widespread and very difficult to reverse. Waiver-authorized welfare reform, therefore, had a distinct, if temporary, political advantage over federal reform.

The federal waiver program freed state governments to experiment with welfare reforms. The benefits of such experiments for the governors were clear. Radically reforming welfare, even if only in small pilot programs, virtually guaranteed them media attention and constituent support. Welfare reform that saved money was also advantageous to the governors, who have to pay a portion of welfare benefits out of their state budgets. The political payoff from the national attention attracted by the pilot programs was also high. The Republican governors most closely associated with state welfare reform, Governor Tommy Thompson of Wisconsin and Governor John Engler of Michigan, were later mentioned as possible Republican vice presidential candidates for the 1996 election. Waiver-authorized welfare reform programs became a vehicle for governors to enter the national spotlight and establish themselves on the frontier of social policy.

Federal Welfare Reform Initiatives and Time Limits

By 1994, time limits on welfare benefits were at the center of most prominent federal and state welfare reform proposals. But there were still deep divisions over what a welfare time limit should entail: the end of all benefits including publicly supported jobs, or only the end of cash benefits. The goal of time limits was also unclear. Was the primary goal of time limits to encourage women to marry and delay childbearing because they could not support children alone, as Christian family groups argued, or to promote work, as the National Governors Association maintained?

Work-Trigger Model Time Limits

Clinton's Work and Responsibility Act of 1994 would have replaced traditional welfare programs with two years of assistance, during which recipients would have been required to begin moving from welfare to work. After the time limit, state subsidized work would have been available for recipients who could not find jobs in the private sector. The Clinton plan also allowed liberal exemptions from the time limit. Months in which an individual worked more than twenty or thirty hours per week (by the discretion of the state), for example, would not have been counted against the two-year time limit. Teen parents would have been exempted from the time limit until they turned eighteen. Recipients who were completing their studies toward a GED or other education and training programs could have received extensions of twelve to twenty-four months. People with learning disabilities, a language barrier, or other serious obstacles to employment would have been exempted from the time limit. States would have been required to grant exemptions to persons who had reached the time limit but had not been granted access to the appropriate government programs, e.g. the JOBS program. Finally, recipients who had exhausted the two-year "lifetime" limit but who left welfare for an extended period would have been eligible for up to six months of additional public assistance.

Benefit Termination Model Time Limits

The Work and Personal Responsibility Act of 1995, proposed by House Republicans, was the first important federal example of a benefit termination model of time-limited welfare. The aim of this bill was to change the reproductive behavior of the poor, particularly black, inner-city, unwed adolescents:

[T]he likelihood that a young black man will engage in criminal activities doubles if he is raised without a father and triples if he lives in a neighborhood with a high concentration of poverty; and the greater the incidence of single-parent families in a neighborhood, the higher the incidence of violent crime and burglary; and in light of this demonstration of the crisis in our Nation, the reduction of out-of-wedlock births is an important government interest and the policy contained in the provisions of this title address the crisis.[63]

At the core of this proposal were provisions to stop nearly all assistance to young women who had children out of wedlock. The guiding philosophy was that if young women could not afford to raise children on their own, out-of-wedlock childbirth would decline.[64] Teenage girls would be more careful not to become pregnant, and those who did would have a greater incentive to marry their babies' fathers. Young men would be more inclined to marry the mothers of their children because they would feel a greater sense of responsibility now that the state would no longer assume the role of breadwinner in their absence. The bill also included a five-year lifetime limit on receiving welfare, contingent on the recipient's participation in a work program after the first two years. Each state could grant "hardship" exemptions, for which there were no clearly defined criteria, to up to 10 percent of its caseload.

After Clinton vetoed H.R. 4 twice, once as a freestanding bill and once as a part of the Omnibus Reconciliation Act of 1996, congressional Republicans changed their strategy to reform welfare. Their goal shifted from discouraging single-parent families to getting welfare recipients to work. In March 1996, the National Governors Association, led by Wisconsin's Governor Tommy Thompson, drafted a bipartisan welfare reform plan. This plan focused on welfare-to-work programs and benefit termination time limits. Preventing out-of-wedlock childbirth took a backseat to encouraging work. The Christian Coalition and the Eagle Forum, along with Representatives Tim Hutchinson (R-Ark.) and James Talent (R-Mo.), headed a small campaign expressing dismay over the shift in the direction of Republican-supported welfare reform. The Ways and Means Subcommittee on Human Resources held a hearing on the relationship between welfare and illegitimacy to appease the Family Values faction of the Republican party. Critics who argued that welfare did not promote illegitimacy pointed to the lack of evidence of a direct correlation between welfare payments and out-of-wedlock childbirth. They noted in particular that the rise in out-of-wedlock childbirth happened across class lines and in all industrialized Western countries, not in the United States only. Those believing that welfare did promote illegitimacy maintained that the impact of welfare was diffuse.[65] Ultimately, the advocates who emphasized work over marriage won. It was not until the 2002 reauthorization debate that concerns over out-of-wedlock childbirth would again dominate the welfare reform agenda. Largely, this was a rhetorical victory. There was little difference in the specific policies advocated by the promarriage faction and the prowork faction. The Republican-sponsored plans all made benefit termination time limits their primary reform.

Defining Success

Surface agreement over the desirability of time limits made it difficult for Republicans and Democrats to argue in favor of their preferred policy models on ideological grounds. Since the two sides seemed to be so close to agreement, grand arguments over why *this* type of time limit was better than *that* type of time limit looked technical and wonkish. A more powerful rhetorical strategy for each side was to argue that its plan *worked*. Bolstering this approach was the fact that the experimental waiver programs were required by law to be set up as experiments, "tests" of the policy ideas. Rather than arguing over the merits of various models of time-limited welfare, political actors could point to the fact that particular pilot programs "worked" and were succeeding.

The success of a welfare program could be measured in any number of ways: decreased poverty, fewer families on assistance, more mothers at home, more mothers working, freedom for poor women to raise their children alone, fewer single-parent families, and so forth. In the debates, the goal of welfare reform was often a contentious issue even among policymakers who essentially favored the same reforms. The target of welfare reform was never simply the program itself. It was the behavior and lives of recipients and their children. Controversies over the goal of welfare reform reflected the diverse ambitions and desires of reformers. Ultimately, however, the success of welfare reform was measured by one criterion: caseload decline.

Declining Caseloads

In the mid-1990s, one statistic quickly became the primary measure of success: caseload decline. Clinton / Gore 1996 campaign materials on welfare reform boasted: "President Clinton's effort to assist [welfare] reform in 38 states is working. . . . Welfare caseloads have declined by 1.4 million since March 1994—a 10% drop. Participation in the food stamp program has dropped by 1 million people (from October 1994 to October 1995)—saving taxpayers over $800 million."[66] The *New York Times* noted that the governors were also claiming credit for caseload reductions: "As the nation's governors gather here [in Washington, D.C.] this weekend for their winter meeting, many are crediting their programs for the reduction in caseloads."[67] By measuring the success of welfare reform in declining caseloads, administrators and politicians could tap into the generalized distaste for welfare—if welfare is bad, then the fewer people on it the better—without getting into the stickier issue of what the ultimate social goal of welfare reform should be. With more than half of Americans believing that welfare did more harm than good, the decline in welfare seemed to indicate that former welfare recipients were better off, if only by virtue of no longer being on welfare, and that the states were doing a better job than the federal government had done. Declining caseload size also freed up government dollars, which is always a popular accomplishment.

Representative E. Clay Shaw (R-Fla.), commenting on the decline in caseloads, suggested that "People are seeing that welfare reform is a certainty and that they had darn well better take responsibility for pulling their lives together." He added that "the law is working. And it's working right from the beginning."[68] In other words, if the caseload declines before people hit the time limit that is evidence that merely sending the message of welfare reform is enough to make people find other ways to support themselves.

Caseload decline, however, can be achieved in a number of ways. Wisconsin, a state that had one of the biggest caseload declines, established "a program of bureaucratic incentives that measures caseload reductions and threatens lagging offices with a loss of money."[69] It is not hard to imagine that offices might find official and unofficial ways to reduce the caseload under these circumstances. In Florida, during the debates over the Family Transition Program (FTP), one representative suggested a performance-based pay incentive "if you're a field worker and you can get folks off welfare."[70]

The expectation that successful welfare reform would result in fewer people on the welfare rolls was rooted in a cultural understanding of the nature of poverty. Every piece of legislation is partly the result of a cultural model or "policy paradigm" of how the world works, including ontological assumptions of who relevant actors are and their causal interrelations.[71] The policy paradigm underpinning the benefit termination model of time limits has been central to American poverty discourse for years. It is, as Katz has articulated, that the poverty of the

poor "is to some degree a matter of personal responsibility, and its alle-
viation requires personal transformation, such as the acquisition of
skills, commitment to the work ethic, or the practice of chastity."[72] This
model is especially salient in the time-limited welfare debate: if long-
term poverty in general is a matter of choice, then continued poverty
after completion of a new welfare program designed to offer numerous
ways out of poverty would be unquestionably a matter of choice.

Florida's Family Transition Act, for example, assumed that all welfare recipients were competent citizens and masters of outside social
forces. The Clinton administration did not share these assumptions.
Nonetheless, the cultural model that shaped the Florida legislation ultimately shaped FTP agency policy. Getting people off welfare within
the time limit was seen as a success in all cases, whether they found employment or not. The "good" welfare recipients, it was assumed, made
the personal transformations to become self-supporting and the "bad"
were smoked out and kicked off the dole.

Measuring the success of welfare reform by caseload reduction also
served bureaucratic needs of administrators and politicians searching
for clear evidence of success. Policymakers and administrators often favor easily measured, simple to understand, quantitative evidence of
agency success, such as dollars saved or number of workers back on the
job after injury. Whatever a program's goal, quantitative measures are
likely to frame the debates about the legislation that brought the program (or agency) into being.

Quantitative measures of agency success are useful tools in public relations. Numbers are simple to report and easy to compare. They fit into
the limited space of newspaper columns and can be grasped quickly by
the public. The drive to produce statistics with public relations value,
however, not only affects which aspects of a program's performance are
emphasized; it can also shape agency policy and create the very outcomes it is supposed to measure. As Chapter Four illustrates, administrators in Florida's FTP understood that the nation was looking to them
for evidence that welfare reform could be a success. They did not have
a scientist's view of experimentation. There was only one acceptable
outcome: Time-limited welfare had to work.

CHAPTER 4

Florida's Family Transition Program

[W]e will be the first state in the nation to have time-limited benefits. There are no other states. Mr. Clinton's proposal mirrors what we are doing.

Florida state representative George Albright (24-R), 1993[1]

Between 1992 and 1996, the welfare pilot programs became a shadow institution in policy making. In political debates leading up to the passage of the Personal Responsibility and Work Opportunity Reconciliation Act, the pilot programs served to legitimate the idea of welfare time limits and reshape the politics of welfare at the federal level. By 1996, one could no longer argue that time-limited welfare could not be done because it had been done. Yet the "results" of these programs reported by the media and political actors had more to do with the politics of the welfare reform debate than has been recognized. This chapter and the next focus on how welfare and administrative politics shaped the first time-limited welfare experiment, Florida's Family Transition Program (FTP), on the ground level. Unless otherwise noted, all quotes are from the author's interviews. To protect confidentiality, names have been omitted from most of the interviews.

Florida was a critical pilot program for several reasons. The FTP was the first time-limited welfare program implemented in the United States. It was framed as an empirical test of the policy ideas in time-limited welfare. Would time limits motivate recipients to work? Would they hurt poor children? It was also framed as a test of one of the most fundamental questions of the welfare debate: How many people who made a good faith effort in a time-limited welfare program would be unemployed by the time limit?

The question of how many hardworking families would fail to find jobs by the time limit was at the heart of the policy conflict between the Clinton administration and congressional Republicans. If it turned out to be true that many families involved in time-limited welfare programs had made a good faith effort yet were still unemployed, then the congressional Republican plan to end all benefits after the time limit would be much harder to sell. Conversely, if very few families who made a good faith effort were unemployed when they reached that time limit, then the Clinton plan to provide public jobs would appear costly, unnecessary, and counterproductive to the message of independence many policymakers hoped to put forward with reform. The following chapters highlight the inevitability of political influence on policy implementation, particularly in high stakes, high profile pilot programs.

The FTP on its surface was one of the least partisan pilot programs. Wisconsin's welfare experiments—policy showpieces for then-Governor Tommy Thompson (R)—were steeped in politics. Wisconsin's largest welfare experiment, Wisconsin Works, known as W2, was designed under heavy secrecy. Leading conservative reformers including Andy Bush and Anna Kondratas from the Hudson Institute, Jason Turner, a former Bush administration official, and Jean Rogers, a former Republican party activist, drafted the W2 in the "war room," as it was referred to by those involved.[2] The goal of W2 was not only the reform of welfare for Wisconsin recipients. It was also part of a larger political debate about the devolution of policymaking and states' rights. Thompson never pushed the idea that W2 was implemented to build the knowledge base of social policy, as the waivers had originally been designed to do. Thompson took the position that the states had a right to run their own social programs and that severely restricting welfare benefits was good social policy. The waivers were simply a cumbersome means to that end.

In contrast, the Florida legislation grew out of a very open process. A number of political and professional interest groups were involved in a study commission for reforming welfare that preceded the bill. The report issued by the commission became the foundation of the Family Transition Act, which authorized the FTP. In its final report, the study commission offered several key recommendations.[3] First, it endorsed time-limited welfare both as a practical means of cutting costs and as a social message. The report emphasized the importance of making welfare assistance transitional, rather than a long-term support program. A number of social service providers were involved in the commission, and their views were reflected in the commission's recommendations of intensive social services during the period of welfare receipt. The commission's report was reminiscent of the early Kennedy administration's ad hoc committee recommendation to increase the role of social workers in order to offer "the total resources of the community to meet the total needs of the family to help our less fortunate citizens help themselves."[4]

The political strategy for welfare reform in Florida was inclusive. The legislature sought out the views of diverse interest groups and formalized participation of these groups in the policy-making process through the study commission and its report. By involving groups that could potentially oppose welfare reform in the policy-making process, the state legislature minimized the opposition to the FTP. In the legislature itself, there were open and wide-ranging debates among members that helped to promote strong bipartisan support for the bill.[5] Florida's open and inclusive bipartisan process was a stark contrast to the closed and deeply political Wisconsin process of developing welfare policy in "the war room." Following the openness of the political process in Florida, the FTP legislation provided for community oversight of the program and the evaluation component of the pilot was taken very seriously. Florida, therefore, was not only the first time-limited welfare experiment; it was also a welfare experiment that seemed to fit the evaluation model of pilot programs outside of partisan politics. Building the knowledge base of social policy was one of the goals of the FTP. There were, however, political and ideological goals as well.

Florida's Family Transition Program

Florida had not historically been an innovator in social policy. With the FTP, however, Florida became the first state in the nation to test welfare time limits. The summary of the bill, passed in 1993, noted that the FTP was to be a model for national welfare reform: "This bill establishes the Family Transition Program (FTP). FTP is a national trend-setting program that provides short-term intensive services designed to move a person from welfare dependency to employment and self-sufficiency."[6]

The Family Transition Act established two models of the Family

Transition Program, one in which client participation was voluntary and the other in which client participation was mandatory. The voluntary model was implemented in Alachua County, which includes Gainesville. The mandatory model was implemented in Escambia County, which includes Pensacola. The voluntary program attracted few participants and was almost immediately abandoned by Florida as a model for welfare reform.[7] Because of the small size and political marginality of the voluntary model, the federally mandated evaluation of the FTP focused on the mandatory model.

In 1994, the success of the FTP was politically important for incumbent Florida governor Lawton Chiles. Widespread public dissatisfaction and even anger over AFDC made advocating welfare reform politically useful, particularly for "New Democrats" who sought to distance themselves from the more liberal social policies of their predecessors.[8] One journalist noted right before the 1992 election: "Bill Clinton's call for time limits on AFDC benefits hits the right political notes and places him in the forefront of an emerging political consensus."[9] In 1993, advancing welfare reform was a powerful political position.

During the tight 1994 gubernatorial race between Chiles and Jeb Bush, the *St. Petersburg Times* ran a series of articles based on the "Voices of Florida," a project sponsored by several Florida newspapers. Voters were asked to let the newspapers know what issues were important to them. In response, the *St. Petersburg Times* published the candidates' positions on the top ten issues that readers ranked as being important. Welfare reform was the second issue covered. Chiles pointed directly to the FTP and its leading role in welfare reform in his response: "We have two of the largest welfare reform pilot programs in the nation under way in our state. . . . The Family Transition Program provides the tools that men and women need to get off welfare and get a real job."[10]

According to a source in the Clinton administration involved in the waiver negotiations, the officials in the Department of Health and Human Services (HHS) were sensitive to the importance of the FTP in the gubernatorial race. HHS moved quickly to approve the waiver, although not without first insisting on some significant modifications.[11] In 1994, a year when Democratic incumbents lost in historic proportion, and in a state that was shifting to the political right, Chiles defeated Bush in the gubernatorial election by a slim margin. Welfare reform was an important part of that win.

The Waiver Negotiations

In 1993, AFDC was still federal law and in order to implement the FTP Florida had to apply to the federal government for waivers from aspects of the Social Security Act. Numerous governors complained about having to go to Washington and "Kiss the King's Ring" in order to move forward with state welfare programs.[12] The key sticking point between officials in the HHS and the state of Florida was the presumption that all welfare recipients would be employed by the time limit if they "played by the rules" and actively sought to become independent. This difference encapsulated the national debate between work-trigger and benefit-termination time limits. For many members of the Florida legislature, firm time limits were a necessary "stick" to make welfare reform work. The time limit was part of a larger message about personal responsibility. As one Florida state representative commented during debate on the Family Transition Act:

We are trying to put in, or at least send out, the message that there is a limit. We're gonna give you increased benefits, we're gonna give you the carrot, the extended Medicaid, the childcare provision, the extensive training. . . . We are gonna give you everything we can to get you back on your feet. But you've got to understand as a part of that contract that we get you on your feet, there is going to be an obligation on your part and that's that we can no longer afford to fund you coming back on the program unless there is truly an extraordinary circumstance.[13]

At the end of the two-year time limit, participants in the FTP were supposed to be self-sufficient.

Representative Cynthia Chestnut (23-D), a sponsor of the bill, emphasized the importance of making the participants "whole" before the end of the time limit in order to avoid the need for assistance.

Within the twenty-four month period, there will be six month periodic check ups with the caseworker so that the caseworker is aware of what the person needs to make them whole, if you will. So then the caseworker will be providing those services. If a person has gone through a training, a community college, they are about to finish . . . to graduate four months from now, we would then be able to extend those benefits. That would be the case-by-case review and then the Review Panel would have the option of looking at that information and extending [the benefits]. We don't anticipate a lot of those extension cases.[14]

Chestnut's use of the term "check ups" reflects a therapeutic understanding of the FTP that permeated the language of Florida politicians.

Her comments suggest that with proper "treatment" FTP participants would be self-sufficient by the end of the time limit. Chestnut envisioned situations, largely the result of mismatched administrative calendars, in which a participant might need additional time to complete a course necessary for her employability. Her vision of welfare reform, however, was that, done rightly, it would place welfare families in jobs without encountering significant problems. This reflected a marked turn away from the structural understanding of poverty that had dominated welfare policy since the War on Poverty.

The premise of the FTP was that two years of public assistance was enough. The Family Transition Act stipulated that participants in the FTP could not receive public assistance for more than twenty-four months in any sixty-month period, or thirty-six out of seventy-two months for recipients who were considered to be particularly disadvantaged.[15] During the two to three years of assistance, the participant and the department were to establish and execute an "employability plan" that would enable the participant to be self-sufficient by the time limit.[16]

The Citizen Review Panel formalized the role of external interest groups in the FTP in much the same way that the study commission had formalized the role of interest groups in the policy-making process leading up to the passage of the Family Transition Act. The panel was established to hear cases of participants who were failing in the FTP. The review panel members were to evaluate whether the FTP was providing failing participants with sufficient social services to help them reach self-sufficiency.

By law, participants failing to meet the FTP requirements were to be sent to the review panel every nine months. The law also gave the review panel the authority to grant two four-month benefit extensions to participants who had "substantially" met the requirements of the program and were having "extraordinary" difficulty obtaining employment. It was left to the review panel to determine the meanings of "substantially" and "extraordinary"; these terms were not defined in the law. If the panel found that the agency had not provided a participant with sufficient services, the law granted the panel the power to void or modify the participant's time limit. All determinations by the panel were to be made independently of the welfare department.

Officials in the Clinton administration's HHS did not share the state of Florida's faith that all FTP participants who worked with the program would be self-sufficient by the end of their two-year time limit. In

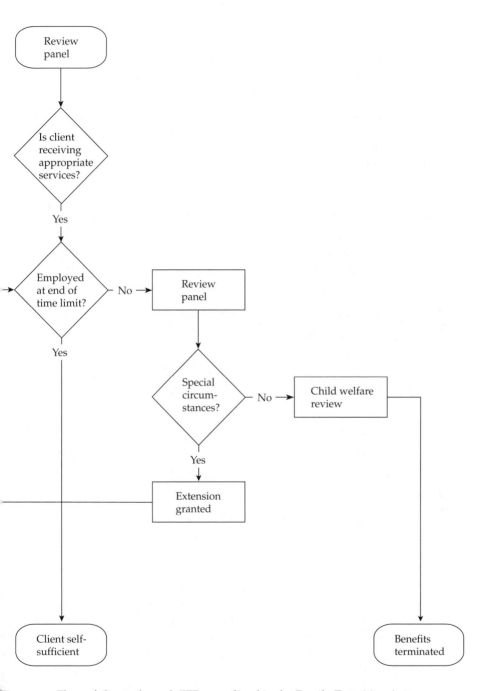

Figure 4.1 Flow of clients through FTP as outlined in the Family Transition Act

a letter to James Towey, secretary of Florida's Department of Health and Rehabilitative Service (HRS), Mary Jo Bane wrote:

[T]he principal issue for us is the question of what happens to people who participate fully and in good faith with all the program's requirements but are still unable, through no fault of their own, to find a job before the time limit expires. We are concerned about the prospects of such individuals and would like to discuss whether Florida would agree to adding a job guarantee to the demonstration.[17]

In 1993, HHS was still not approving waivers with benefit-termination time limits. Wendell Primus, former deputy assistant secretary for Human Services Policy in the Office of the Assistant Secretary for Planning and Evaluation, explained, "We resisted all through '93 and '94 approving waivers that weren't 'play-by-the-rule'"[18] The Clinton administration was firmly committed to advancing work-trigger time limits.

"Self-sufficiency" was defined as a participant earning the welfare grant plus ninety dollars (AFDC + 90), $393 a month for a family of three.[19] The rationale behind setting the standard for "self-sufficiency" at this level was that former welfare recipients who were earning at least what they had received in their welfare grant, plus ninety dollars for work expenses, would be able to maintain their standard of living without public assistance if they were earning a comparable amount. One problem with this definition of "self-sufficiency" is that it did not take into consideration the monetary value of the loss of time for welfare recipients who moved into the paid workforce.[20] For example, the ability of mothers to exchange baby-sitting and other in-kind goods and services may be reduced when they go to work. An assessment of lost in-kind exchanges as well as work expenses would have been useful in determining a minimum "self-sufficiency" income. Within the FTP, however, "self-sufficiency" was defined simply as earning at least AFDC plus ninety.

In a fax to the U.S. Department of Health and Human Services Administration for Children and Families, the Department of Health and Rehabilitative Services for the state of Florida raised some concerns over the HHS's request that a job guarantee be incorporated into the FTP. "In the initial response to Florida's waiver request, the Administration for Children and Families raised the question of the state's willingness adding [*sic*] a job guarantee to the program. . . . [T]he Act received broad bipartisan support from the legislature. A job guarantee provision could be a very divisive issue and could erode legislative support. It is not at all certain that a modification requiring legislative approval would pass."[21] In addition to changing the character of the FTP, the transitional employment program was potentially expensive. Although the waiver identified the ideal transitional employment as being based in the private sector, some sort of employer subsidy or public jobs program would almost certainly have been necessary for such a program. Participants who were unable to find or be placed in jobs prior to reaching their time limit would most likely not be good candidates for placement in private, unsubsidized employment after the time limit.

Budgetary Constraints

Florida's concern about guaranteeing employment to compliant participants was rooted in fiscal realities. If, over the five-year demonstration, the FTP cost more than traditional AFDC would have, the state of Florida would have been financially responsible for the surplus costs—a provision known as cost neutrality. The federal government imposed this requirement on waiver-authorized pilot programs to contain the cost to the federal government of experimenting with welfare reform.

Going over budget is never good for the reputations and careers of program administrators, but it would have been particularly bad in the FTP. As with many welfare reform efforts in the early 1990s, saving money was an explicit goal of the FTP. The FTP handbook for review panel members lists "[l]ong range cost savings to the state and federal government" as one of the four primary objectives of the FTP.[22] The job guarantee mandated by the federal government, therefore, potentially held both political and financial costs for the FTP.

In correspondence with the Department of Health and Human Services Administration for Children and Families (HHS / AFC), Florida officials expressed concern that a mandated job guarantee would make it impossible for the FTP to meet the cost neutrality provision. "Any job guarantee that is based on continued AFDC eligibility (for example community work experience with continued AFDC receipt) would not meet the parameters of the state law. Even if such an extension were possible, it would affect the ability of the demonstrations to meet federal cost neutrality provisions."[23] Not persuaded by Florida's objections, the federal government stuck to its position that no family on welfare should completely lose its benefits if the parent was willing to work and was cooperating fully with the welfare agency.

With little choice but to accept the federal request for what was in effect a job guarantee, the state of Florida developed a strategy to ensure that as few compliant participants as possible reached the time limit without adequate employment. Florida suggested, and the federal government agreed, that any person reaching the end of the time limit could be designated as "hard to place" and therefore eligible for JOBS-funded employer incentive payments. One appeal of this approach was that JOBS money is both capped and separate from the money used to fund the FTP. In other words, by using JOBS money, the state of Florida shifted limited federal resources away from other AFDC recipients to provide more services in the FTP without increasing the cost of the FTP on paper or affecting the program's cost neutrality. Ultimately, the state of Florida agreed to add a "work opportunity," but avoided the term "job guarantee," for compliant participants who reached the time limit without being self-sufficient. The term "work opportunity" was a rhetorical retreat from the contentious "job guarantee" but it amounted to the same thing. Florida agreed to give compliant participants who reached the time limit without a job "an opportunity to work" for which they would be given money. The details of the "work opportunity" were not specified. With that concession, however, the HHS approved the waivers for the FTP.

The budgetary importance of not allowing too many FTP participants to receive benefits past the time limit was also a factor in the procedure developed by the FTP for granting four-month benefit extensions. The state of Florida's concern that too many extensions could jeopardize cost neutrality is explicitly outlined in an internal HRS memo on the procedure for extension requests.

Two other factors that come into play with extensions are the FTP performance indicator and cost neutrality. Our FTP performance indicator states that 85% of FTP participants will be off AFDC prior to their assigned time limit. For any case going beyond the time limit due to an extension we are affecting our cost neutrality. Cost neutrality is measured by comparing the money spent assisting participants in achieving self-sufficiency against money saved by getting them off AFDC.[24]

The extension procedure memo also suggests that the program administrators recognized that the agency itself, not the review panel, would be primarily responsible for keeping the number of extensions granted low. "The only reason for giving the above information [on cost neutrality] is to emphasize the importance of carefully reviewing extension requests prior to concurring. Once we concur, as representatives of the program, the panel is most likely going to agree with granting the extension."[25] By explicitly linking the financial integrity of the FTP with the actions of FTP administrators and staff involved in the extension procedure, ostensibly the domain of the review panel, this memo defines granting extensions as an agency failure. It also assumes that the panel is not going to play a large or independent role in granting extensions.

These communications on post-time-limit jobs and benefit extensions show that preserving cost neutrality was a central concern for the administrators of the FTP. Granting post-time-limit benefits in any number could be expensive and undermine both the cost-saving goal of the program and the "message" that the FTP was a new program with reciprocal obligations and a firm time limit. It would also run counter to the program's performance indicator, which set the benchmark at having 85 percent of welfare recipients off welfare *before* they reached the time limit. Yet the federal waiver accepted by the state of Florida was clear: Post-time-limit benefits were to be provided to compliant participants who were unable to find adequate employment by the time limit. This tension within the FTP between the benefit-termination model of time limits and the work-trigger model would ultimately be up to the FTP administrators to resolve. Arguably, FTP evaluators had an obligation to clearly report how administrators resolved this tension and to clearly identify exactly *which* policy idea the FTP was testing, work-trigger or benefit-termination time limits. If policy evaluators borrow the clinical tools and language of experimentation, for example having treatment and control groups, in order to assess the outcome produced by the treatment, then the nature of that treatment must be clear. The precision of experimental methodology makes no sense if the nature of the treatment is obscured. There may be a political value in having hard numbers on the outcome produced by a vague and shifting policy "treatment" but it is a bastardization of the experimental method.

The waiver itself reiterated the role of the review panel, outlined in the law, in granting benefit extensions. It states that the review panel shall recommend extensions when:

[The] participant has substantially complied with the FTP plan and either (a) the state has substantially failed to provide sufficient services as specified in the FTP employability plan, (b) the participant would benefit from additional education and training in a way that is likely to contribute significantly to her (or his) immediate employment prospects or (c) the participant has encountered extraordinary difficulties in obtaining employment or in completing her (or his) employability plan.[26]

The terms and conditions of the waiver also stipulated that the state had to provide jobs, preferably in the private sector, to FTP participants who had "diligently completed" the employability plan but had been unable to find employment.

The state, in conjunction with businesses in the pilot counties, will design a transitional employment program to provide private sector employment opportunities for each FTP participant who has diligently completed her (or his) self-sufficiency plan but has been unable to find employment at the end of the AFDC time limit. . . . If private sector employment is insufficient to meet the needs of the program, the state will provide the opportunity for public sector employment.[27]

This provided the job guarantee for participants who "diligently completed" their employability plan.

Finally, the waiver modified the panel's authority by stipulating that the district administrator would have the final say on benefit-termination. This provision addressed concerns that a citizen panel should not have the sole power to extend or terminate government benefits. As one person involved in the negotiations on behalf of Florida explained:

There was an attorney, of course, on the fed side that had a lot of those types of questions [about having a citizen panel make the final determination on benefit-termination]. And we met with Mary Jo Bane and company in one of the tables, you know, longer than a ship. We figured that [having the district administrator make the final decision on benefit-termination] was no big deal because the DA's gonna go along with the recommendation of the review panel. . . . [28]

The district administrator had to sign off on all review panel recommendations, limiting its power in theory. The assumption during the waiver negotiations, however, was that in practice the district administrator would routinely approve panel recommendations, leaving the power with the review panel.

In a letter to Assistant Secretary Mary Jo Bane dated October 26, 1993, Mark Greenberg, senior staff attorney for the Center for Law and

Social Policy (CLASP) expressed the concern that the safeguard was insufficient.

The state has incorporated a set of ostensible "safeguards" by providing for review of cases by private citizens and the District Administrator. These "safeguards" would ultimately result in a system in which a family's ability to receive continued assistance would largely depend on a parent's ability to persuade private citizens of her worthiness, or on her ability to accurately and sympathetically describe why loss of cash assistance would have a catastrophic effect.[29]

Greenberg articulated the fear that the radical decentralization of authority in welfare administration—in this case away from the federal government and into the hands of ordinary citizens—had the potential to bring back the worst aspects of discretion. Implicit in Greenberg's letter is the fear that racial discrimination might play a role in the panel's decisions. The history of welfare administration in America provides substantial examples of discrimination in welfare administration. It is remarkable that one of the first programs to break away from the centralization imposed on AFDC by the courts as a result of discrimination placed discretionary power in the hands of local citizens in the rural South. There is no evidence that this was a part of any thought-out political strategy. It appears to have been almost accidental. Symbolically, however, it was a powerful turn away from post-civil right concerns and toward states' rights politics that rejects racism as a relic of the past.

The FTP, as modified through the federal waiver, provided three ways for a participant to receive benefits after the time limit: (1) four-month benefit extensions, (2) Transitional Employment (publicly provided jobs), (3) voided or modified time limits. The first two provisions were dependent on the participant's "substantial" and "diligent" cooperation with the program—vague terms not defined in the law or the waiver. The third provision was only for use in cases where the FTP had not provided appropriate services.

Before the FTP even began, it was at the nexus of competing views on the nature of poverty. The Clinton administration believed that some people who played by the rules would still be unable to find a job and become self-sufficient. The administration wanted to enforce work and encourage independence. It was willing to see families cut off the rolls for failing to cooperate with the program, but it did not view continued financial need or dependency as a sign that a family was "undeserving."

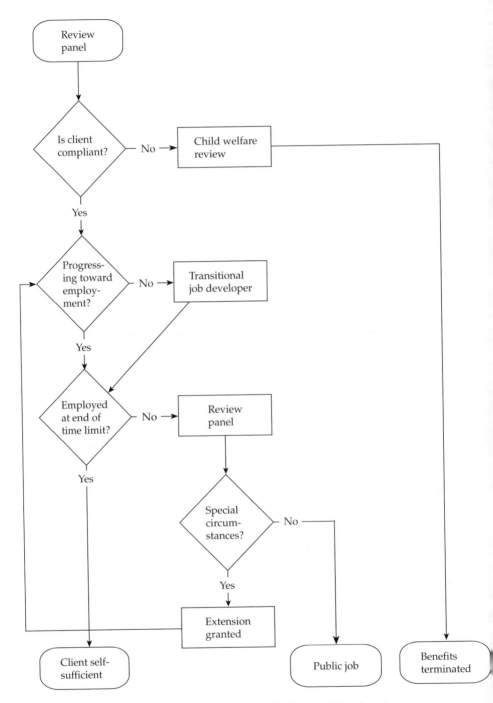

Figure 4.2 Flow of clients through FTP as amended by the federal waiver

In the Florida legislature, a mix of ideologies brought about the firm time limit in the Family Transition Act. There were some conservative members of the legislature who believed the fewer people on welfare the better, period. Others focused on the pragmatic aspects of the pilots, such as meeting federal cost neutrality requirements. Liberal members of the Florida legislature appear to have been willing to trade off enriched services for time limits. Yet there was little concern expressed during the debates by any member, liberal or conservative, over what would happen to families once they reached the time limit. Unlike the Clinton administration, the prevailing view within the Florida legislature was that anyone could fall on hard times for a short period, but that long-term dependency was a choice and, particularly if the state provided enriched social services for a period, evidence in itself that an individual was "undeserving." The Florida legislature thought that long-term poverty was a choice that welfare recipients could be discouraged from making.

Was long-term poverty a choice? Would some people need help after the time limit? These questions were at the heart of welfare reform. And they were not simply empirical questions. They were tied to the ideological politics around welfare that would become even more heated after the 1994 Republican takeover of Congress. Fundamental questions around the nature of poverty and the role of the state could not fully be resolved in the waiver negotiations. They would be sorted out in the street-level implementation of the pilots themselves.

Implementation

The Clinton administration's approval of Florida's experimental welfare program was widely covered by the media. Media coverage emphasized the similarities between the Florida program and the president's proposal for welfare reform. The *Los Angeles Times* reported: "The Administration approved an experiment in two Florida counties Thursday that will give poor people a taste of the reforms that President Clinton is advocating for the entire country. The experimental programs will put a two-year time limit on public assistance benefits and require recipients to work, two of the basic principles of Clinton's welfare strategy."[30] The same day the *Orlando Sentinel* reported, "A senior administration official said that Florida's demonstration project is significant because it mirrors President Clinton's. . . . "[31]

Similar stories ran in the *Oregonian*, the *New Orleans Times-Picayune*, and throughout the country. A few weeks after the FTP's approval, the *Washington Post* ran an in-depth article entitled "North Floridians Are Pioneers In Clinton-Like Welfare Program."[32] The FTP was "Clinton-Like" because the architects of the Clinton plan were also in charge of approving state waivers. They had inserted aspects of the Clinton plan, notably the job guarantee, into the FTP.

The FTP received a lot of media attention, much of it emphasizing the connection to the Clinton plan and the experimental nature of the program. For example, on June 14, 1994, the FTP was featured on CBS's *Eye on America*. Dan Rather introduced the segment. He also emphasized the relationship between the FTP and President Clinton's welfare reform plans: "Earlier in this broadcast, we reported about President Clinton's plan to overhaul the welfare system. A key element in the Clinton plan is a lifetime limit on cash benefits. The key question: Can it work? For answers Congress and the administration may be looking to Florida."

The FTP began under intense public scrutiny. A high-level Escambia County administrator explained, "It was an almost instantaneous spotlight involved from the very first client. The media cranked. The politicians cranked. . . . That is always an amazing thing that in one month one could expect welfare reform to have anything. But those are the kinda things we face. I mean, almost boom, instantly."[33] The FTP began very quickly. It had numerous start-up problems that were widely acknowledged by administrators and staff.[34] As one top administrator explained: "The governor all of a sudden one day said this is the day we'll start. We took in our first participant. I know you've heard that old story. We didn't have the computers. We didn't have the space. . . . "[35] Top state and federal officials had spent considerable time and effort negotiating the waivers, the governor of Florida had campaigned on the program, major media sources ran prominent stories on the program, and yet there were not enough computers or space for the program to operate.

The FTP was driven by politics, not the needs of experimental design. A senior FTP administrator commented on the political nature of the FTP's early start:

[I]n the political arena you really can't do anything 'til the politicians pull the triggers. And we have all said that we began in February of '94 and we really should have started in May or June of '94. But we were told to start in February

'94 and we started in February '94. And it's somewhere around September ['94] before we have the first wave of employees. So it was somewhere around September of '94, having started in February '94, before we really had the space used and the personnel on board in place.[36]

Despite the start-up problems, on October 31, 1994, right before the gubernatorial election, Governor Lawton Chiles proposed to expand the FTP beyond Escambia and Alachua Counties to other Florida counties, proclaiming in the *St. Petersburg Times* that "[t]he Family Transition Programs have been nationally recognized for their successful, aggressive reform."[37]

In the media spotlight and underprepared, the FTP began operating in February 1994, just one month after the federal waivers had been granted. It was not until May 1994 that the FTP was established well enough to begin taking in significant numbers of participants. As the FTP staff and administrators struggled to build a new program, they were constantly being asked to provide information to the media and politicians. A report from the federally mandated evaluation noted, "[T]he program has been in the spotlight since its inception, and managers and staff have fielded a continual stream of inquiries and requests for information from legislators, the media, and officials in other counties and states, among others. As one staff member put it, working in FTP is 'like working in a glass house.'"[38] From the beginning, it was clear that the FTP would succeed or fail very publicly. State senator Tom Rossin (D-West Palm Beach) commented, "Hopefully it [the FTP] works. If the expectations are this high, you can really fall off a cliff."[39]

The Program

The FTP law and the federal waivers contained competing visions of welfare reform and the nature of the time limit. On the one hand, the legislative intent was for the program to have a firm time limit. The cultural assumption underlying this vision was that anyone, with hard work and the proper assistance, could become self-sufficient within a couple of years. The program outlined by the federal waivers looked very different. In this program, welfare recipients who cooperated with the FTP were guaranteed a job. The time limit in the waivers was a work-trigger time limit, as the time limit in Clinton's welfare reform proposal had been. The state of Florida had financial and ideological incentives for staying with its original policy. It had agreed, however, to the federal provisions as a requirement for being granted the waiver. Finally, thrown into this mix was a wild card—the Citizen Review Panel.

The review panel had the potential to remake the program. Much like jury nullification, the panel could have decided that *everyone* was eligible for a public job and nullified the time limit. Alternatively, the panel could have decided that only particular situations warranted that a participant be granted a public job. For example, it could have used its discretion to rule out women who did not comply with the "family ethic," which, Mimi Abramovitz has argued, shaped welfare so dramatically in the past.[40] The panel could have continued the racial discrimination—holding black and white recipients to different standards—practiced in many parts of the South before the courts enforced a bureaucratic model of welfare administration in the 1970s. Following the focus of the mid-1990s welfare reform debate and the New Paternalist ideology, the panel could have based its decision on the participants' work efforts. The panel had the power, at least on paper, to define "playing by the rules" in a number of ways, each of which could have had a profound impact on the size and demographic makeup of the public jobs program.

When the program was implemented, however, the panel did not have any impact on who received public jobs. The waiver provision for public jobs was administratively eliminated. There were no public jobs. This was an extraordinary shift in the policy. How did it happen?

The program on paper still had a work-trigger time limit. To implement a work-trigger time limit *without* a job guarantee, it was necessary to define all unemployed clients as noncompliant and therefore ineligible for the job guarantee. If at the end of the time limit, someone was unemployed *and* compliant, they were guaranteed a job; but the FTP defined anyone unemployed at the end of the time limit as *noncompliant*, thereby eliminating the guarantee. Reverting back to the law did not simply void the provision negotiated in the federal waiver. It recast the terms of the welfare debate.

In a front page *New York Times* article on the Family Transition Program, Jason DeParle reported: "[T]he program pledged public jobs to recipients who cooperated by seeking work or training but remain unemployed. Forty-seven out of one hundred and thirty people who have exhausted their limits have shown such cooperation. But to officials' surprise, *not one* has needed a public job."[41] The FTP appeared to be a test of the Clinton plan that provided evidence for the congressional Republican plan. This was a critical point in the welfare debate: How

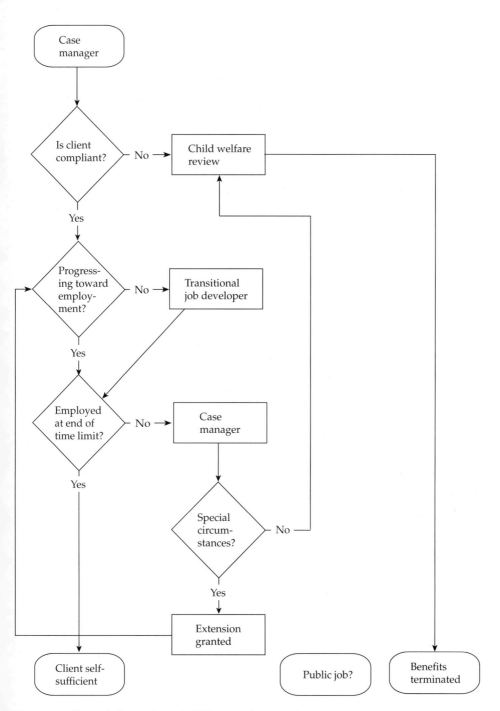

Figure 4.3 Flow of clients through FTP as implemented

many people who acted in "good faith" and "played by the rules" would need continued assistance after the time limit?

As Kent Weaver has noted, one use of policy research is as "fire alarms."[42] Research can highlight danger areas. I think it is fair to argue that many Americans believe that sounding an alarm is one of the key functions of research, particularly experimental research. In 2002, a large study on hormone replacement therapy was halted because of evidence that the treatment caused harm. Many American women heard this as an alarm bell rung by scientists to alert the public to the potential hazards of hormone replacement. In fact, scientists took the opportunity to address the American public about the risks and benefits of hormone replacement through the media. The absence of negative information in the media can appear to be like a fire alarm that is not ringing, a benign and virtually unnoticed signal that everything is normal.

If a fire alarm has been installed, the fact that a bell is not ringing conveys information. There is no fire. The silence of high profile policy experiments conveys information about the programs; everything is proceeding as expected and there are no adverse consequences to the "treatment." Americans trust scientists to tell us if they are finding anything of public importance. The lawsuits against cigarette manufacturers provide a good example of the faith that Americans have in scientists. One of the greatest sources of outrage is that the industry scientists knew that cigarettes were bad for people's health and yet this information was not disclosed to the American public. Even in the context of corporate science—science performed for the express purpose of increasing companies' profits—the American public held the expectation that the rules of science should triumph over the rules of commerce; all relevant findings should be reported openly.

As FTP participants began to reach the time limits, Jack Levine of Florida's Center for Children and Youth, a child advocacy group, told the *St. Petersburg Times* "[The FTP] is our first experiment, and if there are failures to the project, they will start to show now."[43] On the surface, the empirical test of work-trigger time limits seemed to prove that advocates of benefit-termination time limits were right—everyone who made a good faith effort found a job. The treatment had been fairly applied and the results were being clearly reported. Based on the existing, albeit minimal evidence, time limits appeared only to remove the undeserving from the roles. Thus, it was a fair assumption that the deserving poor would not be hurt by the new welfare law. The alarm bell did not ring. In Florida, however, the wires had been cut.[44]

The outcomes for the first cohort are summarized below. MDRC had not determined the outcome for one participant at the time of the report.

Public jobs	0
Official termination	137
Self-sufficient	90
Protective payee for child	9
Total	237

How the Job Guarantee was Eliminated

In the FTP, "noncompliant" participants could have their benefits terminated at the time limit even if they were unemployed. Therefore, the FTP could avoid the transitional employment provision as long as no "compliant" participants reached the time limit without a job. There were two ways to accomplish this. First, the program could make sure that everyone who reached the time limit had a job. This clearly was the preferred option within the FTP, and both staff and administrators worked very hard at securing a participant's employment. There was, however, a second way for the program to meet the requirements of the letter, if not the spirit, of the federal waiver without providing public jobs. The program could make sure that no participant was both "compliant" and unemployed at the time limit. Having employment could become a criterion of "compliance." Over the five years of the FTP's implementation, no one was both "compliant" and unemployed. No public jobs were provided.

Defining Compliance

There was no formula within the FTP to determine a participant's compliance. FTP supervisors described the process of making these decisions with generous use of equivocating phrases such as "I guess" and "basically." Some cases, according to staff, were clearly noncompliant; these included participants who missed the majority of their appointments and generally refused to cooperate with the staff. There were, however, cases where a participant's compliance was not clear-cut. As one supervisor explained:

Some of them you have to weigh them, do they have more compliance or do they have more non-compliance. For some of them, it is really hard to say. And a lot of times they do have non-compliance, but they are good cause [noncompliances], but it [the participant's compliance] is still doubtful. So sometimes you have to weigh it.

One key factor in determining a participant's compliance was whether she had been sanctioned. Welfare recipients were sanctioned for not participating in mandatory programs, such as job training. When an FTP participant was "sanctioned," her portion of the family's grant was removed. AFDC and FTP grants were based on family size. Therefore, a sanctioned family of three would receive the amount of money typically given to a family of two.[45] Sanctioning was used in both the traditional AFDC program and in the FTP. FTP participants, however, had more requirements than did AFDC recipients. There were therefore more opportunities for the participants to miss appointments and receive a sanction.

Being sanctioned in the FTP did not automatically mean that a participant was classified as noncompliant. As one supervisor noted:

Basically, if the person is sanctioned for one time, if they're pretty much compliant with us and that might have been just a slip up or just a one time thing, normally we don't [take them to the panel]. Basically we try to look at the number of non-compliances and no-shows and non-cooperations in comparison to cooperation. That is the biggest factor that we look at. When there is any doubt, we normally take them [to the review panel].

Review panel members, although officially responsible for determining a participant's compliance status, were also unsure about the criteria for compliance. For example, when asked whether the meaning of the term "compliance" was clear to him, one panel member responded:

No. And the reason it is not is because it depends on the case manager and the caseworker. I've seen—yesterday I saw two cases that I know if the case manager and the case worker that I had heard prior had had those two cases both of those persons would have some problems, there would be some sanctions. . . . [I]t is just a matter of the luck of the draw.

In addition to being unclear on the criteria for compliance, review panel members, as illustrated by the above quote, tended to view compliance as being established by the case managers, rather than by the panel itself. As discussed further in Chapter Five, panel members, including the one quoted above, often used the terms "sanctioned" and "noncompliant" interchangeably. There was a high level of confusion over the meaning of compliance.

Sanctioning took place before the time limit and affected recipients' grants. Compliance was an assessment of a person's overall work with the FTP—whether they made a "good faith" effort and "played by the rules"—that determined their eligibility for a public job at the time limit. Case managers were sometimes unable to sanction a participant, for example, because she was pregnant, but still felt that the participant was noncompliant because of her actions or attitude.[46] One supervisor explained:

> As far as the panel is concerned a lot of factors are looked at, OK? It is the compliances outweighing the non-compliances. It is the attitude, basically, of the client. If the client, to me, does not want to participate, they are showing no interest whatsoever, they are just refusing, they want to do what they want to do, they are not working with us. I say that's a good reason to take them to the panel because the panel needs to see that and it needs to be documented.

As the panel members' use of the term "compliance" demonstrates, the panel did not understand the definitions of key terms within the FTP. Sanctions were a long-time part of AFDC. Case managers determined them in AFDC and the FTP. The review panel had nothing to do with that procedure. Compliance, however, was a critical term in the new welfare pilot program—it determined a person's rights after the time limit. The review panel had a central role in determining compliance. But most members of the panel did not know that.

Establishing Noncompliance

Bringing participants to the panel evolved into the means of establishing "noncompliance" within the FTP. Every month, case managers, career advisors, and their supervisors held "prestaffing" meetings to discuss problem cases, identified by a case manager or career advisor, and to decide which cases should be sent to the review panel. Participants who were approaching their ninth, eighteenth, or (for participants with three-year time limits) twenty-seventh month received the most attention. Overwhelmingly, participants were sent to the review panel for not complying with the FTP. According to staff, a few participants who were complying with the program but not making sufficient progress were also sent to the review panel. "Compliant," nonprogressing cases, however, do not appear to have been treated any differently by the review panel than "noncompliant" cases. A review of review panel recommendations found that all participants who came before it were advised to reassess their noncompliance and warned that their benefits could be terminated. Six months before the time limit, noncompliant participants in the FTP were sent back to the review panel in order for it to recommend that the participant's benefits be terminated at the time limit.[47] Staff assessments of a participant's compliance status were always supported by the panel. In practice, therefore, the staff decision to bring a participant to the panel established that participant's noncompliance.

Employment and Compliance

Participants earning the self-sufficiency level income (AFDC + $90) in fairly stable jobs were brought to the review panel less frequently than those without steady employment because those participants would not be eligible for an extension or public job regardless of their compliance status. One supervisor noted, "If they are making the grant plus ninety, then they shouldn't go to the panel because when the grant ends, they will just roll right off." In contrast, the FTP staff often brought participants to the review panel who were reaching the end of their time limit without adequate employment. One supervisor explained, "If they are progressing with no job, that is scary. We will probably staff them [in preparation for the review panel]." Supervisors were extremely concerned about having a client reach the time limit without earning AFDC + $90 or appearing before the review panel. When asked what would happen if a client who had not been to the review panel reached the time limit without adequate employment, one supervisor seemed unclear about the ramifications of such a case. She knew, however, that she did not want to find out: "I wouldn't want to be the supervisor on that case. Let's put it that way. Oh God, I don't know what would happen. I would not want that to happen." This supervisor's comments are striking. The federal waiver made clear provisions for such clients—they were to be placed in a post-time-limit job by the state. The state of Florida agreed to this provision but would not use it.

The review panel served as the mechanism through which the FTP administratively eliminated the job guarantee. The panel members accepted this role unquestioningly. The composition of the review panel, which was weighted toward social service professionals, the personal networks used to recruit people to the panel, and the administrative methods of funneling information to and from the panel—discussed further in Chapter Five—all contributed to a review panel that served more as a rubber stamp than a safeguard. In the end, the review panel obscured the administrative choices made by the FTP.

Testing Time Limits?

The FTP was publicly set up as a test of "Clinton-like" work-trigger time limits. As Dan Rather told the nation, the FTP was going to answer the question: Can it work? In practice, though, the program did not have a work-trigger time limit. A central part of what it was purported to test was not there. How could this be?

The administrative elimination of the job guarantee is easy to understand by looking at the program in its political context. The Florida legislature never wanted the job guarantee. The Transitional Employment provision was forced on them by the Department of Health and Human Services. The explicit and approved goal of the FTP was to get participants off the welfare rolls—85 percent of them *before* the time limit. If time-limited welfare was not truly time limited, that would risk the perception that there was a flaw either in the premise of the policy as it was designed by the state legislature or in its implementation at the local level. Both interpretations would threaten the legitimacy of the program.

Additionally, in order to implement the post-time-limit "work opportunity" for any number of participants, the FTP would have had to create a public jobs program. To build such a program would have been both practically difficult and politically dangerous. In 1994, the Republican revolution of smaller government, not larger government, occurred. Finally, post-time-limit benefits could jeopardize the fiscal integrity of the program. One of the stated goals of the FTP was cost savings. Therefore, granting post-time-limit benefits in any number would have undermined the program at three levels: ideologically, structurally, and fiscally. Ideologically, it would cast doubt on the premise of time-limited welfare embedded in the Family Transition Act— that anyone who tries can become self-sufficient in a few years. Structurally, it would have required the creation of an untested public jobs program that might not be viewed as legitimate state action. Fiscally, the expense of providing post-time-limit benefits would have jeopardized the FTP's cost neutrality.

There was a policy feedback loop between state programs that trumpeted their ability to get people off welfare with little to no increased human suffering by the time limit—often before the time limit—and policies based on the idea that such goals could reasonably be achieved. The political reasons why the "work-trigger" time limit in the FTP was in fact a "benefit-termination" time limit, therefore, are clear; the state legislature, local administrators and, by 1996, Congress, were all backing benefit-termination time limits. In a political framework, what happened administratively in the FTP is easily understandable. But by looking at the FTP in its political context, we violate the assumptions underlying the notion that the pilots were a *clinical test* of welfare reform ideas. We assume that the *treatment* is subject to political pressures.

In the FTP, the "treatment" on paper was work-trigger time limits. In practice, the "treatment" was benefit-termination time limits. It is inconceivable to have a pharmaceutical trial in which the treatment on paper is penicillin and in practice is erythromycin. It is not inconceivable, however, in social policy to have a program appear to be quite different in practice than it is on paper. It is inevitable. How then, should we evaluate social programs? Do evaluators have an obligation to make clear the nature of the "treatment" in a social experiment? How does one objectively determine the "treatment" when informal administrative procedures shape a program as much as or more than formal policy? In introducing a greater emphasis on the subjective aspects of policy evaluation, do we go down a slippery slope? Is there a risk to the professional authority of evaluators and social scientists? Will everyone simply "be entitled to his or her own statistic" or can we maintain the reputation of rigorous research while turning away from the ill-fitting metaphors of clinical science?

The following chapter examines the day-to-day realities of decision making and administration in the FTP. In many ways, it is a case study of administration rather than of politics as the term is usually understood. Yet as I have argued throughout this book, administration and politics cannot fully be separated. The political environment shapes the ideological context and incentive structures in which key administrative actors operate. The actions of these actors—and the policy outcomes they produce—then shape the broader political debate. The divide between politics and administration, particularly in a high profile pilot program, is fiction.

This is the knot of the problem for social scientists and policymakers.

Policies have a real impact that, at least in theory, can be measured objectively. Politically neutral research, therefore, should be possible. However, programs cannot be isolated from their political and cultural context. Context shapes every contour of a program's administration; there is no "pure" effect of a policy. As the following chapter illuminates, the day-to-day workings of the FTP were inextricably linked to broader political and social environments. Administrative practices supported a distinctive political agenda without overt political manipulation. Although it is unwise to generalize from a single case, the FTP does show specific mechanisms at work that are worth explicating. In particular, the case identifies the ways in which people actualized a specific policy constrained by time and knowledge. It provides an empirical example of how bringing aspects of social policy that are often ignored in policy evaluation into view sharpens our understanding of the political process and of policy outcomes.

CHAPTER 5

Street-Level Policymaking

[T]he staff has to "educate" the Board constantly and persistently and it certainly does choose elements of education which lead toward the conclusions of which the staff approves. In other words, we tell them how to vote and they vote and we call that process "the Board sets the policies of the agency."

Executive of a family service agency, 1956[1]

[W]e are doing nothing more than what they [the FTP staff] have already done in large part, which is formalizing the process. We're putting a rubber ... not a rubber stamp on it really, but a seal of approval from the community on the work and the recommendations that they have basically already made.

FTP review panel member, 1996[2]

The story of how the first test of Clinton-style work-trigger time limits emerged with a *firm* time limit is a story as much about administration and street-level bureaucracy as one about national politics. In Florida's Family Transition Program (FTP) administrators were pragmatic. They sought to create a program that "worked." The credibility of the program hinged on minimizing the number of participants who were "playing by the rules" but still reached the time limit without being employed. From the administrators' perspective, it was better to have all of the "compliant" participants employed at the time limit and all of the "noncompliant" participants thrown off the welfare rolls with ritualized community approval than it was to have participants who did everything right still needing assistance after they had reached the time limit.

The Review Panel

The review panel had a remarkable amount of power in the FTP as written into law and amended in the waiver process. In practice, however, the panel played a largely symbolic role, serving primarily to ratify the decisions of the FTP administrators. Why did the review panel exercise so little of its apparent power? As outlined in the last chapter, the FTP administrators had considerable incentive to minimize the discretionary powers of the panel and to limit the number of extensions granted. If a significant number of compliant participants reached the time limit without being "self-sufficient," the credibility of the FTP could have been undermined. Additionally, the expense and difficulty of providing post-time-limit benefits could have jeopardized the fiscal integrity of the program. The FTP's procedures were shaped by the program's need to maintain its legitimacy and to be a demonstrable "success." In this context, the actions of the FTP administrators seem logical. Why, however, would the panel members defer to the needs of the program? Why would the panel willingly give up its power? Why would ordinary citizens with little at stake in the welfare debate respond to the needs of administrators?

One of the larger issues raised by the actions of the review panel is whether ordinary citizens are comfortable exercising power without the justification and support of an external authority—in this case the FTP administrators. The experience of the FTP panel members suggests that many people may not be comfortable with such power. Two key reasons emerged for why the citizen volunteers who were vested with such power chose not to exercise it. First, in the FTP, many panel members did not know the extent of the powers that they had. They relied on the FTP staff to define their role and, not surprisingly, the staff defined the panel members' role narrowly. Second, many members expressed discomfort with making judgments about what should happen to particular families. They felt that they were unqualified to exercise such a power. There was an implicit belief in the technical judgment of experts, in this case welfare workers who often had limited formal education and training and relatively few years of experience in the welfare system. Middle-aged professionals who espoused a strong belief in the importance of community standards and flexibility in welfare administration deferred to welfare caseworkers in their early twenties on the basis of their "expert" authority. If there is a fundamental discomfort among Americans with assuming power without professional authority, there are great ramifications for the politics of citizen participation. Specifically, it may facilitate an increase in agency power with a decrease in agency accountability as a latent function of citizen panels and boards.

It is important to distinguish between expressing broad, abstract political views and even policy recommendations, which many panel members felt comfortable with, and rendering judgments and forcing actions in specific cases. This is akin to the difference between voicing support for the death penalty and administering a lethal injection. Harold L. Wilensky and Charles N. Lebeaux articulate a similar distinction nicely by dividing policy issues into "big policy" and "lesser policy" issues. In their research, Wilensky and Lebeaux found that lay boards tend to be more concerned with "big policy" than with "lesser policy." "Big policies" are policies that affect a large number of people and resources and "lesser policies" are technical issues and policies affecting only a small number of people.[3] This was true of the review panel. Panel members expressed considerable interest in influencing state and national welfare policy, but they were not interested in—and in fact were often quite uncomfortable with—influencing the outcome of individual cases in the FTP.

It is a mistake, however, to view the passivity of lay boards as an indication that they do not have an impact on policymaking and implementation. As Wilensky and Lebeaux argue, lay boards perform a legitimating function rather than an instrumental one. A fundamental reason for this, illustrated by the quotes that begin this chapter, is that board members, being nonprofessionals, must be "educated" by agency staff. In the process of educating the board, staff transmit their views to board members. There is not necessarily any intention on the part of the staff to bias the process. The staff may simply provide the board with the necessary information as they understand it. The "education" of the board by the staff, however, provides the means through which institutionalized facts can be transmitted from the agency to the board. For example, in the FTP, review panel members were told that the participants who came before the panel were noncompliant. The panel members accepted this definition because the staff providing it were the "experts." When welfare recipients came before the board, the panel members accepted the staff's assessment of "noncompliance" and never questioned the agency's classification of participants. "Compliance," in the eyes of the panel members, was something that only experts could determine.

In the process of "educating" the board, the agency can gain significant strength. As outsiders begin to see the situation as the agency defines it, the agency view begins to spread out into the community. It is no longer only insiders who hold a particular view of the agency's work, it is also these "outsiders"—such as the panel members—who have become, through the process of their orientation, partial insiders. In addition, the agency gains power and legitimacy because there appears to be an external check on their actions. The circle therefore works something like this: members of lay panels, being nonexperts, must turn to administrators and staff in an agency in order to learn what that agency is supposed to do and what it actually does. Administrators and staff then define the agency's role for the panel members. At minimum, the agency representatives will provide information based on the dominant agency perspective. They may also, quite reasonably, consciously choose not to highlight issues and areas that it is not in the agency's interest to highlight. Of course, it is possible that a lay board could actively choose to educate itself or even be hostile to the agency altogether. The key point, however, is that the default position of lay boards, that position that requires neither active support nor active hostility toward the agency, will be biased toward the agency by virtue of the structure of the information flow to the board members. The structure of information flow promotes a proagency bias. As a result, the agency may gain the legitimacy of external validation for its actions when judged by criteria that it has defined itself. The political ramifications of this are that lay boards may appear to open agency activity up to external scrutiny, whereas in fact they do little more than provide political cover for agency actions.

Origins of the Review Panel

The Florida legislature established the review panel as an independent, community-based panel to review cases that were not succeeding in the FTP. The review panel was also to serve an advocacy role for the FTP participants, ensuring their fair treatment in the program. During the legislative debate over the Family Transition Act, the review panel was framed primarily as a safeguard, ensuring that no participants in the FTP would have their benefits terminated if the agency had failed to provide them with adequate services or if they were facing extraordinary circumstances. Representative Cynthia Chestnut explained that the safeguards in the FTP would include "review by an independent panel to determine if any unforeseen emergency merits modification of the plan and to ensure that the department has provided the services called for in the plan."[4] As a part of these safeguards, the legislature gave the review panel the power to grant short-term extensions and to void or modify a participant's time limit if the department had been negligent or the participant faced extraordinary circumstances.

The review panel had seemed so powerful on paper that the Washington-based Center for Law and Social Policy wrote to Mary Jo Bane, assistant secretary for children and families at HHS, to express concern that post-time-limit welfare benefits would be granted solely to those individuals who could sympathetically articulate their cases to the panel.[5] The legislature, however, may never have intended the panel to be as powerful in practice as it appeared to be on paper. One high-level administrator in the Florida welfare department noted that the power of citizen-based boards is generally dependent on the goodwill of local departments: "Actually, these local boards, whatever they are, have about as much power as the local department is willing to give them. And that varies from district to district." The power of the review panel may have been implicitly understood by FTP administrators to be limited by the welfare agency.

At the time that the Family Transition Act was passed, Florida was in the midst of creating numerous citizen-based panels and boards. Another Florida administrator explained that the passage of the Family Transition Act took place during a time "when Tallahassee, the legislature, the governor and all was really pushing community involvement." A central reason that Governor Lawton Chiles and the Florida legislature wanted to institutionalize community involvement with social service agencies was to increase public awareness of and support for social welfare programs. As one administrator noted, "The public perception of what we do is real skewed. But when people become involved with us, they become advocates. . . . What Governor Chiles tried to do, which I fully support, was tried to localize this with the creation of the boards." The same administrator went on to note that boards and panels played an important role in building political support for social service agencies and individual programs, such as the FTP.

I think the major advantage [of the review panel] is a political advantage, and that is it gives you a certain amount of built-in community buy-in. From both points of view, from either a very conservative point of view or a very liberal point of view. You still have that community buy-in. Either you have the community protection of the poor people or you have the community looking at all these bleeding heart social workers. And to me, of course, that makes my job that much easier in dealing with the public and the media.

The review panel did create community buy-in for the FTP. Panel members felt that they were a part of the welfare reform process and that they were witnessing firsthand the good work of the FTP.

The review panel was a result of a broader movement in Florida to bring members of local communities into contact with the social service agencies. The central mission of this movement toward localization was to increase community "buy-in" and political support by making members of the community partners in the provision of social services. The apparent power of the review panel on paper, therefore, must be understood in the context of a concerted effort by Florida government officials to increase political support for social service programs and government initiatives more generally.[6]

The review panel also provided a forum for individuals and groups to air their concerns about the FTP. Interest groups were important in the review panel as legislated. The Family Transition Act very explicitly stipulates that each review panel must "consist of seven members and must include a member of the local Health and Human Services board, a member of the private industry council, a participant or former participant in the Family Transition Program, two members of the local business community, one member of the education community and one member at large."[7] Clearly, the intent of this level of specificity was to assure members of various groups that their interests would be represented by the panel.

The FTP, despite considerable effort, was never able to put together panels that met the requirements of the law. Even assembling a review panel that consisted of three or four warm bodies from any segments of the community proved to be a difficult task. Everyone wanted their interests represented, but considerably fewer wanted to do the day-to-day work. It is possible that one reason there was so little effort by interest groups to influence the implementation of the FTP was that there had been an exhaustive effort to solicit input from interested parties before drafting the Family Transition Act. Interest groups may have felt that their agendas had already been adequately encoded in the law and that their representation on the review panel would assure that their concerns would continue to be addressed in the program's implementation. This assumption was wrong. There was no perceptible influence of any interest group on the panel. This was largely due to the fact that interest groups did not take advantage of the opportunity to sit on the panel that they had pressed for in the legislation; interest groups did not follow through by providing representatives to sit on the panel.

Situating the review panel in this political context helps us to understand both why the review panel on paper was such a prominent and powerful part of the FTP and why the local welfare department largely dismissed the panel's authority. By formalizing the role of various nongovernmental groups in the administration of time-limited welfare, the institution of a citizen-based review panel helped to build support for the FTP and allay fears about the potential negative impact of time-limiting welfare. At the same time, because the proliferation of community-based boards and panels was widely understood by government agencies as being primarily a political strategy for building local support for government programs, administrators had good reason to take the stated powers of lay boards with a grain of salt. In the FTP, the top administrators tended to view the review panel as more of an advisory board than a decision-making body. This interpretation may not square with the legislative language of the Family Transition Act, but it fits quite well with the probable legislative intent as understood in the broader political context.

It is difficult to say why interest groups did not push to see that their interests were upheld in the FTP. A simple answer is that there was a geographical mismatch. Florida's political nexus is in the center to eastern areas of the state, areas such as Tallahassee and Miami. Pensacola, and the panhandle more generally, although ideologically conservative, are not centers of organized political action. Had there been a comparable review panel in Miami, one can imagine that interest groups might have been more involved in the day-to-day operations of the program. Arguably, interest groups, like many political actors, have also overlooked the importance of implementation, assuming that the written law will be more or less translated into agency policy. Despite the fading attention of interest groups and political actors, however, the review panel remained a central, if only symbolic, part of the FTP.

Review Panel Hearings and Benefit Termination

The review panel was the final stop for FTP participants. It was the body that was supposed to determine who was compliant and who was noncompliant. It was to determine whose benefits would be terminated, whose would be extended, and who would get a public job. On paper, it held the participant's fate in its hands. In practice, the situation was very different. Exactly how the review panels would run was not outlined in the Family Transition Act or the federal waiver. The law provided that the FTP would provide support services to the panel; however, it did not specify in detail what those services would be. The procedures that were ultimately used by the FTP to screen review panel members and to run the hearings were developed ad hoc by the program administrators. As one high-ranking administrator explained: "[W]e just started to develop different kinds of forms . . . just like we have done everything in the program. We developed a form and redeveloped a form and redeveloped a form, until we finally got something as we gone along." The procedures that the FTP administrators developed enabled the program to eliminate the job guarantee administratively while retaining the public relation benefits of the review panel.

The Hearings

The review panel hearing rooms were set up to mimic a judicial hearing. The panel members sat at a large table in the front of the room; two smaller tables faced the panel. At one, the "prosecutor's" table, the FTP case manager and career advisor sat. Behind them sat their supervisors. At the other, the "defendant's" table, the participant sat. Observers sat in the back. One panel member explained the room setup the following way: "[I]t's kind of like a court martial. . . . I am behind the big table, there's a whole expanse of floor and you [the participant] are behind this table. The case manager's over here behind another table. The participant is a little bit isolated. And then there're all these strange people in the back of the room. I would think it would be very intimidating." The setup of the review panel hearing room was often remarked on by the panel members, and was commonly referred to as the "judge and jury thing." FTP administrators generally liked the room setup, feeling that its legal overtones helped to get the participant's attention. Many of the review panel members also thought that the room setup helped to convey the seriousness of the participant's situation. As one panel member noted:

You [the participant] walk into that room, two people over there, a panel of people that you've probably never seen and then you have people in the back—supervisors, et cetera, et cetera, et cetera. It's an unsettling, I think, experience. You kind of understand that this is different. This is not just you and the case manager, some personality conflict that you may or may not have. This is a whole room of people that you need to now explain why you have or have not done what you are supposed to do.

Some review panel members, however, did not like the room setup:

I personally don't like the setup, the physical layout. It is like a tribunal. You have two counselors over here, the career advisor and the case manager. The board is at this—like the Nuremberg trial—long table and there is five or six of us sitting there. And the individual sits alone at a table in the front.

I would like to have been in a different room setup in there, because I felt just like the judge. Judge and jury, right here, hallelujah.

By using images of a "tribunal," "the Nuremberg trial," and the religious invocation of "hallelujah," these panel members expressed discomfort with the power and supremacy of the panel members implied by the room's layout.

One panel member suggested that the hearings might have been more effective if the room setup was not so intimidating:

The intimidation factor of those people [participants] walking into that room and here is a panel of five or six people sitting there. And another table with a couple of people sitting over here. It's like, am I on trial here? So, I think we need to lighten up from that aspect. Bring 'em in and offer 'em a cup of coffee or a donut or a co-cola. You know and let's just talk about what your problems are. And we are here to help you. We don't want to get into your business, but sometimes it is necessary.

Those who liked the room setup tended to think that a legalistic approach to the hearings served as a "wake-up call" to the participants. Those who did not like the room setup tended to fear that isolating the participants would only further alienate them.

Review panel hearings generally ran a little under a half hour. First, the panel members introduced themselves, and then the case manager and career advisor read over a short summary of the participant's activities, highlighting activities that the participant did not attend, often half or more of those that had been scheduled. These summaries were sent to the panel in advance of the hearing by the review panel liaison.[8] The panel members would then ask questions or request additional information from the staff. All of the information that the panel had access to came through the FTP staff. The information provided by the staff therefore had tremendous weight. As one panel member commented: "We don't have access to anything. All we have is information that is fed to us by the case manager and the client, if the client comes. Other than that we don't have nothing. We don't have any knowledge of anything." If the participant attended the hearing, she was given a copy of the summary during the hearing. Participants were not sent the activity summaries in advance, and many spent the hearing simultaneously trying to read over the summaries of their cases and answer questions from the panel.[9]

During the hearings participants were typically asked if they had anything to say. They often brought up personal issues, such as problems with a child. The panel typically addressed these issues by offering advice to the participant. The panel members also discussed career goals with the participants, not always in gentle terms. At one review panel, a panel member leaned over the table and rhetorically asked a participant, "You have less than a ninth grade education. What are you going to do with your life, young lady?" Another panel member reported that, during the hearings, he sometimes challenged participants' assertions that they cannot find work:

I've gone through the newspaper and I've cut clippings out and carried them with me and I've asked the client what do they want to do and they'll say this and that. Why aren't you working? Well, there's no jobs. And [I will] turn around and hand them the newspaper. Say, you know here are the jobs, the same thing you were looking for. But the other panel members think that is funny. To me it is serious.

For many panel members, the hearings were as much an opportunity for "tough-love" interventions with FTP participants as they were fact-finding hearings.

The participants were sometimes angry or upset during the hearings, though many showed little emotion at all. The participant's demeanor appeared to be important to the panel members; defiant, unkempt participants elicited the most unfavorable responses from the panel, whereas polite, well-groomed participants were more favorably received. The following excerpts from the author's field notes illustrate how the participant's self-presentation influenced the panel. Both of these cases were heard on the same day by the same panel:

[The participant] was a slightly overweight white woman with bleached hair in her early 30s. She was wearing reflective sunglasses, a green T-shirt and tight black bike shorts with flip-flops. She was very "butch" looking and had a very hostile attitude. This woman was very slow functioning. Her test scores were around third grade level, though from [what I could judge] hearing her, she probably functioned above that. She read her "summary" and got very angry when she saw that she was described as "unstable." She was hostile, cried, never took off her sunglasses. Said that she was taking it one day at a time when the panel tried to get her to think long-term. When the panel asked her if she understood what she had to do to be considered compliant, she said sarcastically, "Yeah, I got to do everything they say."

In fact, there was nothing this participant could have done at this point to be considered compliant by the time limit. Once she appeared before the panel, she became ineligible for an extension, a public job or any other benefit reserved for "compliant" participants. Her chance "to do everything they say" had passed.

Another woman seen the same morning was received differently:

[The participant] is a very beautiful young woman. . . . Her mother is white and her father is black. She alternated between charming the panel and sobbing. She is 22, had a four-year-old-child, is caring for her mother who is dying of AIDS, and is actively rejected by her father who lives in the area. A few months ago, she and her baby were in a car accident. Both suffered injuries but recovered. She was brought before the review panel for failing to bring a doctor's note verifying her medical problems in time. She agreed with the panel on everything they said. When she left someone [a panel member] noted that "she was a success story."

It was unclear what, other than appearance and attitude toward the panel, made the first participant a lost cause and the second "a success story." Panel members, however, seemed to view a good attitude and appearance as manifestations of an almost spiritual transformation that is the foundation for escaping from poverty.

In general, the panel members' reactions to the cases that they saw had far more to do with the appearance and demeanor of the participants than with the contents of their cases. In some ways, the panel members' responses to participants were in line with the new paternalist argument that Americans want the poor, those who receive state aid in particular, to adhere to culturally accepted norms of behavior. The review panel did not take a rights-oriented, legalistic view of compliance. They did not determine on a fact-by-fact basis whether a participant had upheld her contractual obligations to the state and whether the state had upheld its contractual obligations to her. Instead, the panel judged participants by far more subjective standards. Did her manner of dress show respect for the panel? Was she polite and soft-spoken? Did she express responsibility and remorse for the actions that had brought her to the welfare office? The review panel members judged the merits of each woman more than the merits of each woman's case. Did she embody any of the ideals of American womanhood?

The Role of the Review Panel

When asked in a survey what the main role of the review panel was, the greatest number of panel members, 35 percent, answered: "To validate case managers' and career advisors' decisions that clients are noncompliant or need to progress." This answer was followed closely by "To advise the case managers and career advisors on ways to help the clients comply before they reach the time limit," selected by 32 percent of respondents. In contrast, very few panel members selected "To make decisions about which clients have their benefits terminated and which are granted extensions" as the main role of the review panel.[10] Overall, the panel members viewed their role as assisting and supporting the FTP staff.

An internal memo written by an FTP administrator supports the review panel members' assessment of their role as marginal and primarily supportive of the case managers' decisions regarding the participant's behavior and the appropriate agency response.

In general, the findings / recommendations are mostly the same as the recommendations contained in the summaries submitted to the Review Panel. Activities that the panel recommend the client be scheduled for are the same activities that the client has been scheduled and re-scheduled for numerous times. (Usually the reason that the client is now sanctioned.) We don't receive any new ideas or information from the Review Panel, they just end up saying what we have been saying, and trying to get the client to do for the past nine or eighteen months.[11]

In interviews, review panel members emphasized the therapeutic value of the review panel for the FTP participants and expressed the belief that they were helping the FTP participants by listening to, caring about, and often confronting the participants. Many panel members viewed the hearings as a chance to "reach" a client and help her turn her life around. Even marital advice might be offered during the hearing. One panel member mentioned a case where another panel member had advised a participant to leave her abusive husband. Although the panel member expressed his concern that this was beyond the purview of the panel, FTP administrators actively supported the second panel member's intervention and minimized the other panel member's concerns. According to the first panel member:

[The participant] mentioned that she has some personal problems. It turns out that the personal problems were an abusive spouse. And that was documented. Basically, a member of the panel told her that basically what she needed to do was get a divorce. I thought that was way, way, way out of line. I didn't say anything, but when we deliberated, I said, I didn't think that you should be suggesting to anyone: divorce your spouse or anything that drastic. That is a personal decision and I don't personally feel comfortable and I don't think that we as a panel need to be making those types of recommendations. One of the higher-ups were there and they felt just the opposite—that, hey, this is a big problem in her life and maybe that is something that she needs to consider. I said maybe it is but I don't think that we need to be suggesting it. I see some problems, what if she goes and does that and that is what we tell her to do and then what? What are we going to do for her? Nothing.

Although there was some disagreement about the level of personal advice that was appropriate for them to dispense, most of the panel members viewed counseling participants as a central part of their mission. This view of the panel was strongly supported by the FTP administration. The FTP administrators' support of a counseling role for the panel had the effect of encouraging the panel members to feel like they were doing something without the FTP losing any real authority over the program.

Very few review panel members saw determining whether a participant had been compliant with the program as primarily being their responsibility. In fact, many review panel members were under the impression that only noncompliant participants were brought to the review panel, and that by definition a participant before the review panel cannot be compliant. One panel member noted, "We don't see the ones that are in compliance. We seldom talk about them. Once in a while word comes out that out of 100 people, ninety are in compliance and ten are not. But you never hear about the ninety, you only hear about the ten." In a similar vein, another panel member explained, "All we know is the people who are not doing what they're supposed to do. That's the reason they come before the board, if they are not compliant."

Forty-five percent of the review panel members reported that they had never seen a compliant client come before the review panel. The other 55 percent reported that they had seen compliant clients. Of the panel members who reported that they had seen a compliant participant come before the panel, 78 percent knew that the participant was compliant because the FTP staff had *informed* them of the client's compliance. The review panel never made the decision of who was compliant but merely accepted the FTP staff's decisions. A review of cases sent to the panel revealed that none had been classified as being fully compliant.[12]

Confusion

Panel members frequently confused a participant's being "compliant" with being "sanctioned." For example, when one panel member was asked whether a participant's compliance status was clear-cut or not, she replied, "It's clear-cut. . . . If they've come in and done their ten days, whatever, and had their sanction lifted, then they are in compliance." The ten days of compliance with program requirements were necessary to lift a participant's sanction, but they did not make a participant "compliant." Sanctions are a tool used in welfare to make participants adhere to particular behavioral expectations, primarily attending appointments. They had no impact on what happened at the end of the time limit in the FTP. They only affected the amount of money that a participant received in a given month. Compliance, on the other hand, had no impact on what happened to participants before the time limit—cash grants were not affected by a participant's "compliance" status. A participant's compliance status affected her eligibility for benefits only after the time limit, at which point compliant participants were guaranteed a job. In short, sanctions affected the amount of cash received *before* the time limit, whereas compliance affected participants' eligibility for benefits *after* the time limits.

The confusion between sanctions and compliance may have been a result of the fact that FTP staff talked about whether a participant was complying with the program, meaning currently fulfilling the program requirements. Complying in that way, however, was not the same as be-

ing "compliant." Being "compliant" was a status, and once a participant became officially "noncompliant," she retained that status even if
she complied with the program from that point on. When asked why
participants were brought to the review panel, one panel member explained "because they are going to sanction them for not attending the
programs that they have been assigned, they make appointments and
they don't keep 'em. So they sanction them and bring them to the
panel." Given the complexity of the FTP's sanctioning procedures, the
multiple uses of the term "compliance," and the lack of criteria for
defining "compliance" as a status, panel members' confusion over the
issue was understandable. Nonetheless, because the panel was responsible for determining a participant's overall compliance status, and thus
the state's obligation to her, this confusion had serious ramifications for
the program.

Panel Recommendations

Once the panel heard a case, observers would be asked to leave while
the panel discussed the case and made recommendations. The recommendations were then written up by the review panel liaison. A panel
member explained the procedure in the following way, "We make recommendations to the liaison that sits there and then he writes it up and
then he gives the recommendation to the case managers and the career
advisors." The first finding in the review panel's "Findings and Recommendations" was always that the participant was noncompliant. As another panel member explained:

We first find that the participant is not in compliance and we describe how they
are not. Then we, second, always say that they need to come into compliance by
doing thus and such. And oftentimes, that's something like they need to get
with the Welfare Child Support Enforcement Agency. They need to do the ten
days and consistently and get on track and that's often the ten days are an issue.
Get their immunizations up-to-date. That's basically the peripheral stuff, but
it's usually they gotta do something for ten days. They got to make their appointments.

After finding the participant noncompliant, members of the panel
made the remainder of their recommendations based on what the case
manager and career advisor had already recommended.

Panel members reported almost no disagreement within the panel
on participant recommendations. In part, this was due to what they felt

to be their limited options. A panel member likened the process to ordering from a menu: "It is like I said, there is a menu here. And if you stick to the menu there is not very much [to disagree on]. I mean, you have to answer the question. You don't get into variables. And that is what causes disagreements." Another review panel member commented that she felt limited in the kinds of recommendations that she was allowed to make, "When we are making our recommendations, we should be able to make some recommendations that's not in the box." The images of working from a "menu" or being confined to a "box" suggest a high level of constraint on the panel that was not implied in the law or the waivers. The composition of the panels, drawn overwhelmingly from social service providers, also encouraged conformity. They did not reflect the diversity of interests as had been planned because the different interest groups did not get involved in the process.

The review panel findings and recommendations were, in fact, extremely uniform. They were form letters in which the participant's name and a few other individualized bits of information had been inserted. One panel member, when asked about the almost identical language in the review panel recommendations, explained: "[The FTP staff] put it into their own words. . . . They will word it the way that it is supposed to be." Occasionally, the FTP staff did more than structure the panel's recommendations. One review panel member recalled a time when, as chairman of a hearing, he found that the findings and recommendations contained something not recommended by the panel.

Recommendations will always be based on a finding that we have . . . that gets hand written, initially. Then it is typed up and the chairman gets called over and reads and initials and makes certain that what is typed now is exactly what was said, as opposed to something. . . . Sometimes things get typed up that aren't correct. I had that problem once. And I mean, it is an honest mistake. And it is hard sometimes because you don't recall. Some things, you can recall and you make that a correction and you sign off.

The additional recommendation, however, may not have been accidental. One high-level administrator admitted to occasionally adding recommendations to those of the panel: "I started to add some things every once in a while [to the review panel's findings and recommendations] and then I . . . When the review panel chairperson signs off, I just hope they approve my changes." As the review panel member's comment suggests, it may not always have been easy for the chairperson to remember exactly what recommendations the panel had made.

The review panel did not have the power that it appeared to have on paper. The administrators not only ran the program with virtually no interference from the review panel, they also had the additional legitimacy and strength conferred by the appearance of community oversight. Much of this shift in power was the result of administrative procedures that structured the information flow to and from the panel members.

Benefit Termination

Recommending that a participant's benefits be terminated or extended at the time limit was the central task of the review panel according to the law and waiver agreement. In practice, however, many review panel members were not even fully aware that they made recommendations on benefit termination. One noted, "I guess if the people do not comply, and after the end of the twenty-four months, I guess it's automatic termination. And I guess it does not have to come back before the panel." In the words of another review panel member, participants terminate themselves. "The person automatically—it looks to me as if they terminate themselves. The review panel does not terminate a person, the person terminates themselves by not complying." The use of qualifiers such as "I guess" and "it looks to me" were indicative of the uncertainty among the panel members about exactly how benefit termination works.

Panel members who did recognize that the review panel had a role in benefit termination downplayed its importance. For example, when asked if the FTP staff had told him how the review panel would handle recommending terminating or extending benefits, a panel member answered, "I believe they told us how that, you know kinda it's, we would make recommendations and it would go in front of somebody else. That we wouldn't actually sit there and go, hey you are off of benefits and so on and so forth." When asked what the role of the review panel was in terminating benefits, another panel member responded, "We can't. It's not up to us. All the panel does is make recommendations. We have no authority." Other panel members commented that whereas the panel made recommendations, the final decision to terminate benefits rested with the district administrator. For example, one panel member noted, "We make recommendations. The DA really has the dirty work to do because he is the one who has to do the terminations. I would not want that job." Similarly, other panel members emphasized that the panel did not decide on benefit termination.

[W]'re not hearing officers in the terms of we come to a conclusion or a jury and we, you know, we find the defendant guilty type thing. We would find that the applicant either was or was not in compliance with the program and then we would identify those certain elements where the applicant was not in compliance and we could make some recommendations, but it was not our job. I mean, what we recommended wouldn't necessarily be what was put into force. That went up the chain of command that was approved and we were simply serving as an advisory group if you would.

I didn't think that we would make the decision [to terminate benefits]. I knew that it was HRS and the state of Florida, the state had to say so. All we were going to do was make recommendations of what our opinion was. I didn't go down there with the intention of saying "This person isn't doing this, you're off." I knew I wasn't going to have the say to do that. And really I don't want it. I think that should be up to the state.

These panel members not only felt that they did not have the responsibility for deciding to terminate a family's benefits, they also did not want that responsibility.

When the district administrator was asked how he made the decision to terminate a participant's benefits, however, he reported relying quite heavily on the review panel recommendations.

We follow the process as put out by the, as in the law, we try to do that very faithfully. We use the citizens' panels, which makes a recommendation to me, I believe when there is three months left. . . . I've only had a couple of occasions to even ask major questions. When the material gets to my desk, it is pretty well gone through. And you know, we have case managers, we have the review panel, we have child welfare look at it.

The system of checks that the district administrator referred to was limited. The FTP staff was required to bring all participants who were failing in the program to the panel, and the Child Welfare Review only determined the likelihood that children would *immediately* be put into substitute care, such as foster care, as a result of benefit termination. The review panel had the responsibility for looking at the whole case and determining whether benefit termination was appropriate. The review panel, therefore, was primarily responsible for making the decision to terminate a participant's benefits, though many panel members were unaware that this was true.

A number of review panel members were also confused about the nature of benefit termination. When asked if they were concerned about the effect that benefit termination would have on children, several panel members incorrectly explained that the children's benefits would not be terminated.

Some of my concern was, if you take benefits away, you know and when the general public hears that, [and thinks] oh how can you do that. And of course I did learn that, no you don't take benefits away from the entire family. You're not going to put them in the street. So I learned a lesson there, that only a portion of it is going to be taken away.

Well, they're not going to cut . . . well, the parents, the mother or father won't get anything but the children will get [benefits].

In fact, children's benefits were continued through a protective payee only in those rare cases in which the Child Welfare Review determined that full benefit termination would likely result in the children being placed in foster care.

The panel members' understanding of the short-term benefit extension procedures was, if anything, foggier than their understanding of the benefit termination procedure. In response to questions about their role in extending benefits, several review panel members expressed considerable confusion. A few even seemed to be unaware of the extension procedures. One woman noted, "I think they did [mention the extension in the Review Panel training]. I don't remember the details of that." Another looked back blankly and stated, "No. I am not aware of them."

One panel member pointed to the external political influences on whether the program provided benefit extensions. He highlighted the influence of the Florida legislature and the FTP's need to respond to the national trends generated by the other states' pilot welfare programs. He stated, "I think it's kind of been a wait and see kind of process from the legislature and what we are doing and what other pilot programs are doing and how they are handling it." It is particularly interesting that this member of the review panel pointed to the fact that the welfare pilot programs were both responding to *and* creating a consensus over the meaning of time-limited welfare. Rather than viewing the FTP as a test of work-trigger time limits, this panel member viewed the FTP as a living and dynamic program creating, and being created by, the larger political context.

Other panel members answered questions about what would happen to those participants who reached the time limit by citing the written policy more accurately:

If they have like we call it legal reason, perhaps you were sick or something and you couldn't comply with what you're supposed to and your time ran out then you can be given an extension. But the participants are not supposed to be told about that up front. Cause if they do, that just makes them, well I got twenty-four months, I still got another six months I can go. So they're not supposed to be told that.

Yeah, they talked briefly about it and they talked about it, just you'd have to take into consideration what the circumstances were. . . . We talked about one last time we were there. She needed to extend for either one or two months, because her schooling had added some more courses to, before she could graduate. So she had to take these. And that wasn't a problem. That is what this is all about.

A majority of review panel members reported that they had the authority to grant short-term benefit extension—as opposed to public jobs—even if the FTP staff opposed it, but none reported having done so. The benefit extensions were useful to the FTP staff, although they still were encouraged to use them selectively. The extensions smoothed over administrative mistakes, such as permitting a participant to enroll in a college course that extended beyond her time limit, without fundamentally altering the program. It is telling that the panel did not exercise the power to extend benefits, even though panel members were aware that they could. This suggests that even if panel members had known that they determined compliance, and thus eligibility for post-time-limit public jobs, it might not have made much difference in how the FTP operated. Why were the panel members so reluctant to exercise any authority?

Who Was on the Panel?

There was considerable diversity among review panel members. Forty-one percent of the panel members were male and 59 percent were female. Approximately 75 percent of review panel members were white and 25 percent were black. Household incomes were also diverse. Twenty-four percent of review panel members reported household incomes under $30,000, 42 percent reported household incomes between $30,000 and $69,999, and 33 percent reported household income between $70,000 and $149,999.[13] No one reported an annual income of over $150,000. Most review panel members were or had been married. Seventy-eight percent reported being married, and 15 percent reported being divorced. Only 6 percent reported being single or never married. Almost all of the review panel members had some college education. Fifty-seven percent of the panel members reported having at least a bachelor's degree, with a notable minority, 39 percent, holding advanced degrees. None of the review panel members reported having less than a high school degree.

Because service on the review panel required that members be able to take at least half a day off every few months to serve without pay, many of the people who volunteered were service professionals who were able to incorporate review panel service into their jobs. When asked how he got involved with the review panel, one panel member cited a request from a superior at work, "Our assistant executive director asked me to apply and there was some kind of an application. And I submitted my application and I guess about two months later in the mail I received notification that I was going to be on the panel."

Other factors played a role in panel members' decisions to participate in the panel. For example, the same panel member who noted that the assistant executive director where he worked had asked him to apply also spoke in detail about the personal reasons that he had for wanting to serve on the panel.

Probably I wanted to sit on the panel because I'd been there before; I'd been on welfare before. It's been a good many years ago. I know what the program is about. I know what it is supposed to be used for. To me it is not being used the correct way. I think that it was originally written to subsidize a person's income for a short period of time, not for a lifestyle. When I was on it, I was on it for a short period of time. . . . I wanted to see what these people were doing. I know how I did it, and it lasted for three months.

Most of the review panel members held mid-level "pink collar" jobs such as administrative assistant. The second largest groups represented were white-collar job holders and retirees. There were also several blue-collar workers and former FTP participants on the panel.[14] A few panel members expressed concern that the panel was too heavily weighted toward professionals. As one panel member explained when asked if she thought that the review panel was representative of the community, "There were not too many housewives, just plain housewives. I know when I started, there were only two [FTP] participants on the review board panel membership, because nobody wanted to do it. . . . Not many blue collars, you know, not many grunts, people that were out there maybe a little more closer to the situation." The image of the panel being made up primarily of professionals was probably enhanced by the fact that most panel members, regardless of the nature of their employment, dressed very professionally for the panel hearings. The panels therefore appeared to be even more dominated by white-collar workers than they actually were. An appearance of judicial formality was important to the panel.

Finally, a considerable number of review panel members had some personal experience being on welfare. Twenty-seven percent reported having received public assistance, defined as AFDC, Food Stamps, SSI, the food assistance program Women, Infants, and Children (WIC), or Medicaid, and 55 percent reported that they had close family or friends who had received public assistance. Twenty-one percent reported that before their review panel service they had never had regular contact with anyone on public assistance.

Attitudes

The panel members as a group supported a New Paternalism approach to welfare reform.[15] Paternalists advocate a supervisory approach to poverty, requiring that welfare recipients fulfill particular social obligations in return for support. They emphasize the obligations rather than the rights of welfare recipients and accept some intrusion into the lives of welfare recipients (and others) by government. As noted previously, New Paternalists differ from their predecessors in that they focus primarily on obligations related to work and school rather than on obligations of family and sexual behavior. There is considerable evidence that the New Paternalist's approach to welfare had popular support in the middle 1990s. Americans were willing to require work in return for benefits. Public opinion polls at the time of the FTP consistently showed strong support for work requirements.[16] Americans were also concerned about behavioral issues, such as out-of-wedlock childbirth, and supported some ideas, such as "family caps," which deny additional benefits for children born while the mother is on welfare. But they hesitated about other proposals, such as denying all benefits to unwed teenage mothers, framed as potentially sending children into foster care or orphanages.[17]

The review panel members held views about welfare that were very much in line with the New Paternalists and national public opinion of the time. Panel members were much more concerned that FTP recipients work than they were about how recipients conducted their private lives. Although there was some concern over women who had children out of wedlock, particularly by multiple fathers, panel members focused on the obligations of welfare recipients to work. There was overwhelming support among panel members for the idea that people on welfare should fulfill social obligations in return for their benefits. Panel members also supported time limits on welfare benefits. Yet, mirroring the debate between benefit-termination model time limits and work-trigger time limits, the panel members were divided on whether benefits should be continued to welfare recipients who were unable to find adequate employment. Some panel members simply did not believe that anyone was incapable of finding employment, and therefore did not think that terminating benefits would cause undue hardship. Other panel members argued that a mother who is unable to support herself is not fit to raise her children and that terminating a family's benefits might force the children into a better situation. This is not far from the "family breakup" policies pursued in the 1870s and 1880s, which aimed at getting children out of the poorhouses and succeeded in filling the orphanages with children of living parents.[18]

Although somewhat uncomfortable with the issue, several review panel members brought up the possibility that state-run orphanages might be a necessary component of time-limited welfare. Other panel members believed that no one willing to work should be denied the opportunity. These panel members tended to favor individualized time limits and benefits, with a few even mentioning long-term supported work. The vision of time-limited welfare articulated by review panel members was of a temporary assistance program containing reciprocal obligations. Beyond these two core principles, however, there was considerable dissensus. Divergent views on the nature of poverty and the appropriate role of the individual and the state led different panel members to argue in favor of very different time-limit policies. Notably, there was very little correlation between demographic variables and attitudes.

The Nature of Poverty and Welfare

Fifty-one percent of review panel members thought that if everyone "played by the rules"—worked or looked for work, did not have children out of wedlock, etcetera—there would be about half as many children in poverty in the United States as there are today. An additional 19 percent thought that 75 percent of child poverty in the United States could be eliminated if everyone "played by the rules." The majority of review panel members thought that child poverty was the result of personal choices by adults. Having children out of wedlock was viewed as a consequence of irresponsibility and immorality. Working to support those children became almost a form of absolution.

The panel was more divided over whether most welfare recipients really needed their benefits. About a third of panel members thought that almost all of the people on the welfare system really needed help. An additional third answered "about 75 percent" and slightly under a third answered "about 50 percent." A few review panel members took a harsher view of welfare recipients, viewing only 12 percent or fewer as truly needing their benefits.

The majority of panel members thought that a lack of job readiness was to blame for welfare receipt. Thirty percent of panel members responded, "[T]hey don't have the education or training they need to get a job" when asked why most people were on welfare. "They don't have a strong work ethic" was chosen as the second most popular explanation for why most people are on welfare, cited by 18 percent of panel members. Tied for third, with 9 percent each, were "they have learned 'to work the system,'" "not enough jobs," and "they have children out of wedlock." None of the panel members cited substance abuse, domestic violence, or mental health problems as being the primary reason that people are on welfare.

Review panel members viewed a substantial amount of poverty as being the result of personal choices. In general, however, they meant economic choices rather than moral choices. The panel did not focus on out-of-wedlock childbirth, drug use, or other "behavioral" causes of poverty. Rather, they focused on employment issues, on commitment to the work ethic, and preparedness for the job market. They did not believe there was a lack of jobs available, but they did believe that welfare recipients might not have the human capital to find and sustain employment.

Time Limits

Review panel members overwhelmingly supported time-limiting welfare. In response to the question, "In general, do you think that putting a time limit on welfare is a good idea?" 94 percent answered yes. Panel members viewed time-limited benefits as a way to help people who are truly needy without creating welfare dependency. Thirty-three percent of review panel members reported that the primary benefit of time-limited welfare was that "it helps people who temporarily hit hard times without supporting people who just don't want to work." Sixty-seven percent viewed this as being one of the top three benefits of time-limiting welfare. "It breaks the cycle of dependency" was the next most often cited reason for supporting time-limited welfare, cited by 21 percent of respondents as the primary benefit of time limits. Panel members did not, in any number, choose "it discourages out-of-wedlock childbirth" or "it saves the taxpayers money" as the primary benefit of time-limited welfare.

Although steadfast in their support of time limits, panel members did express some concerns about time-limiting welfare. Ninety percent of review panel members reported being concerned that "some people may not be able to become self-sufficient because of personal limitations." One panel member commented:

[Y]ou can't take a person who has a third grade reading level and teach them to read in two years. I am sorry, it just can't be done. You can take a child and teach him to read in a couple of years, but you can't take an adult. I've seen too many people in the business that I am in come in with these low reading scores. They either can't learn it. Don't have enough time. Don't have enough desire. You know, you're just not going to get real good work if you read on a third grade level.

A number of respondents came close to describing a supported work system of welfare, in line with the Clinton plan, rather than a benefit-termination model, when they articulated a vision of what should be done for welfare recipients who did not find adequate employment by the time limit, as the following comment illustrates.

We need to bring in some industry here. We need some jobs here. We do need the training. But we need the jobs to put the people in. Don't jerk the welfare away from them. Don't take the Medicaid away from them. Let the people work and gradually take it away. If they make five dollars an hour to start with, take part of their benefits away. And then when they start making six dollars, take a little bit more of their benefits away. . . . [I]t may take five years to get where all their benefits are gone but [by then] they are making nine or ten dollars an hour and you can live on that around here.

Conversely, a few panel members, echoing Charles Murray, did not believe in welfare of any kind.

I do not believe in welfare for people who are able to work because I believe that anybody can find a job, I really do. No matter what their education is there is work out there. See you can't even get anybody to mow your yard nowadays. Clean your house at minimum wage an hour. Now you say that isn't much but it is better than someone giving you something. I guess that is my background. I was taught you need to work for what you get, you don't expect people to give you things.

Finally, 39 percent of respondents reported being concerned that "children may be hurt when families lose their benefits."

I wrestle with the idea about the benefits for the children, because I know that they all [welfare recipients] get a lot quicker wake up call if we turn off the benefits for the children. That's almost anti-American, you know. You don't let the children suffer and yet, that's a terrible moral dilemma there. I think about it a lot and I struggle with it and I don't have an answer for it.

Other review panel members were not concerned that benefit termination would hurt the children. One panel member noted on a survey, "We go limp when we face the issue of kids, so we are held hostage by them. If kids are affected by termination of benefits. One, there will be fewer kids on benefits. Two, the threat of benefit termination will have real meaning." Another panel member speculated that children in families whose benefits had been terminated would not suffer because they would be taken care of by "grandparents, neighbors, churches. It's not going to affect the children." A third panel member expressed concern for the adults in these families, but not the children. "I am sure the children will be taken care of, but I really don't know [what will happen to the adults]. We may be seeing more people on the streets than we see now." Very few panel members reported being concerned about the well-being of children whose families lost their benefits in the FTP in cases that *they* had reviewed. Only 14 percent of review panel members reported that they had recommended benefit termination for a family and been concerned about what would happen to the children.

Although review panel members held a variety of views on how a time limit should ideally be implemented, virtually all strongly felt that welfare recipients who were not cooperating with the system should lose their benefits, even before reaching the time limit. Only 6 percent expressed an unwillingness to cut off benefits prior to the end of the time limit under any circumstances. The panel members supported time-limited welfare. For most, time-limiting welfare was a means of ending the entitlement system, which nearly all panel members viewed as destructive.

Beyond broad agreement that the entitlement to welfare should be ended, panel members held diverse views on how welfare should be administered. Panel members who viewed welfare as unnecessary thought that two to three years of assistance was more than sufficient for everyone. Other panel members supported the time limit as more of a metaphor than a reality, as a statement that government support is not unlimited, but not as the end of the social safety net. These panel members supported case-by-case time-limit modifications or some form of assisted employment after the time limit for welfare recipients unable to make it on their own and willing to work with the Family Transition Program.

Although the review panel members held strong views on how time-limited welfare should operate in the abstract, they did not attempt to bring their convictions into the day-to-day administration of the FTP. For example, the review panel members who supported flexible time limits in the abstract did not advocate that particular FTP participants have their time limits modified. Although comfortable making policy suggestions in theory, review panel members seemed considerably less comfortable making decisions on individual cases. "Big Policy" issues were their domain; "Little Policy" issues—those that affected individual participants—belonged to the experts. It was, however, the "little policy" issues that defined the program. The devil, as always, was in the details.

Interpreting the Review Panel's Confusion

As the preceding discussion illustrates, there was considerable confusion among panel members over issues of FTP policy. The review panel members were not stupid or negligent. Welfare policy is a labyrinth even for those with experience in it. Despite the concentration of social service professionals on the panel, there were very few panel members with experience in welfare policy. The majority of panel members came to the program knowing very little about the details of welfare, such as

and administrators was not only the result of the panel members' lack of technical knowledge but also of their discomfort with making the final decision to terminate a family's welfare benefits. Many seemed to share a feeling of relief at not having to make the final decision on benefit termination. This feeling was particularly well articulated by one panel member, who noted "At least you're off the hook, when [the district administrator] has to terminate someone you can say, oh yeah, it might have been our recommendation but it was his decision." The widespread misinterpretation that children continued to receive benefits if they were in any danger of suffering as a result of their family's benefits being terminated may have reflected the desire to believe that no harm could come to children from the new program.

The FTP very effectively eliminated the discretion of the review panel. Because noncompliant clients were not eligible for the short-term benefit extensions or the post-time-limit work opportunities, two out of the three possible ways for the review panel to grant "unsuccessful" clients post-time-limit benefits were essentially eliminated. The only remaining way for participants to be granted benefits after the time limit was if the panel found that the program had been negligent. Of the three possible ways of extending benefits past the time limit, this was by far the most threatening to the agency—a direct statement by the panel of agency incompetence. It was also the least likely to be utilized for many reasons. First, many members of the review panel were recruited through the personal and professional contacts of administrators in the FTP. The county in which the program operated was small and personal and professional networks were strong. In many cases, personal and professional ties would have been strained or broken had a panel declared that the program had incompetently handled a case and the time limit had to be voided. Second, panel members tended to identify themselves with the FTP staff, for example, using the pronoun "we" when referring to the FTP. This may have been related to the strong network connections between the program and the panel. Most panel members saw themselves as being a part of the FTP experiment and were committed to its success. Undermining the program would not have contributed to that end. Third, the FTP itself supplied the panel with its information on the FTP's obligations to participants. The agency therefore defined both its obligations and its actions for the panel. Not surprisingly, it did not present its actions as errors.[19]

The review panel members could have contested the FTP's interpretations of either a participant's behavior or the law. However, because the FTP trained the review panel, the FTP personnel were able to define the policy. The inherent noncompliance of participants who came before the review panel was institutionalized. This institutionalization was bolstered by the fact that many of the participants brought before the panel were clearly *not* cooperating with the program. In cases that fell into a gray area, however, the automatic noncompliance of participants before the review panel remained. In the few cases observed in this research where panel members seemed uncomfortable with the termination of a client's benefits, there was a sense of fatalism about terminating the benefits, a sense that no other option was possible. The panel members, however, never felt the full burden of terminating a family's benefits because they believed that the final decision-making responsibility lay somewhere else. Panel members overwhelmingly believed that someone else with more knowledge and power than they had was looking out for the families and children before making the final decision to terminate benefits. They wanted to believe in powerful, almost omnipotent, expert judgment. In fact, however, this responsibility lay with the very human members of the review panel, even when they chose to abdicate it.

Why There Were No Public Jobs

State and local politics clearly hindered the construction of a public job component of the FTP. There were political costs to having participants who complied with the program fail to find a job by the time limit. For the FTP administrators, therefore, running a successful program meant running a program in which compliance and success were synonymous. The FTP trained the review panel members to see their own role in the program in a distinctive way. The panel was defined by administrators and panel members primarily as a way to provide a "wake-up call" to participants. This role had resonance and value in the therapeutic culture that was venerated (some might say denigrated) on daytime television shows in which dramatic confrontations were portrayed as an important first step toward personal redemption. It provided a powerful and apparently emotionally cathartic role for panel members to play without affecting the administration of the program.

The FTP staff and administrator defined the meaning of compliance and even the character of the women who came before the panel. In the fifteen minutes or so allotted for each hearing, the panel members could gain little independent information about participants. Moreover, the precious little time that the panel did have was framed as an opportunity for the panel members to engage in what amounted to a community intervention, bringing each participant's attention to her problems and maintaining that the hearing represented a critical opportunity for her to turn her life around. It became a "fact" in the FTP that only noncompliant participants came before the review panel and that the hearing was an opportunity to shake some sense into them.[20] No one questioned it.

In his classic work on administration, Philip Selznick discussed how "organization doctrine" is transmitted in the process of training of people in an organization for particular tasks.[21] Organizational doctrine goes beyond the technical facts that people within an organization need in order to complete the tasks and functions that they are assigned. It also contains particular ways of viewing the work that is being done by the organization and even the broader social conditions in which the organization operates. The transmission of organizational doctrine, therefore, is the transmission of particular values and perspectives as well as facts. It provides a specific framework for making sense of the world as it relates to the work done within the organization. This kind of indoctrination, Selznick notes, is particularly important when policies are new. In order to maintain coherence, an organization must develop administrative ideologies, which help to build a consistency within the staff, boost morale, and rebuff outside claims and criticisms.[22] Without a unified sense of mission, a new policy and even the organization itself are vulnerable to fragmentation and the loss of internal and external support.

The biggest threat to the fiscal and political integrity of the FTP was the review panel. Outsiders could have easily come in and developed a vision of the program that did not fit within the developing organization doctrine. This would have been threatening to the FTP not only because it would have challenged the developing administrative ideology necessary for launching a successful new policy, but also because that administrative ideology was *directly tied* to broader political interests. One of the hallmarks of institutional structures is that they do not always have to be tied to instrumental goals. In other words, sometimes ways of accomplishing tasks or envisioning the mission of an organization develop historically in a way that is detached from any rational interest or efficiency goal; things are done in a particular way because they have always been done that way. But in this case, the administrative ideology that developed within the FTP and that was actively promoted by administrators was directly tied to political expectations and the broader political environment. There was no bright line between administrative politics and governmental politics.

The organizational dynamics and politics were not solely shaped by external political factors, however. Clearly, the time constraints and personal network ties of the panel members promoted acquiescence with the administrators' definition of the panel's role. Governmental politics, in the traditional sense, cannot fully explain the actions of the panel members, who had little reason to cede their power to administrators. The panel's actions can be explained best by looking at two factors. First, administrative procedures effectively indoctrinated the panel members and limited the information that they received. Second, the panel members did not want to exercise the power that they had. Many viewed the active exercise of power as a morally charged act. The passive refusal to exercise power, regardless of the consequences that it might have, was not viewed in the same moral terms. In short, the panel members were very concerned about sins of commission, but not sins of omission.

By controlling the information that flowed to and from the panel, FTP administrators were able to maximize their influence over the panel's recommendations and make sure that the panel "worked." They gained the benefits of having a citizen panel with few of the risks. The appearance that the review panel had considerable discretion to extend the benefits of worthy individuals helped to build support for the program; who could argue that the program was cold-hearted when a citizen group was looking out for the participants? At the same time, the administrative procedures that essentially eliminated the panel's discretion helped to ensure that the program met the politically defined criterion for success: Every participant who complied with the program became self-sufficient.

The confusion of the review panel members over policy issues and their reluctance to take responsibility for terminating or extending participants' benefits highlight some of the limits of decentralization and community control. Although it may be tempting to grant considerable power to citizen boards when programs or agencies are potentially controversial, the ability of these boards to be truly independent should be questioned. These boards may not have, or feel that they have, the technical knowledge necessary to make the decisions that they are assigned to make. As a result, they may rely entirely on information provided to them by the agency, thus compromising their independence. Asking people to make professional judgments without sufficient training may not increase the objectivity of the decisions, but merely mask the role of the agency in the decision-making process.

Arguably, this is the same dynamic noted by Deborah Stone in her analysis of the process of determining eligibility for disability benefits, albeit with inverse results. Stone's research demonstrates the political utility of discretion in determining eligibility for disability benefits. Flexibility in disability determination, Stone found, allowed legislators and agencies to respond to conflicting and often rapidly shifting political demands.[23] By relying on expert discretion, disability programs were able to balance the public desire that all who can work should work with the imperative that provisions be made for those who cannot work. Drawing an explicit distinction between those who can and cannot work would invite political battles over the definition of disability. Such battles are minimized by a reliance on professional judgment in determining disability. In other words, discretion can be used as a political tool to blur lines that might be controversial if sharply drawn.

In the FTP, the judgments of nonprofessionals were supposed to insure that the new law did not unfairly hurt anyone. In practice, however, the review panel served the political function of symbolizing fair treatment and thus defusing political criticism of the program without actually altering the program's administration. Building on Stone's insights, one lesson from the FTP is that decisions that appear to be discretionary may be particularly susceptible to political influence. The veil of individualized treatment may allow agencies to implement policies with overt ideological slants without appearing to lose their expert neutrality. As Chapter Six details, the pilot programs themselves provided a veil of neutrality that covered overtly political programs.

What is incontestable is that the reality of the FTP bore no resemblance to a laboratory study of work-trigger time limits. It was messy, human, and subject to political and administrative imperatives. For anyone familiar with social service programs or policy evaluation, none of this is surprising. But these realities fell out of the public discourse around waiver programs. Even more importantly, key facts that emerged from the street-level implementation of the FTP were buried not only by political actors with an interest in promoting particular outcomes but also by evaluators apparently without such motives. There are two key factors, which I will return to in Chapter Seven, that I believe account for why the FTP evaluators did not highlight the administrative shift from work-trigger to benefit-termination time limits that took place as a result of administrative actions. First, and I think primarily, the administrative practices that eliminated the job guarantee were viewed as "soft" and subjective. As noted in Chapter Two, professional evaluation has defined itself as a hard, objective science. The question of whether or not the FTP eliminated the job guarantee *is* a subjective one. It is possible, although I believe not plausible, to argue that the FTP would have been happy to provide public jobs had anyone qualified. The empirical evidence against this perspective is strong. The FTP's administrative procedures to define compliance were circular and airtight; anyone who was failing in the program went to the panel and anyone who went to the panel was noncompliant. No public jobs were ever granted and no system for providing jobs was ever put into place. Nonetheless, no one can definitively rule out the possibility that the FTP would have, under some circumstance, provided a participant with a public job.

This is the catch for evaluators. The evidence that the job guarantee was administratively eliminated is overwhelming, the political consequences profound, and yet there is no statistical test to prove that it is true. On the surface, the most defensible action in terms of the integrity of evaluation research might be to do what the FTP evaluators apparently chose to do, which was to provide documentation of some of the procedures that created this outcome but not draw attention to it. But is it ethical to minimize a profound change of the "treatment" in a social experiment? Does that not violate all of the assumptions of experimental research? These questions are, I believe, further complicated by the structural position that evaluation corporations find themselves in as contractors to the states whose programs they evaluate; there is an inherent incentive not to dig too deeply into areas that might cast a bad light on the states.

There are therefore, I believe, both legitimate intellectual reasons for the reticence of evaluators to look too closely at subjective issues of administration and more dubious reasons tied to conflicts of interest perpetuated by the evaluation system as it is currently practiced. I will return to both of these issues in Chapter Seven. For now, Chapter Six turns to the broader political role of the pilot programs in legitimating the idea of benefit-termination time limits and creating the structural conditions necessary to demolish AFDC and replace it with state-based welfare programs.

CHAPTER 6

Revolution in the States

> [I]n the last three years my administration has granted thirty-eight states welfare reform waivers, clearing away federal rules and regulations to permit the states to build effective welfare reform of their own. The state-based reform we've encouraged has brought work and responsibility back into the lives of 75 percent of the Americans on welfare. . . . America is in the midst of what the *New York Times* has called "a quiet Revolution" in welfare reform.
>
> President Bill Clinton, 1996[1]

In his radio address to the nation, President Clinton proclaimed that the pilot programs were reforming welfare even as the White House and Congress bickered over the federal law. There was clearly a political strategy motivating Clinton's statements. The 1996 presidential election was approaching, and Clinton wanted to be on the right side of welfare reform. Clinton had vetoed welfare reform on January 9, 1996, and his political opponents were poised to attack him for breaking his campaign promise to end welfare. In addition to positioning himself politically, however, Clinton pointed to a real and profound change in the American welfare system that had taken place outside of the normal policy-making channels. Between 1992 and 1996, waivers had changed everything about welfare in the United States. Families on public assistance were receiving a multitude of different services and facing new requirements under a tapestry of welfare pilot programs that covered the country. The vague promises to "reform" welfare and to "end welfare as we know it" had morphed into time-limited benefits and effectively ended the entitlement to welfare that had provided a national safety net for poor families.

Few, if any, political actors viewed the waivers in purely experimental terms. Although individuals within HHS were interested in promoting the use of experimental methods in the waiver programs to build the knowledge base of social policy, the pilots were fundamentally deals brokered between the states and the federal government. They were tests of the political legitimacy of policy ideas—and a tool for expanding that legitimacy—far more than true experiments. Yet, however clear the political and ideological aspects of the waiver programs may have been, the Clinton administration framed them as empirical tests of new ideas. The HHS press release announcing the approval of Florida's FTP, for example, emphasized the rigorous research that would be conducted on the program. In the press release, HHS secretary Donna Shalala stated, "I am confident the Florida demonstration I am approving today will add to our knowledge of how welfare can most effectively be reformed."[2] The press release went on to trumpet the research value of the project: "Florida's demonstration will include a rigorous evaluation using random assignment to control and experimental groups."[3]

The language of experimentation and social science provided important political cover for the pilot programs. In addition to being legally necessary—federal law would not otherwise have permitted such a dramatic restructuring of AFDC—setting up the pilot programs as empirical "tests" of welfare reform was politically advantageous. The governors were able to implement new welfare programs that they felt better reflected the social, financial, and political needs of their states while gaining overwhelmingly positive media attention as welfare reformers. The Clinton administration similarly was able to claim movement toward welfare reform even as its own welfare reform plan lost steam. Finally, the media got a policy story with irresistible, and uncharacteristic, drama: "Can welfare reform work, stay tuned. . . . "

For many of the governors, Wisconsin's Tommy Thompson in particular, the experimental components of the waiver programs appear to have been viewed as a minor benefit at best and an obstacle to true reform at worst. At its root, this perspective probably grew out of the pragmatic orientation toward politics and social policy of most elected officials. Elected officials have rarely seen social science as the key to better public policy. Funding, political power, administrative competence, and other issues of resources—rather than knowledge—are dominant. Political work is chaotic. Reflexive academics often impute strategies where political actors see only individual decisions. There may be, however, an implicit and emergent strategy or pattern in the actions of these actors as they respond to rapidly changing environments and demands that they do not recognize at the time.

The use of experimentation as political cover for waivers that were, in fact, being used to reform policy falls into the category of ad hoc actions that, in retrospect, followed a pattern. There is little evidence that President Clinton set out to undermine the structure of AFDC and legitimate new policy ideas using the waivers. Yet it was clear from the start that he viewed the waivers as an opportunity to extend flexibility to the states. It is also clear that he understood the political value of claiming that the waiver programs were successfully reforming welfare. For research-oriented political actors in the Clinton administration, such as Mary Jo Bane and David Ellwood, perhaps it appeared that the pilots could serve two functions, they could respond to political imperatives and, at the same time, produce rigorous and valuable research. David Ellwood noted at the time, "We really see the states as laboratories. There's so much we've learned by watching the states. . . . Some things are better to observe on a small scale."[4] Emphasizing the evaluation component of the waivers sent a signal that the Clinton administration wanted research to be taken seriously, though the message was sent by HHS more forcefully than by the president himself. Although few political actors ever believed that the pilot programs were truly about experimentation, the experimental frame made the programs both legally and politically viable. It also, however unwittingly, encouraged the perception that the pilots were empirical tests of welfare reform that would scientifically assess what "works" in welfare.

Returning Power to the States

One critical effect of the waiver process was that it shifted the locus of welfare reform from the federal government to the states. From the 1960s to the mid-1970s, the movement in welfare had been toward the centralization of authority in the federal government. From the mid-1970s to the early 1990s, bureaucratic consistency in welfare administration was the rule.[5] The court rulings and changes in administrative procedures discussed in Chapter Three reduced the states' ability to restrict welfare use to categories of recipients. By the mid-1990s, the centralization and bureaucratic consistency of welfare was viewed by many as its weakness.

Centralization of authority in welfare came in response to abuses in welfare administration in the 1940s, 1950s, and 1960s. Discriminatory policies and practices were widespread during this time and ranged from the elimination of welfare benefits during cotton-picking season in southern states to the purging of "undesirable" families from the welfare rolls.[6] "Suitable home" rules required that women keep "moral" and orderly households in order to receive benefits. Although not always discriminatory at face value, these rules were used overwhelmingly against African American women, particularly in the South. In 1960, for example, Louisiana passed a suitable home law; 95 percent of the 24,000 children removed from the welfare rolls as a result were black.[7]

"Man in the house" rules, which made women who cohabited with men ineligible for benefits, led to midnight raids on families who received welfare. Even a single article of clothing could be used as evidence that a man lived in the house and thus the family was ineligible for benefits. Similarly, seasonal employment rules, which might not appear to be discriminatory prima facie, disproportionately excluded African Americans from the rolls. In part this was because, as Winifred Bell wrote, "seasonal employment policies emerged in areas where seasonal employment was performed by non-white families."[8] Race was a defining factor in discretionary welfare practices. African Americans received very different treatment than whites under the law in the 1940s, 1950s, and early 1960s.[9]

In the 1960s, there was a dramatic change in the role that race played in American social policy. Centralization of power at the federal level and the removal of discretionary powers from the states became hallmarks of social reform.[10] The passage of the 1964 Civil Rights Act and the Voting Rights Act two years later were critical turning points in American domestic policy. The Civil Rights Act in particular reversed the balance of power between the states and the federal government. As R. Shep Melnick explains: "In two short years the political logic of race had been reversed: previously objections from southerners had prevented the federal government from touching matters—such as education and welfare—with racial implications; now race became the rationale for federal control of the most fundamental elements of state government, including election laws and spending patterns."[11] These laws fundamentally changed the relationship between the states and the federal government.

Legal Services brought numerous lawsuits against the states that sharply limited the states' role in welfare.[12] In combination with the order from the Department of Health Education and Welfare (HEW) that separated the income support aspects of welfare from its social work activities, these legal challenges changed the nature of welfare. By the early 1970s, discrimination and discretion gave way to bureaucratic consistency across the states. States still set benefit levels, but they did little else. The bureaucratic model of welfare dominated. There was little individual treatment for welfare recipients. This minimized discrimination, but it also made the welfare system appear to be unresponsive and stagnant; welfare agencies focused purely on determining eligibility and cutting checks.

Other social changes were also shifting the dynamics of welfare politics. In the early 1960s, the Great Society programs were sowing the seeds for the explosion of the welfare rights movement that would take place in the late 1960s and early 1970s. Sponsored by the Office of Economic Opportunity (OEO), storefront welfare rights offices opened and promoted the aggressive use of welfare services and of litigation when applicants were denied services. These offices had a powerful effect on the size of the welfare rolls. For example, one study examined the impact of a newly opened welfare rights center and found that in one year the AFDC caseload in the surrounding area increased by 36.6 percent in contrast to the 8.6 percent increase in the city as a whole.[13] The changes in the 1960s and 1970s expanded the welfare caseloads and decreased the states' authority in the welfare programs. From the late 1970s to middle 1980s, the welfare rolls were fairly stagnant. In the late 1980s, the rolls began to explode again and the governors had little flexibility to respond. Not surprisingly, by the early 1990s, governors were chafing at the bit to change welfare.

The Early Waivers

The governors had been attempting to take a leading role in welfare reform since the middle 1980s. The National Governors Association, led by Bill Clinton, for example, had been active in advocating for increased work provisions in the 1988 welfare reform, the Family Support Act. Increased state control of welfare appeared to the governors to be a good idea both financially, since a portion of the money to fund AFDC came out of state coffers, and ideologically, since states' rights have an inherent appeal to those who govern the states. In 1986, President

Ronald Reagan created an opportunity for the governors when he centralized the authority to grant waivers in the White House-based Low-Income Opportunity Advisory Board (LIOAB). Reagan's centralization of power in the White House-based LIOAB smoothed the way for state programs to be approved and signaled that state initiatives in welfare would be welcomed by the administration.[14]

Newly elected Wisconsin governor Tommy Thompson quickly picked up on the potential to use waivers as a part of a broader political strategy to reform welfare. In what Michael Wiseman has termed Thompson's "first wave" of welfare reform waivers in 1987, Thompson developed a series of initiatives that reshaped welfare in Wisconsin. These initiatives included increased work requirements and incentives in addition to the well-known experimental "Learnfare" provisions, which required that children remain in school as a condition of welfare receipt.[15] Thompson also expanded existing welfare programs such as the Work Experience and Job Training Program (WEJT), which put adult welfare recipients to work and provided job training. A key component of the WEJT was the Community Work Experience Program (CWEP), which put welfare recipients who failed to find paid employment into unpaid jobs. The waiver process under the LIOAB expanded what the governors could do with their welfare programs, but there were still considerable limits. Federal AFDC regulations remained restrictive.

As innovative as Thompson's first wave of initiatives were, they were also clearly in line with the intention of Section 1115 of the 1962 Public Welfare Amendments, which aimed to encourage programmatic experimentation to increase the well-being of families and children on AFDC. Learnfare, for example, tested the idea of school attendance requirements, but kept AFDC a state / federal partnership with considerable federal authority. Although these early waiver programs were important—both in creating support for the policies they contained and in foreshadowing the role of the waivers in the policy-making process—they do not constitute the fundamental turning point at which the waiver programs became an institutional channel for policymaking. The experiments were still tinkering at the edges of welfare. With the early waivers, Thompson attempted to make changes in the lives of welfare families, particularly by encouraging behaviors such as school attendance and work. He did not, however, attempt to use the waiver process to fundamentally restructure the relationship between welfare recipients and the state. The true shift in the function of the welfare waivers came in 1993.

The Clinton Waivers

By January 1993, when Clinton took office, the governors wanted the states to have real power and discretion again: local problems, they argued, need local solutions. Thompson was not the only governor who found welfare reform to be a powerful issue. Electoral pressure encouraged even the less entrepreneurial governors to advocate for welfare reform. By 1996, the politics of gubernatorial elections demanded that candidates take a stand on welfare reform. In a 1996 survey of state policymakers, 61 percent of governors' staffs reported that their governor was forced to publicly defend his or her position on welfare policies during the election.[16] David Bloomquist, a New Jersey reporter, noted "Garden State Republicans discovered during the early 1990s that welfare made a highly effective 'sucker punch issue' with which to fight Democratic Governor Jim Florio, who was narrowly defeated by Christine Todd Whitman in 1993."[17]

Similarly, a study of gubernatorial leadership on welfare reform in the Midwest found that Governor John Engler of Michigan had "linked his political capital to the success of welfare reform," and that "Governors Thompson and Engler clearly utilized their informal powers to garner press attention and eventually public acclaim for their [welfare reform] efforts. Both were active in Washington debates and were cognizant of their roles as leaders in federal and state welfare reform efforts."[18] The waivers gave the governors a chance to take back some of the power that they had lost in the welfare rights court cases, and to score some political points with constituents.

The governors used the waiver process to set the political agenda in welfare reform.[19] Thompson was particularly astute in using the waivers to influence the political debate. Months after Clinton's inauguration, Thompson submitted a request to run a small pilot program called Work Not Welfare (WNW). WNW required that welfare recipients work for their grants. The number of hours a participant had to work was determined by the dollar amount of the grant divided by the minimum wage. The heads of larger families would be required to work for more hours than the heads of smaller families, up to a maximum of forty hours a week. The work requirements were demanding and a radical departure from AFDC. In an even more significant departure, WNW contained a time limit on benefits. Recipients could only receive assistance for twenty-four months. No cash assistance would be available for thirty-six months after the twenty-four-month time limit was reached.[20] This definition of time-limited welfare was markedly different from the definition of time limits in the Clinton plan, which only sought to institute work requirements after the time limit, not to end benefits.

Wisconsin's WNW program was symbolically important. It was an attempt to define time-limited welfare before the president put forward his plan. As Thomas Kaplan explains, "The Work Not Welfare waiver request was widely viewed, when submitted in July 1993, as the governor's attempt to beat President Clinton to a time-limited welfare system."[21] Michael Wiseman articulates WNW's role in advancing a particular vision of welfare reform even more strongly.

Work Not Welfare was a political coup. Other states, most notably New Jersey, had already instituted benefit cap projects. But in 1993 WNW seemed to be yet another dramatic leap forward. It was a concrete proposal that specifically incorporated the features most often discussed by the president in the course of his campaign: a two-year time limit on benefits. Moreover, Governor Thompson managed to get his plan before the public well in advance of delivery of the administration's own scheme. Like earlier initiatives, while the WNW proposal received massive national publicity, its planned scale of implementation was small.[22]

WNW was small, serving only about one thousand participants over its entire lifespan. It was too small to have an impact on a large number of welfare recipients. The program was not designed with a rigorous evaluation component, and it took an inordinately long time for it to be implemented, which suggests that the policy statement made by the waiver request was at least as important as the program itself.

WNW was politically and symbolically important because it defined the term "welfare time limit." In an ironic twist, the Democrat-controlled Wisconsin legislature attached a provision to the WNW legislation that called for the elimination of AFDC in 1999. This provided the Republican governor with an opportunity to focus more resources and attention on welfare reform that aimed specifically at dismantling AFDC. The opportunity provided by the Wisconsin Democrats was noted outside of the state as well. Michael Wiseman writes: "The opportunity thus presented was widely recognized: The Hudson Institute, a conservative policy analysis organization with home offices in Indianapolis, promptly opened and funded an office in Madison [Wisconsin] that was specifically charged with providing technical support to the governor's reform task force. The Hudson Institute solicited and received financial contributions for its support effort from other foundations, most notably the Annie E. Casey Foundation of Baltimore."[23] The plan that the team developed in Wisconsin, Wisconsin Works, also known as W-2, created "the first fully articulated plan for what a state welfare system might look like in an era of block grants."[24]

Of all of the welfare waivers, those emanating from Wisconsin were among the most overtly targeted at changing welfare through an alternate policy-making channel. WNW was not primarily an experimental program to test time-limited welfare in order to determine if it was effective social policy. Rather, WNW was a tool to shape the debate in welfare reform by defining the term "time limit" and to pave the way toward eliminating AFDC. Even more dramatically, W-2 later was designed specifically to replace AFDC. Yet when the Department of Health and Human Services (HHS) announced its approval of WNW, the press release emphasized the evaluation component of the program. WNW was framed as an empirical test of time limits. HHS deputy secretary Walter Broadnax was quoted as saying, "Our approval of Wisconsin's demonstration shows that the Clinton administration is serious about providing the states with the flexibility needed to test innovations. . . . This is one of several state demonstrations designed to test the concept of time-limited receipt of AFDC benefits."[25] The press release went on to emphasize the research component of WNW by noting that "[t]he demonstration will be carefully evaluated. . . . "[26] The emphasis on the evaluation component seems curious considering that Wisconsin had fought against having a rigorous randomized evaluation. As an HHS report notes, "DHHS and the state of Wisconsin agreed that an experimental evaluation of WNW was inconsistent with the demonstration's emphasis on communitywide changes in the culture of welfare; it was feared that random assignment would dilute the cultural change sought. Consequently, Wisconsin received approval from the federal government for a quasi-experimental 'matched comparison county' design for the WNW evaluation."[27]

Wisconsin officials may have requested the omission of an experimental design from the pilot program for several reasons. First, as Wisconsin officials argued, a control group might have diluted the message for participants in the test county by leaving a half-changed welfare system. If random assignment meant that only some welfare recipients received the new "treatment" program, it very well might have undermined the sweeping changes in culture and practice that Thompson thought were central to true welfare reform. Second, they may have objected to the experimental design because they did not want to cede any control over the program to evaluators. Finally, evaluations with experimental designs notoriously produce small positive outcomes, even for the most successful programs. Since Thompson was trying to change a culture and shift a political debate, increases of 5 to 10 percent in employment rates, numbers that would be in keeping with prior successful reform efforts, could have dampened the impact of the program. Thompson wanted WNW to make a statement to welfare recipients, policymakers, and the American public. He did not want to dilute that statement with the conditional successes associated with rigorous policy evaluation.

Thompson was politically savvy and profoundly committed to the idea of reforming welfare. He was arguably the political actor most responsible for turning the waiver process into a policy-making channel. Thompson clearly recognized that welfare experiments were a way to get welfare reform done, and one that Clinton would support even when he disagreed with the content of the policy. David Ellwood recalled, "if the governor called the president [to facilitate a waiver request], he would say yes. . . . Tommy Thompson figured this out real fast. Therefore, Tommy seemed to do pretty well in this process."[28] Policy evaluation, in this context, was beside the point.

Florida's Family Transition Plan (FTP) also worked around policy evaluation in order to make a big statement about welfare. In the case of Florida, rather than reject the evaluation, administrators provided alternative numbers that defined the program's "success" both for its participant and for the broader policy audience emphasizing, for example, that "not one" participant who complied with the program needed a job at the time limit. Florida used administrative procedures, as discussed in Chapters Four and Five, to define compliance as having a job by the time limit. This made it impossible for a participant to be unemployed and compliant when she reached her time limit and thus eliminated the job guarantee pushed by Clinton. More importantly, it permitted Florida to claim that no one who had been compliant with the program reached the time limit without a job. WNW and the FTP were not only or even primarily about testing new welfare ideas; they were political tools.

There were also waiver requests that were clear responses to immediate political demands within the states. For example, the state of California, in the middle of a budget crisis, requested a waiver to test the effect of statewide cuts in welfare benefits on recipients' work efforts. David Ellwood explains,

The state of California comes and asks for a waiver to test whether or not reducing benefits increases work effort. Now the reason they needed a waiver to reduce benefits was that there was a rule that you could not reduce benefits. . . . So, the state of California comes in and says they want this [waiver]. What is really going on is that the state of California has this massive budget deficit, just a huge problem. They have among the highest [AFDC] benefits in the country. . . . So, the state comes in and says, "we want to do a statewide experiment to see if lowering benefits increases work effort." It takes a really generous interpretation to believe that this is really about social science, whether this is an experiment.[29]

The California experiment was ultimately approved by HHS and a small "control group" was pulled out for the purpose of the evaluation. The average family's benefits were cut by a few dollars a month.

Fast Track

In August 1995, Clinton announced that he would "fast track" welfare reform by simplifying the waiver process. This marked a transition point in the use of the waivers as a channel to reform welfare. The fast-track policy enabled a state to submit welfare reform waiver requests that had at least one of five components: (1) a work-trigger time limit, (2) new work requirements, (3) requirements that minor mothers live with their parents, (4) improved child support collection, or (5) the use of welfare money to subsidize the hiring of welfare recipients by private employers.[30]

Announcing the "fast-track" program, Donna Shalala directly acknowledged the policy-making function of the waivers: "The Clinton Administration is helping the governors right now carry out real welfare reform, even as Congress delays on national legislation."[31] Mary Jo Bane similarly acknowledged, "We are encouraging states to use this quick and easy process to end welfare as we know it."[32] The fast-track process was not only an effort by the Clinton administration to create the appearance that it was leading the efforts for reform; it was also an attempt to harness the political power of the pilot programs and steer them back toward advancing work-trigger time limits.

Before August 1995, many high-profile waiver programs had been small, symbolic programs, such as Florida's FTP and Wisconsin's WNW, that attempted to set the welfare reform agenda by defining the meaning of welfare reform and the term "time limit." After August 1995, the waivers were increasingly used to structurally undermine the AFDC programs in the states and to make national reform inevitable. The tone of the HHS press releases also shifted after August 1995. They began to acknowledge that the waiver programs were not testing reform but were themselves a part of the reform process. This was also a tacit acknowledgment that the waiver demonstration programs were defining the meaning of welfare reform in the public eye. The Clinton administration did not announce that it would fast track all waiver applications, only those that fit with its own vision of welfare.

HHS explicitly acknowledged the political role of the welfare experiments even as the momentum of the welfare experiments shifted toward benefit-termination time limits and away from work-trigger time limits. In November 1995, announcing small grants to innovative welfare programs, Shalala stated: "President Clinton is committed to signing a welfare reform bill that will help move people from welfare to work. . . . This administration has provided 35 states the ability to *enact* welfare reform with waivers. Even while Congress debates, these grants will help states change local welfare offices one office at a time"(italics added).[33]

Agendas, Legitimacy, and Bureaucratic Structure

The waiver programs served two functions: a symbolic, agenda-setting and policy-legitimating function, and a structural alteration function. Interestingly, the types of waiver programs that served each function were different. Small, high profile programs, like Wisconsin's WNW and Florida's FTP, played a primarily symbolic role. They defined the meaning of time limits and helped to set the welfare reform agenda. Not coincidentally, these programs were tightly controlled to minimize the financial and political risks. These programs were about image, not fundamentally restructuring the welfare bureaucracy. It was politically important to demonstrate that time-limited welfare programs could exist without catastrophic consequences. The first important step was to define time limits, as WNW did. The FTP then provided evidence that a time-limited program did not have to be cruel; community representatives ensured that the program was fair. Together these programs defined and embodied the idea of time limits.

In contrast, the larger statewide programs, such as the Illinois Work and Responsibility Program, fundamentally restructured the welfare bureaucracy. The Work and Responsibility Program contained a firm time limit of two years for all recipients whose children were thirteen years or older.[34] Wisconsin Works (W2), which was implemented after the 1996 welfare reform passed, was expressly designed to replace AFDC. The Virginia Independence Program (VIP), phased in over several years, also contained a two-year time limit on benefits.[35] There were earlier statewide waiver programs, notably Michigan's To Strengthen Michigan Families (TSMF) and California's Assistance Payments Demonstration Project (APDP), both implemented in 1992. These programs, however, did not fundamentally restructure welfare in their states in the way that later ones would. Instead, they tended to tinker with more minor policy areas, including work incentive formulas. In the later statewide programs, the public perception mattered. Thompson put W2 forward as an example of what the states could do if block grants replaced welfare. But they also aimed at restructuring welfare from the ground up.

By 1995, the true target of reform became the bureaucratic structure of AFDC and the institution of welfare itself. As Bane explains, the waivers "moved from being a situation where the experimental group and the control group would be a similar size—and both small—to being statewide with the exception of a control group that was pulled out for the purposes of evaluation."[36] The air and ground attacks—the symbolic and structural challenges—demolished AFDC even before federal legislative action.

As noted in Chapter Three, early in 1996, Elisabeth Boehnen and Thomas Corbett wrote, "Waivers are no longer granted merely to learn new things to inform national policy; they are increasingly used to circumvent national policy."[37] In fact, the waivers went beyond circumventing national policy and became an institutional channel for policymaking. An editorial from the Institute for Research on Poverty made the point starkly: "Even if Congress does not pass legislation ending the open-ended entitlement to welfare, the rapid pace at which states are requesting waivers means the eventual dismantling of the current welfare system."[38]

The waivers were also physically changing welfare offices. To emphasize these structural changes, many states, including Florida and

Wisconsin, painted their welfare offices and put up motivational signs to signal the changes brought about by the pilot programs. Pictures of ticking clocks emphasized the time limit. Drawings of working women in business suits conveyed the new expectations of work. These were efforts to change the institutional culture of welfare offices and to convey to both recipients and staff the message that welfare had changed and that reform was real. In addition to the physical changes in the welfare offices, many pilot programs dramatically altered the services provided to welfare recipients. The rules of welfare changed, most notably with time limits. Social services, job placement, and "diversion"—discouraging families from applying for welfare—became central to welfare offices that had previously determined eligibility and cut checks.[39]

These changes were not taking place on the margins of social welfare. They were restructuring welfare throughout the country. Between 1992 and 1995, forty states sought waivers to reform welfare.[40] A full year before the Personal Responsibility and Work Opportunity Reconciliation Act (PRWORA) passed, thirty-five states had welfare waivers.[41] Even more strikingly, individual waiver demonstration projects had grown dramatically in scope. In 1992, most states requested waivers for only a few federal rules. By 1995, pilot programs often requested waivers from forty or more federal requirements. There were not only numerically more welfare reform demonstration projects—individual programs were increasingly complex and ambitious.

By mid-1995, nineteen states had approved waivers for time-limited pilot welfare programs. New Jersey, Georgia, Virginia, and eight other states had waivers to test family caps, which excluded children born more than ten months after the mother began receiving welfare from a family's grant. States including California, Massachusetts, and Wisconsin also modified their earnings disregard. This allowed families on welfare to keep more of the money they earned. Under AFDC, earned income over a certain level was "taxed" dollar for dollar and deducted from the welfare grant, which critics claimed meant work did not pay for welfare recipients. Thirty-one states had waivers that permitted requiring welfare recipients to work or engage in job training as a condition of benefit receipt. Numerous other policy areas were also covered by the waiver requests.[42]

The scope of the welfare waivers undercuts the claim that the pilots were ever intended to be tests of welfare reform. If the goal had truly been to test welfare reform ideas, it would have made far more sense to have different programs test particular ideas and then to determine which policies had a positive effect. Michael Wiseman, in an assessment of the welfare reform experiments in the 1990s, wrote,

Objective evaluation of this avalanche of novelties is difficult. A defensible summary is that few will ever produce any results usable in the process of policy development. In general the interventions were too poorly planned, the number of program changes too large, and the evaluation schemes too limited in scope to encompass the range of possible program effects. In some ways this outcome was politically desirable. In state welfare reform initiatives, the political payoff from demonstration activism may be more important than the modest gains in knowledge that might be attained. Moreover, in most cases the political payoff seems to come early, while assessment is postponed virtually indefinitely.[43]

The primary goal of the waiver programs was not to test and learn about reform. It was to reform welfare from the bottom up and to define the terms of the debate. The political payoff of the demonstration programs came early. Symbolic political payoffs could come as early as the *announcement* of a program and certainly came by the early implementation. The structural advantages also came early—at the moment that the institutional structures of AFDC were dismantled and replaced with those of the waiver program. There were additional political benefits to be gained from the pilots over time, but many of the greatest benefits came almost instantaneously.

How did the waiver programs shift the political debate around welfare reform? Few Americans were involved in the reform efforts themselves. Many of those who were involved at the higher levels were ideologically committed to the idea of time-limiting welfare or of requiring work. Recipients, certainly, were aware of changes in their benefits, and recipients were one audience targeted by reformers. Sending "the message" to welfare recipients that welfare had changed was a fundamental goal of reform in Florida, Wisconsin, and other states. However, given the low voter turnout among the poor and their limited political power, reformers had to target two other audiences in order to build support for their particular version of welfare reform—voters, to garner broad-based political support for reform, or at least to avoid widespread public opposition, and federal lawmakers.

When PRWORA passed, there was no public outcry that this was not the desired reform. By 1996, the work-trigger model of time-limited welfare was politically dead even though it was, as Kent Weaver noted, "probably closer to the views of the mythical 'median voter' than the welfare provisions of the Contract with America."[44] There are several reasons why such a large shift in social policy was met with so little public comment; two of them have been widely discussed and the third largely overlooked. The simplest explanation for why the public did not object to the triumph of benefit-termination time limits over work-trigger time limits is that by 1996 animosity toward the AFDC program was so great that almost any program that replaced it would have been greeted favorably. Considering that in 1995, 56 percent of Americans thought that the welfare system did more harm than good, it is not surprising that the replacement of AFDC with Temporary Assistance for Needy Families (TANF) did not prompt rioting in the streets.[45] In addition to nurturing the widespread public perception that anything would be better than AFDC, Clinton had artfully maneuvered to claim as much credit as he could for the policy.

Many of the president's closest advisors, including Peter Edelman, David Ellwood, and Mary Jo Bane strenuously objected to the bill. Whether the president signed the bill out of political opportunism or moral conviction is widely debated. In August 1996, when Clinton signed PRWORA, the 1996 election was quickly approaching. The devastating losses of the 1994 midterm elections were still fresh. Welfare reform had been one of Clinton's strong points in 1992. He did not want it to be a liability in 1996. Signing PRWORA would take away one of the Republicans' weapons and fulfill a campaign promise.

"Today, we are ending welfare as we know it,"[46] Clinton said as he signed the welfare reform legislation. By evoking the phrase, "ending welfare as we know it," Clinton framed the new welfare law as the fulfillment of his reform plan rather than its defeat. Clinton's opponent, Republican candidate Bob Dole jabbed, "After two vetoes of similar welfare reform bills, Clinton knew he couldn't afford a third strike."[47] But Clinton's political victory was won. Others have speculated that Clinton, despite disliking aspects of the bill, did view TANF as better than AFDC and signed it because he thought that it was good policy as well as good politics. Wendell Primus speculates on the president's motives: "I think he truly believed that welfare was hurting people. . . . I know he didn't have a problem with the block grants. I know he didn't have a problem with the loss of entitlement. . . . I don't think there were many things that disturbed him in this welfare bill . . . there was a lot more substance [to signing the bill] than just the political."[48]

Thus, two factors help to explain why the American public expressed so little concern over a fundamental restructuring of the welfare state: (1) AFDC was so reviled that any reform was welcome, and

(2) Clinton took enough credit for TANF to create an impression of bipartisanship despite the fact that many Democratic members of Congress voted against welfare reform. Related to Clinton's credit claiming, there was a third often-overlooked factor that encouraged public acceptance of benefit-termination time limits. The pilot programs had legitimated benefit-termination time limits because the time-limited programs were widely defined as successful. The credit that Clinton was claiming when he signed PRWORA was not only for signing federal welfare reform into law. It was also for instigating the process that led to the dramatic rise in the scope and number of welfare experiments and creating the conditions that made reform possible. Clinton would go on to state that "we know welfare reform works"—a claim he based on the falling caseloads that resulted, at least in part, from the existence of the pilot programs.

The media played a role in the legitimization of benefit-termination time limits.[49] The governors could not have used the welfare experiments as a political issue if the media had not provided coverage of the issue. Newspaper coverage provides a means of transmitting information to voters and policymakers alike. In every congressional office, one of the first tasks of the staff in the morning is to comb through the national and local papers and bring important articles to the Congress member's attention. Media are very important in defining the terms of public and political debates by highlighting particular issues. Issues not covered by the media can lose their place on the political agenda.

Legitimacy

Why do some ideas become powerful whereas comparable ones do not? What makes a policy idea legitimate at one point in time? John David Skrentny, in his 1996 book *The Ironies of Affirmative Action: Politics, Culture, and Justice in America*, makes the point that preferences for veterans have long been considered acceptable whereas preferences for racial minorities and women remain contested.[50] What made benefit-termination time limits an acceptable choice in 1996 when they would have been almost unthinkably radical a decade earlier? Neo-Institutionalist scholars, in discussing organizational behavior, have argued that when actors face choices, they often look to others' experiences and decisions for guidance.[51] Perceptions of illegitimate choices can have powerful impacts on policy change. Environments affect institutions.[52]

In the welfare reform experiments, what the governors were doing affected the choices of other governors and their states. Once a policy idea, such as benefit-termination time limits, was approved for one state, other states followed suit. As Bane explains, "in the states there was a dynamic going on, of the states copying each other and wanting to compete with each other."[53] This was true for two reasons. First, having seen that the federal government was willing to approve a type of waiver, other states rightly recognized that the path had been paved for them to receive approval for the same policy idea. Second, once a policy idea had been approved and was on its way to being implemented, the idea itself gained legitimacy. Once one state did it, it became an acceptable policy option.

Political Institutionalists, who typically study policy adoption more directly than their organizationally focused Neo-Institutionalist colleagues, often subsume the effects of culture within the preferences of state actors when explaining policy choices. This is reasonable. Culture does not float freely in the air, influencing policy through osmosis. Culture is mediated through individual actors who have various degrees of power and abilities to shape policy. But how do collective social realities emerge? Just as language and vocabulary encourage isomorphism—the convergence to a single form—in organizations, perhaps the common definition of terms by the media can influence the meaning of concepts in social policy.[54] Media in the middle 1990s may not have had a great effect shaping public opinion regarding welfare; the American public was resolutely against AFDC to start. Media coverage of the time-limited pilot programs, however, may have helped to define welfare reform *as* time limits and time limits *as* benefit-termination time limits.[55]

Trends in Media Reports and Waiver Requests from 1987 to 1995

Brian Gran and I have conducted research on when the tide shifted from work-trigger time limits to benefit-termination time limits in the states and in the media. When looking at the media and state policy choices, it is difficult to determine the direction of the relationship observed. Did media accounts shape innovations in state policies? Or did innovations in state policies shape media accounts? Were media accounts and state policies changing in response to an unidentified third factor, which influenced each independently? Although it is impossible to sort out the nature of the relationship by following trends alone, the trends are striking and suggest that benefit-termination time limits won the welfare reform battle well before 1996. The patterns we found show the triumph of benefit-termination time limits over work-trigger time limits by 1995. Media trends suggest that it was not only the ascendance of the Republicans in Congress in 1994 that brought about PRWORA: there was also a more broadly based shift, reflected in the media and in the states, toward benefit-termination time limits.

In our research, we traced indicators of the quality and quantity of welfare reform ideas at the state level and the quality and quantity of elite newspaper accounts on welfare reform efforts, specifically in the *New York Times* and the *Washington Post*. As a measure for policy innovation, we used applications from the states to the federal government to test welfare reform ideas. This was a good measure of policy ideas in welfare reform from the late 1980s to mid-1990s. We began our analysis in 1987 in order to place the high activity period of 1992 to 1995 in a broader context.

What we termed "a waiver" is technically a package of waivers submitted together. For example, a welfare reform plan might have a time limit *and* permit participants to keep a greater portion of any income they earn. Each of these provisions would require a waiver. As long as these two requests were submitted at the same time and as a part of the same program, we counted them as being a part of the same "waiver." We opted to count packages of waivers rather than individual waivers because we felt that this better reflected the spirit of the pilot programs. A time-limited program that also included a "learnfare" provision or a type of sanction that required the Department of Agriculture's approval was not proportionally less of a time-limited program than one with no other provisions that required waivers. We then coded the waivers as having a benefit-termination time limit, a work-trigger time limit, or no time limit.

For the media analysis, we gathered articles on welfare reform from the *New York Times* and the *Washington Post* from 1986 to 1995. Although the *New York Times* and *Washington Post* are clearly not representative of mass media reports, they are good indicators of policy-relevant, elite information and framing. We did not review insider political publications, such as *The Hill*, because they represent a specialized knowledge we did not view as external to the legislative process. We also omitted small local newspapers, many of which provided too little policy detail to address the question in which we were interested. The *New York Times* and the *Washington Post* were a midpoint between the highly specific policy-oriented publications and more popular, arguably less influential media.

We conducted a search on the Lexis-Nexis service for any articles on "welfare reform" and then excluded editorials and op-ed pieces. After collecting the articles resulting from this search, we analyzed 379 articles for content. We separated the articles into one of four categories: "No mention of time limits," "Benefit-termination time limits," "Work-trigger time limits," and "Ambiguous time limits." A few articles clearly mentioned both benefit-termination time limits and work-trigger time limits; these articles were coded as both. Articles that mentioned time limits but did not make clear whether they would be of the work-trigger model or the benefit-termination model were coded as ambiguous. For example, articles frequently stated that after a time limit, welfare recipients would "have to work," but did not specify whether the state would provide employment or simply terminate benefits. These articles were coded as "ambiguous." Articles that did not mention time limits were often referring to time-limited programs. In these cases, the articles often focused on another aspect of a time-limited welfare program or, particularly in the spike of media attention in 1995, on a political battle. The policy models implied by the articles were not always correct. For example, some work-trigger programs were reported as having benefit-termination model time limits. This analysis therefore indicates the quantity of media attention to welfare reform over the given period and traces the emergence and definition of time limits in elite northeastern media accounts.

Waivers

From the mid-1980s to 1991, the number of waiver requests was fairly small. At this point, the waiver program was operating as a minor experimental component of the largely stable and entrenched AFDC program. In 1992, when Clinton pledged to "end welfare as we know it," President George H. W. Bush responded to Clinton by expanding the power of the states to deviate from federal AFDC rules through the federal waiver program. As a result, in 1992 there was a surge in waiver applications.

Waivers

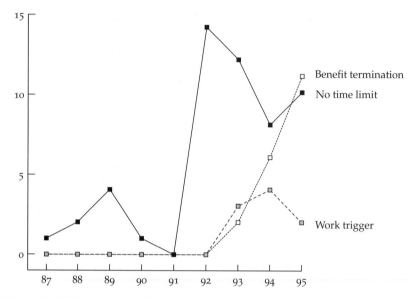

Figure 6.1 Waiver requests by type of time limit, 1987–95

Competing with the "work-trigger" policy model, which provided a job guarantee to all welfare recipients who "played by the rule" but were unable to find a job by the time limit, was the "benefit-termination" model of time-limited welfare, which simply terminated benefits at the time limit. In the states, the number of "benefit-termination" model time limits surpassed "work-trigger" model limits in 1994. Other proposals for welfare reform dropped. By 1995, the benefit-termination model dominated and there were markedly fewer applications for "work-trigger" programs, despite the Clinton administration's attempt to "fast track" such applications.

Media Coverage

The non-time-limited welfare reform initiatives of 1992 garnered little media coverage. In 1993, when welfare reform became a battle between the two time-limited policy models, media attention began to intensify and continued to do so through 1995.

There was considerable ambiguity over the nature of the time limits

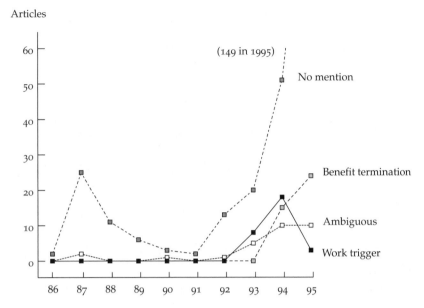

Articles

Figure 6.2　Types of time limits specified in articles on welfare reform, 1986–95

in media coverage. It was common for articles to note that after reaching the time limit former welfare recipients would be "forced to work" or "have to find a job." For example, a 1994 *Washington Post* article reported that "Welfare mothers, other than those with a disability or who care for disabled or infant children, would be required to find work within two years of enrolling for Aid to Families with Dependent Children."[56] The article does not specify whether or not the women would have access to public jobs. By omitting this information, the article seems to imply that welfare recipients would have to find jobs on their own. The Clinton plan, the subject of the article, did require that welfare recipients go to work, but it also provided a job guarantee for those who made a good faith effort but could not find employment. The 1995 spike in articles that did not mention time limits reflected the intense media attention given that year to battles on Capitol Hill over welfare reform. These articles typically mentioned the political players involved in welfare reform but not the details of the policy ideas that they were advocating.

In local papers, the distinction between work-trigger and benefit-termination time limits was also often lost.[57] A 1994 article in the *Orlando Sentinel* introduced readers to the FTP in the following way:

> Mad that the number of Floridians on welfare more than doubled during the past 10 years? You're in crowded company. Welfare reform is destined to be the hottest of political fashions. Already, the issue is being grabbed by everyone from Newt Gingrich and President Clinton to Lawton Chiles and the state Legislature. But if you think that Florida has done nothing about its 648,691 women and children on the dole, you're wrong. This year, Florida began telling some welfare recipients in Escambia County that their benefits will be cut off after two years. . . . In exchange for the two-years-and-out restriction, the women in the "Family Transition Program" are getting help in becoming ready to take and hold down a job.[58]

In December 1994, by all appearances, the FTP would have a work-trigger time limit. Yet the *Orlando Sentinel* article not only presents the FTP as having a benefit-termination time limit; it also obscures the political battles over welfare by calling it a fashion that everyone from Bill Clinton to Newt Gingrich was following.

There were few articles that conveyed the deeper issues and conflicts involved in welfare reform. Jason DeParle, in a uniquely detailed and accurate 1993 article, notes, "Time limits have the appeal of sounding cheap: Two years and then people will have to work. But work where? Some will find private jobs, but many will not, especially in an economy with 8.3 million out of work."[59] Deparle highlighted the question of where the jobs would come from and how former recipients would find them. More often, however, journalists simply noted in passing that the recipients would have to "find work within two years or lose their benefits."[60] Although there is no reason for journalists to mention policy details in every article, the effect in the case of welfare reform was to obscure the difference between the work-trigger and benefit-termination models of time limits so that a casual reader might think they were essentially the same. By the time Clinton signed welfare reform, time-limited programs were ubiquitous and the term "time limit" had been defined as the benefit-termination model.

Thus, in reaction to the political imperative created by Clinton's campaign pledge to "end welfare as we know it," there was a flurry of policy innovation from 1992 to 1996. The media, building on Clinton's 1993 catch phrase "two years and you're off," reported relatively few details of the policy debate until time-limited welfare emerged as a viable policy model. Moreover, in 1994 at the political height of Clinton's work-trigger plan, media coverage that specifically mentioned time limits implied that the time-limit policy would be work-trigger and benefit-termination in roughly equally proportions. And by 1995, there was virtually no mention of work-trigger time limits in the media at all.

Pushing the Envelope

The state welfare waivers facilitated the transition from work-trigger to benefit-termination time limits. Each waiver pushed the envelope a little bit further. Because the welfare experiments were more about advancing welfare reform than testing welfare reform, each program set a precedent. Officials in the Clinton administration were aware of this, although they were divided over the desirability of setting policy precedent in areas such as firm time limits and family caps. As Mary Jo Bane notes,

The states did not see the waiver process as a learning process. The states saw the waivers as a flexibility process for themselves. So the dynamic in their heads was not "they are doing that experiment over there, therefore we will wait and see what the outcome of that experiment is." The dynamic was "they are doing that experiment over there, we want to do that, too." So that was one of the reasons that you had to worry about [setting precedent with] even the small ones.[61]

As noted earlier, David Ellwood similarly explained, "Our fear was as soon as you were there in the waiver process. As soon as you had indicated that you had no line in the sand, no stopping point on waivers, that legitimated [those policy ideas] or made more difficult the process of drawing lines in the sand on welfare reform nationally."[62]

Members of the administration were concerned that approving waivers was legitimating policy ideas—giving them a stamp of approval, even if it was conditional approval, from the administration. Both Mary Jo Bane and David Ellwood supported the idea of letting the states experiment with welfare reform—both are leading academic researchers—but they were also cognizant of the political implications of the experiments. Therefore, there were some provisions that they did not want to approve for experiments. Ellwood explains,

If the leaders of welfare reform were being allowed to [have hard time limits], we knew they were going to be highly influential in the policy debate. So again, that would legitimate a course of policy action that we were not particularly interested in legitimizing. Yet, we had a president who said "we will approve waivers that we do not like." We also know that when Tommy [Thompson] calls up President Clinton, it is going to be over.[63]

HHS ultimately approved the majority waivers the states requested, although some of the more controversial waivers were bogged down in bureaucratic delaying tactics by those within HHS who did not want to see them approved. With so many welfare experiments approved, ideas that might have seemed beyond the pale in the early 1990s entered the political mainstream.

The president's inclination to support governors and his personal ties to many of the most entrepreneurial governors were important factors contributing to the shape and content of TANF. The welfare experiments, however, mattered in their own right. Their approval by the Clinton administration helped to legitimate the policy ideas that they contained. Once they were up and running—and being rigorously evaluated—the debate over time limits left the realm of values and political debate and entered the technical realm of policy questions. The pilots appeared to show that welfare reform "worked." The welfare experiments had pushed the envelope in terms of what policy ideas were viable and minimized the public debate surrounding the desirability of those policies. The waivers had been transformed from a small program for policy experimentation to an institutional channel for policymaking. Through this channel, activist governors and state legislatures reformed welfare and created a revolution in the states.

CHAPTER 7

The Rhetoric and Institutional Politics
of Policy Experiments

> Postal officials rarely introduced new program ideas all at once. Instead, they proposed small pilot programs or used existing administrative machinery to give new programs a trial run without statutory authorization. . . . [D]emonstrating and publicizing program success usually warmed contemporary newspapers and magazines to the idea unless they were predisposed against it. More important, experimentation allowed postal officials to gather piecemeal support for their programs and to build coalitions.
>
> Daniel P. Carpenter, 2000[1]

Aid to Families with Dependent Children (AFDC) ended well before President Clinton signed the Personal Responsibility and Work Opportunity Reconciliation Act (PRWORA). It withered as local welfare offices painted their walls, retrained their caseworkers, and implemented time limits, diversion policies, and a myriad of new policy ideas. The expansion of the waiver process under Clinton opened up new spaces for policy ideas to incubate and then rapidly spread throughout the country. A new set of actors became important in the policy-making process. Caseworkers and local administrators gained a critical position in policymaking as their actions defined welfare reform. They defined the meaning of welfare reform not only at the street level, where clients experienced the new programs, but also in the media, which reported how welfare reform "worked" based largely on local administrative insights and statistics. Across state lines, administrators sought to learn lessons from the state experiments that preceded them. State actors not only defined welfare reform for the American public and federal poli-cymakers; they also defined it for each other. Governors and state legis-lators gained new power to shape the national welfare debate as they used the experimental waiver program to push new policies, many of which would have been unthinkable outside of an experimental rubric. Evaluation itself took on a role in shaping welfare policy, not because the new policies grew out of empirical evidence, as proponents of pol-icy evaluation envisioned, but rather because the experimental pilot programs provided a space for new reform ideas to take root and de-velop into viable policy alternatives.

The end of welfare began well before PRWORA, and the dismantling of the American welfare state will most likely continue long after it. Un-derstanding the unique processes that led to AFDC's demise and their continued relevance in American social policymaking is far more useful than viewing PRWORA as a singularly dramatic event that occurred wholly through normal policy-making channels. The latter is a static view that misinterprets the events that led up to PRWORA, limits our ability to understand the development of the American welfare state, and hinders our ability to predict political strategies and mechanisms for further state building and retrenchment.

Before the 1990s, AFDC had been notoriously hard to change. It grew from a small program that provided money to the children of select "worthy" widows into a comprehensive social safety net for America's poor children and their (primarily single-parent) families. For political conservatives who thought that the New Deal itself was a bad idea, the expansion of AFDC was the welfare state run amuck. Franklin Roo-sevelt himself, conservatives noted, had said that government "must and shall quit this business of relief."[2]

Entrenched social programs, however, are politically hard to end. The demise of AFDC offers several key lessons for understanding con-temporary policymaking and particularly policymaking that is contin-gent on first dismantling the legacy of the New Deal. The first major victory for conservatives who wished to dismantle the American wel-fare state did not take place as a result of considered public debate and a decisive congressional vote. Rather, it occurred slowly and largely through the nonlegislative channel provided by the waiver process; governors and their staffs made deals with the Department of Health and Human Services (HHS), program administrators defined social policy at the street level, the realm of feasible policy choices expanded, and the entitlement to welfare, although remaining the law, was no longer a reality at the ground level.

Dismantling AFDC was certainly facilitated by the program's unpopularity. It may also be true that the program was vulnerable because it was arguably a "semi-entitlement" rather than a full entitlement and therefore had fewer constituents to defend it. AFDC was clearly not an entitlement in the sense that all citizens were eligible to receive benefits based solely on their citizenship. It never had the expansiveness and durability of Western European-style entitlements. Nonetheless, as discussed in Chapter Three, federal court decisions in the 1960s had established that recipients had a firm claim on benefits, often referred to as an "entitlement to welfare," and many in the scholarly and popular debates began to view the program in terms of an "entitlement." Whatever the constellation of factors that made the program vulnerable—and I would argue that the visible failure of the program was one—others had tried to reform AFDC with little success. It took a new political channel to dismantle AFDC, a channel that may be used to dismantle other, more popular entitlement programs.

Although the entitlement to welfare did not officially end until 1996, it had ended in practice at least a year before. In June 1996, before Clinton signed PRWORA, Douglas Besharov, a scholar at the American Enterprise Institute for Public Policy Research, wrote, "[I]n recent months, 25 states have received waivers that go to the very heart of the program. . . . [T]his new round of waivers has the practical effect of ending the unconditional entitlement to welfare and, in its stead, has given administrators and caseworkers vast new discretion in deciding who gets welfare."[3] The pilot programs undermined the bureaucratic structure of AFDC and subtly pushed the envelope of reform far beyond where it ever would have gone without them. The waiver process laid a foundation for the end of the entitlement, returned to the states control and discretion in welfare, and defined time limits as firm time limits.

What facilitated the end of the entitlement to welfare was not the waiver process in itself, but how it was used. The waiver process had been around since 1962 and had operated more or less within its original intent, as a program to test welfare reform ideas. The waiver process, stretched as it was by the Clinton administration, did something different. It permitted the establishment of an alternative, parallel, welfare system even while AFDC was up and running. Between 1992 and 1996, the waiver process was used to replace AFDC. It changed the bureaucratic structure of welfare offices across the country. It made room for administrators and policy entrepreneurs who favored particular forms of welfare, most notably firm time limits, within the official state structures.

There were considerable professional and political rewards to those who were active in state reform efforts. The waiver programs provided an institutional home for advocates of particular approaches to welfare reform. Even within the lower ranks of welfare caseworkers, particularly in early small and high-profile pilots such as Wisconsin and Florida, the waivers provided an institutional structure through which those who energetically backed reform could be consolidated and rewarded. These programs were set up as "model" programs with hand selected staff. In this way, the waiver programs created the ground support and infrastructure necessary to radically and quickly reform welfare. Equally important, this infrastructure was *state specific*; it was different in Vermont than it was in California. This was essential groundwork for turning the welfare system over to the states. Under AFDC, each state had had its own welfare system and so to some extent the necessary infrastructure for returning power to the states already existed. What the waiver programs did was strengthen the internal focus of the state administrative bureaucracies and provide a mechanism for advancing within the welfare bureaucracies those with an orientation toward particular types of state-based reform.

Equally important, the waiver programs began to dismantle the AFDC program at its base. Pilot programs replaced the old AFDC program in very literal and physical ways. The names of the welfare offices and programs changed. In many cases the buildings themselves changed as administrators had offices painted and even arranged for welfare recipients to enter buildings through different doors to emphasize that the "new" welfare program was different from the old one. The message of welfare changed; welfare recipients were told that welfare was time limited and to be used only as a last resort. The pilot programs were, in effect, a Trojan horse. Under the guise of experimentation, new policy ideas were allowed to come in and take root in a system that otherwise would not have allowed them.

Framing the welfare pilot program as experiments was a direct response to the political opportunity in the Public Welfare Amendments of 1962. The "experiment" provision provided a loophole in AFDC. The fact that this loophole was for experimentation, however, and not some other means for the states to build their own welfare programs, facilitated the fast and dramatic movement in policy ideas contained in the waivers. It is very difficult to object to simply *trying out* an idea. Yet as Bane and Ellwood note, once the Clinton administration had authorized a waiver for a particular policy idea, it became politically tricky for the administration to fight against that idea. Moreover, framing the welfare pilots as experiments took them out of the realm of political debate and into the realm of expert knowledge. Only the evaluators could truly say whether or not the program was working because only they had the necessary expertise to scientifically determine the policy's effect. In addition, because of the politics around the waivers, few researchers not affiliated with the federally mandated, and state-contracted, evaluations had any access to data within the programs. Therefore, virtually all of the informed expert knowledge about these programs was located in evaluation corporations.

The result of all of these factors is that the waiver process did something very particular. It both increased and decreased the political salience of the ideas being discussed in welfare reform. On the one hand, the pilots and the colorful governors promoting them received considerable media attention. The pilots thus increased the political profile of welfare reform. On the other hand, the pilots took the reform ideas out of the public debate. Why debate something for which there would soon be an empirical answer? Similarly, because the pilots were "only experiments"—and because of President Clinton's close ties with the governors—officials in the Clinton administration faced pressure to approve waivers. Waiver approvals, particularly those for programs that contained very controversial policy ideas, arguably received less public comment and debate than they would have had they been for nonexperimental state programs because they were for *experiments*. Who can be against learning something about helping the poor more efficiently?

Once a wavier had been approved, however, other states quickly wanted to adopt the same policy. Neither the president nor the Congress was very sympathetic to the assumption of social science that there is little to gain by having twenty-six states run the same "experiment," particularly when each "experiment" is just different enough to rule out even the benefits of replication. Rather, the political view was along the lines of, "if California can do it, then why can't Iowa?" Once approved for a state pilot program, a policy idea instantly became an option for all states. At the same time, the evaluation corporations, dutifully and rigorously collecting data, were, perhaps unwittingly, contributing to the perception that the experiments *really were* experiments.

To summarize, the waivers shaped welfare reform in three ways: First, through the waiver process policy entrepreneurs, such as Governor Tommy Thompson of Wisconsin, were able to push the envelope of social policy and expand the landscape of policy options in welfare reform. The establishment of pilot programs in the states then undermined the bureaucratic structure of AFDC by replacing AFDC policy with new welfare programs that had their own bureaucratic structures. Second, the replication of policy ideas across the states and the rhetoric of scientific experimentation helped to legitimate those ideas by making them appear to be tested and proven well in advance of evaluation results. Finally, the institutional structure of the state pilot programs provided a mechanism for centralizing and supporting welfare experts, administrators, and staff sympathetic to the types of reform being pursued by each state, preparing the groundwork for a return of welfare to the states.

How the Waivers Ended the Entitlement

In the 1990s, the era of big government was over. The governors wanted greater authority in welfare. President Clinton was ideologically sympathetic to the governors and had close ties with many who took a leading role in welfare reform. The stage was set for reform. But policy reform is complex. It does not respond only to public will and presidential disposition. If it did, then welfare would have been radically reformed in the 1980s. Instead, the Family Support Act of 1988 barely made a dent in AFDC. Dismantling federal government programs and returning power to the states is not an easy task. The policy legacy of AFDC had to be overcome. Perhaps even more importantly, the entitlement to welfare had to be eliminated. Both of these facts created considerable structural barriers to reform.

Political Institutionalists have often focused on the origins and retrenchments of the welfare state.[4] Political Institutionalism, sometimes also referred to as Historical Institutionalism, stresses that political institutions shape public policy. Scholars employing this perspective evaluate the relationship between a state's institutional structure and policy outcomes.[5] In this context, scholars typically think of institutions as "both formal organizations and informal rules and procedures that structure conduct."[6] State structures can influence collective action and political alliances in many ways. For example, government systems vary by the degree of centralization of government power. Some researchers contend that, compared to unitary systems, federalized systems permit interest groups to have greater influence on policy development.[7] They hypothesize that federal systems have more points on which pressure may be placed on political decision makers.[8] These pressure points can slow down or inhibit policy formation because political actors must consider more factors and areas of challenge in instituting social policy programs in a federalist system. They also, however, provide numerous access points, which can promote policy adoption.

Political Institutionalism would appear to provide an ideal framework for explaining the rapid ascent of time-limited welfare, but so far it has not provided a definitive analysis. Understanding the institutional role of the pilot programs is the missing piece. The temporary pilot programs broke the policy trajectory of AFDC. Without detailing the institutional role of pilot programs in welfare reform, it is impossible to comprehend the dynamics that made AFDC crumble, eliminating the federal entitlement to welfare. Through the institutional channel of the waiver programs, states were able to define the terms of the debate in welfare reform. Thompson recognized the potential public relations function of the waivers when he submitted his time-limited welfare program—Work Not Welfare—before the president was able to release his program, which would have amounted to a public jobs program.

Thompson gained a "first mover" advantage, because, in what turned out to be a contest to define the meaning of time limits, he drew the first line in the sand quite far to the political right. In 1994 and 1995, other states began to pick up on the fact that they could "do welfare reform" through the waivers. As a result, the states began to apply for waivers to implement statewide "experimental" programs. The waivers defined what was possible in welfare reform. As Clinton's chief welfare reform architects Bane and Ellwood both noted, once the administration approved a waiver, the policy ideas in those waivers became legitimized. Other states would seek to obtain waivers to implement the same policies, and the administration lost some of its moral authority in arguing against the inclusion of these policies in federal law. If the effects would clearly be catastrophic, how could the administration have approved the policy in the first place?

Section 1115 of the 1962 Social Security Act allowed for experimental pilot programs that would otherwise be considered in violation of the entitlement to welfare. The idea of experimenting with welfare reform had considerable public support. As noted in Chapter One, in 1995, 52 percent of the American public favored experimenting with welfare reform compared to 29 percent who favored national reform. But the waiver programs were only secondarily about evaluation and building the knowledge base in social policy. They were primarily an alternate institutional channel for policy reform. In Douglas Besharov's words, "The state-by-state waiver process is an unexpected and unintended way to reform welfare. . . . "[9]

Not surprisingly, as the policy-making function of waiver programs emerged, the nature of policy experiments themselves changed. This change was particularly important for the Manpower Demonstration Research Corporation (MDRC), which had been a pioneer in randomized welfare experiments and had conducted the vast majority of the waiver evaluations. Ellwood explains:

> There was a period early on in MDRC, when they were doing social experiments. But they were social experiments that were conceived of by experts, or scholars or even advocates. Sort of "let's do this, we'll try it in three sites." It was really a top-down kind of thing. During welfare [in the early 1990s], MDRC got into a different mode—and the government did—which is "states, you decide what you want to do. You get invested [in reform] and so forth. But what we'll do is, as you do that, we will come up with a way to do a serious evaluation."[10]

Ellwood views this development as a positive one because it permits more state-level policy innovation while continuing to contribute to the policy knowledge base. The shift, however, did more than shift policy innovation from a top-down enterprise to a bottom-up enterprise. It also expanded the opportunity for the states to use the pilot programs as a tool for advancing welfare reform along particular ideological lines advocated by the governors and state legislatures. Ellwood rightly notes that this is not necessarily a bad development. The states may well be better suited to generating innovative social policy than the federal government or policy scholars. However, it does create a larger policy-making role for pilot programs.

The pilot programs also provided an opportunity to directly undermine the entitlement to welfare. Although the waivers technically preserved the entitlement, in practice the entitlement had been eliminated. Michael Lipsky has termed the loss of entitlement through administrative actions rather than political deliberation and decision making "bureaucratic disentitlement."[11]

Bureaucratic Disentitlement is a mode of fiscal and programmatic retrenchment that takes place through the obscure and routine actions of public authorities. . . . Retrenchment in social welfare policy normally comes to public attention through wholesale legislative cutbacks or highly publicized administrative decisions. . . . In Bureaucratic Disentitlement, obligations to social welfare beneficiaries are reduced and circumscribed through the largely obscure "bureaucratic" actions and inactions of public authorities.[12]

The administrative elimination of the job guarantee in Florida's Family Transition Program is a clear example of bureaucratic disentitlement. The waiver process itself, it is important to note, can be seen as a form of bureaucratic disentitlement. The original intent behind the waiver process was to permit small experiments with considerable safeguards. Most of the safeguards provided in the Social Security Act were disregarded. The experiments included provisions to deny individuals benefits to which they otherwise would have been entitled. Arguably, Congress would have supported the policies contained in these programs, but they were never voted on, and even those involved in the programs admit that they stretched the law as far as it could reach. One of the most dangerous aspects of bureaucratic disentitlement, as Lipsky notes, is that it takes place without public deliberation; it is not a part of the normal policy-making process.

Experimental programs heighten the dangers of bureaucratic disentitlement. If the states view pilot programs as their "way to get reform done," then they may pursue policies that do not include the protections to which recipients are federally entitled. Even if, as was the case in Florida, the Department of Health and Human Services insists that some protections be put back in a waiver program, the states can bureaucratically disentitle recipients. Thus, the entitlement becomes almost a "blue law"—appearing on the books but not in practice. Once this happens, the policy legacy of the entitlement is weakened, making it much easier to do away with the entitlement altogether.

Ironically, some in the Clinton White House had hoped the waiver process could be used to preserve the entitlement to welfare. Bane explains that some in the administration made the argument that federal welfare reform was unnecessary because the goals of reform had already been achieved.

Some of us saw the possibility that the waiver process could be an alternative to a welfare bill. The waivers were reforming welfare with solid federal protections. So, those of us who were trying to hold the line on the entitlement . . . we were trying to do the waiver process in a way that we could say that welfare reform was going on and experimentation was going on and we were learning and we would learn more.[13]

Once the waiver programs were implemented, they changed welfare. The names of the programs changed, walls were painted new colors, and motivational signs were put up depicting working women and ticking clocks. Many program administrators got their first taste of welfare reform through the pilots. Particularly in the entrepreneurial states of Wisconsin and Florida, the welfare departments made a concerted effort to send their staff and clients the message that welfare *had* changed. In retrospect, the states were right. The states began welfare reform before Congress. As Ellwood notes,

> Even if you read the literature, the states that had gotten waivers [are said to have] started welfare reform earlier. That is how it is described. That is how people try and identify the impact of welfare reform—by looking at the states that started earlier rather than later. . . . I think that early on it was about demonstrations and later on it was about how you do welfare reform without having to wait for the Congress to act.[14]

The states began reforming welfare before the Congress acted and they used the waiver programs to do it. For scholars to fully understand what brought about the dramatic restructuring of the American welfare state in 1996 and the loss of the entitlement to welfare, it is necessary to recognize that the waiver programs were not only, or even primarily, experimental programs outside of the political process; they were an institutional channel for reform. Most research on welfare reform cites the Republican takeover of Congress as the decisive factor in welfare reform. Liberal critics of Clinton argue that it was his use of the misleading phrase "two years and you are off" to describe work-trigger time limits and his political pliability. I agree that these were critical factors. Yet the substance of TANF, its emphasis on the states and on policy ideas "tested" through the waiver process, bore a stronger resemblance to the pilot programs that evolved through the waiver process of the 1990s than to previous welfare reform initiatives.

Moreover, the policy entrepreneurs involved in the waiver programs went on to high-ranking posts in George W. Bush's administration. Wisconsin's governor Tommy Thompson became the secretary of Health and Human Services. Andy Bush, a chief architect of Wisconsin's W2, became the director of the Office of Family Assistance. Don Winstead, who had led Florida's welfare department, became the deputy assistant secretary for human service policy at ASPE. Michigan's John Engler was mentioned as a potential running mate for Bush in the 2000 election. Clearly this level of political recognition was not for those who promoted social scientific knowledge. It was for those who helped to turn a small provision of the Social Security Act into an opportunity to restructure the American welfare state.

The Institutional Role of Experimentation

The use of policy experiments as a means to alter the state structure is not new. Daniel P. Carpenter has shown that in the early 1900s, the United States Post Office expanded its domain and political power in large part through the use of policy experiments. This expansion was so dramatic that Carpenter argues it constituted a key moment in American state building; "The crux of the state-building legacy lay in policy innovation. Nothing so separated the Progressive-Era Post Office Department from its past as its ability to inaugurate experimental programs that would later become institutionalized, containing broad and lasting grants of discretion."[15] Echoing a description of what would later happen in the welfare experiments, Carpenter writes that the Progressive Era Post Office Department "developed new programs shrewdly and incrementally, through well-publicized experiments that enhanced political demand."[16]

The Post Office Department in the late nineteenth and early twentieth centuries was able to alter bureaucratic structures through experimental programs, particularly in rural mail delivery. As Post Office experiments were skillfully administered, the programs gained legitimacy. The Post Office Department was able to demonstrate its competence in the areas in which it wished to expand and to build coalitions to support its expansion efforts. Carpenter writes, "As the local presence of the postal state expanded and the array of its services widened, the department's visibility in national social and economic life grew. Its weight was increasingly felt in the very policy debates it had authored, by experimenting with new programs and by building coalitions around them. By developing politically grounded legitimacy, the Post Office Department helped to inaugurate a new mode of institutional change."[17] Although there are profound differences between the case of the Post Office reforms in the early 1900s and welfare reform in the 1990s, both demonstrate clear mechanisms through which experimentation can facilitate policy development by altering the political and institutional context. This goes well beyond the manifest function of experiments providing empirical knowledge on the impact of a policy idea.

Most fundamentally, experiments permit agencies to set up the infrastructures necessary to support a new policy idea. They also permit the dismantling of other structures that may hinder the adoption or implementation of the new policy. For example, the welfare waivers permitted welfare offices to dismantle elements of AFDC in order to implement the experimental programs. Similarly, Carpenter notes that of the Post Offices closed in order to implement the Rural Free Delivery service (RFD), those with experienced, entrenched postmasters were the *most* likely to go; "the more entrenched the postmaster, the *greater* the probability of quick office termination after RFD, . . . [c]learly . . . targeting the old regime" (italics in the original).[18] Experiments provide institutional homes for policy actors who favor particular types of reform. Additionally, experiments provide a focal point for building coalitions and gaining public support through media attention. As Carpenter writes, "Papers reported that the experiments 'awakened widespread interest' in the program, having been 'successful to the point of creating demand for more.'"[19] Similarly, the newspaper accounts of welfare reform appeared to have awakened interest in time-limited welfare and helped to stoke popular demand.

The institutional role of policy experiments, therefore, is not dependent upon policy evaluation, but it is enhanced by the rhetoric of objective, clinical, and apolitical experimental research characteristic of contemporary evaluation. The primary institutional functions of experiments are (1) to build new institutional structures to support a favored policy—these include creating physical infrastructure and professional networks and coalitions—and to weaken or eliminate old structures that might hinder the new regime, and (2) to legitimate favored policy ideas. Policy evaluation is not necessary for either of these functions to occur. The rhetoric of policy evaluation, however, can make the adoption of a policy experiment appear politically benign, washed of politics by science.

Welfare reform was justified in part by the metaphor of the "laboratories of democracy." This suggested that rather than having to make all decisions based on abstract reason, a few states could test a policy before it become national policy and that the other states could draw upon the experimenting states' experiences before undertaking reform themselves. The keystones in the rationality of this project were the evaluation organizations; if the states themselves were in charge of program evaluation they clearly would have incentives to falsely or incompletely reveal the program results. If this happened, other states might pursue approaches whose efficacy they thought had been empirically verified, but that were in fact ineffective. Evaluation corporations seemed to guard against this. The political viability of welfare reform ideas was also strengthened by the claim that these experiments would produce objective and externally verified empirical results. Framing the welfare experiments *as* experiments—a claim bolstered by the Clinton administration and media's emphasis on the evaluation components of the experiments—made it difficult for opponents of the policy ideas that they contained to argue against them. Policy evaluation, therefore, does not make experimental programs political, but its rhetoric can obscure the political origins and functions of policy experiments and bolster the legitimacy of new policy regimes.[20]

The Role of Policy Evaluation

In the preceding chapters there has been an implicit critique of the role that policy evaluation played in the period leading up to PRWORA. Applying objective social science—rigorous social science—to policy questions has been a great advance for both social science and public policy. Bringing randomized experiments to policy evaluation moved policy-oriented research beyond the advocacy role that characterized it before the 1960s. However, there have been unanticipated consequences to the dominance of the experimental model. Among the most important were the political consequences of the claim that programs that are a part of evaluations with an experimental design are objective and scientific. In emphasizing the objectivity of evaluation research, practitioners have contributed to a narrowing of policy knowledge, a winnowing of what is and is not a legitimate object of study. Anything political has been placed squarely outside of the purview of policy evaluation. Yet, as the case of the experimental welfare program of the early 1990s demonstrates, politics shape every aspect of pilot programs. From the policy ideas tested, to the size and scope of pilot programs, to critical administrative practices that shape the policy outcomes, pilot programs are steeped in politics.

The fiction that the welfare pilots were fundamentally a part of an objective, expert determination of effective welfare policy dampened public debate over the ideological issues involved in fundamentally re-structuring the American welfare state. Debating the relative merits of work-trigger time limits and benefit-termination time limits seemed re-dundant when there were experimental programs that—according to the rhetoric of the Clinton administration, state officials, and the me-dia—told us "what worked" in welfare. Most policymakers and citizens never actually see how welfare programs operate; even individuals receiving welfare benefits only see a fraction of the total program. Therefore, policymakers and citizens alike need specialists to do their looking for them. But this means that the public sees only, at second hand, what evaluators choose to look at or determine is significant enough to include in their reports. Journalists and researchers who are not involved in official evaluations can also bring issues to the public's attention. They are, however, often hindered by constraints on their time, particularly in the case of the media, or their access to relevant in-formation within a program. Official evaluators, in contrast, have the access, resources, and expertise necessary to fully examine experimental programs. The legitimacy of the welfare experiments and subsequent national reform, therefore, rested in part on the assumption that the evaluators were looking at and communicating those things that were important for the public to know.

Evaluation corporations, particularly MDRC, were the gatekeepers of objective knowledge on welfare reform. This role, however, was at least potentially compromised by a structural conflict of interest. Evaluation companies contract with the states whose programs they evaluate. Without state contracts, these companies would fold. Given this reality, the evaluation industry has done a remarkable job in maintaining the integrity of its research. There have, however, been troubling cases in which this conflict comes to the fore. In one notorious example, researchers from the University of Wisconsin had their contract to evaluate Wisconsin's Learnfare program canceled when the evaluation found that the program had no effect on school attendance.[21] Learnfare, as previously discussed, had been one of Tommy Thompson's early, and highly touted, waiver experiments. An evaluation was mandated and the Learnfare evaluation design—which it should be noted was not a randomized experimental design but rather a far less optimal matched comparison design—met federal and state requirements. The first evaluation report failed to show a positive effect of the program on school attendance. According to researchers involved in the evaluations, Wisconsin officials demanded that portions of the report be suppressed and then cancelled the evaluation contract when the researchers refused.

On receiving a draft copy of the evaluation attendance study, Wisconsin Department of Health and Human Services staff demanded that the research findings be suppressed and that the methodology be altered according to new specifications developed by the department. When the evaluation report was released without deletions, state department officials attacked the study findings as the product of politically biased researchers and canceled the Learnfare evaluation contract with the University of Wisconsin—Milwaukee.[22]

Without delving into whether or not the evaluation was accurate, the structural conflict here is clear: the states have a conflict of interest in hiring their own evaluators.

In the case of Learnfare, the contract was with a university and this may have provided the evaluators with a layer of protection. University researchers have some independence because they do not rely on evaluation contracts for all of their funding, although this certainly does not make them immune to ideological bias. Research corporations, which have evolved as the primary players in state-contracted evaluation research, are arguably more susceptible to overt and subtle pressures brought to bear by the states. State contracts are their livelihood.

Research corporations must maintain a reputation for accuracy and objectivity at the same time that they win state contracts. They have to maintain their legitimacy with the public and their peers while not being so aggressive that they encourage their employers to drop them for a competitor. The need to maintain a solid reputation among peers along with the professional integrity and public-spiritedness of many of those involved in the policy evaluation industry has led to very little overt manipulation of evaluation findings. The numbers, particularly from the top companies, are accurate. Where the conflict of interest has had an effect, I believe, is in what is studied and how research findings are presented in evaluation reports.

Evaluators take on a narrow definition of their task, focusing on the production of trustworthy numbers while not reporting more politically sticky issues of policy implementation. For example, evaluation corporations tend to stick to impact numbers such as the difference in earning between the treatment and control groups. These are important issues, but I do not believe that they are necessarily more important in understanding the "outcome" of a program than the administrative procedures and political dynamics that shaped the program. By relegating anything beyond the production of "good numbers" outside the scope of their function, evaluation corporations resolve much of the tension between maintaining research integrity and state contracts. But this solution may not serve the public good.

Conflicts of Interest, Tattletales, and Rigorous Research

There is also a personal element to the conflicts of interest that researchers face. Evaluators do not want to play "gotcha" with the administrators and staff of the programs they are evaluating. They do not want to be seen as officious do-gooders setting traps. To an extent, that concern is fair. It is not the role of the evaluator to highlight every Monday morning fumble made by program staff. But there is a line between the normal mishaps of work life and systematic administrative practices that affect outcomes. For example, MDRC's final report on Florida's Family Transition Program does not point out the fact that administrative practices eliminated the job guarantee. Yet in the press release issued by MDRC, Gordon Berlin, senior vice president of MDRC, is quoted as saying, "Time limits were among the most controversial features of the 1990s welfare reform with strong claims on both sides in the debate. With these new results, we are starting to get beyond the rhetoric to see the complex reality."[23] He strengthens the claim that evaluation pushes past politics and provides empirical truth. Only buried deeply in the final report can one uncover the fact that the time limit was changed from a work-trigger to a benefit-termination time limit during the course of the program—a key part of the political context.

The administrative elimination of the job guarantee is not mentioned in the press release, executive summary, or the summary report on the Family Transition Program. Even in the full report, the point is never directly made. Policy issues of that magnitude—particularly those that affect program outcomes in ways that are directly relevant to ongoing policy debates—should fall within the purview of program evaluation. Beyond obscuring relevant information, evaluation research that systematically ignores or downplays information unflattering to program administrators can appear to put a stamp of approval on a program or policy idea that might be more controversial if it were fully understood.

A full discussion of the direction that policy evaluation should take is beyond the scope of this book. The preceding chapters, however, do reveal some fundamental power relationships that must be addressed. First, it is clear that experimental programs create and are created by their political context. It is equally clear that administrative practices play a central role in this political dialectic. It is therefore impossible to evaluate a program without significant attention to the administrative procedures that create the policy on the ground level. Serious attention to implementation and process issues will highlight politically controversial aspects of a program and complicate the role of evaluators. It is not politically, ethically, or intellectually defensible, however, to obscure an important element of the research—such as what the actual "treatment" is in a randomized study—to avoid difficult issues. Second, the structural conflict of interest inherent in the states contracting their own evaluators must be eliminated. If the federal government is going to attach evaluation requirements to programs, then it makes sense for there to be some mechanism for contracting with evaluators that is not so clearly compromised. Finally, if the media continues to present policy experiments as tests of "what works" in social policy, then evaluators need to recognize their role as public experts. If they are funded by taxpayers' money, then they have an obligation not only to those who hire them (currently state officials) and the academic and research communities, but also to those who indirectly pay them and who count on their expertise—citizens.

There are some encouraging examples of this happening. In 2000, Harvard University professor Paul E. Peterson made the rounds on TV news shows stating that experimental school voucher programs were a success. His research had demonstrated that black schoolchildren scored higher in private schools (paid for through vouchers) than the control group had in public schools. In an editorial, Peterson wrote, "The facts are clear and persuasive: school vouchers work."[24] Mathematica, a prominent evaluation corporation that had collaborated with Peterson on the research, disputed this assertion, noting that the gains made came in only one grade, the sixth grade, and only for black students. Latinos and whites from all grades showed no difference between the two groups and blacks from the other four grades being studied showed no difference. Mathematica responded, "Because gains are so concentrated in this single group, one needs to be very cautious."[25]

David Myers, the lead researcher from Mathematica, took the unusual step of making the data in question available to independent researchers.[26] A result, Princeton economist Alan B. Krueger reanalyzed the data and concluded that Peterson had been mistaken; not even the black sixth graders had made significant gains. Krueger found that methodological mistakes—the omission of some 292 children's test scores from initial calculations—had altered the experiment's results.[27] Mathematica's Myers diplomatically called Krueger's findings "a fine interpretation of the results" and concluded that the vouchers appeared to have had no significant effect on any group in the study.[28]

The important point is not who was right about the impact of vouchers on student test scores, Peterson or Myers and Krueger. What is important in this discussion is that Myers and Mathematica entered into the public debate when they felt that the findings from one of their studies was being misrepresented in the media in a way that had important policy implications. Myers in particular recognized the public responsibility of evaluators in public debates. Impressively, Mathematica went so far as to open the database to independent researchers. In this example, David Myers, responding to the public and political aspects of his evaluation research, strengthened the scholarly process by making the data more widely available. Both the political process and evaluation research gained from the open debate and the transparency of the research.

Evaluators and Political Neutrality

Evaluators have replaced administrators as politically neutral practitioners with the technical expertise to determine what works and what does not, all politics aside. Had the states implemented the welfare programs without external evaluation, the program results would have been understood to be influenced by the politics around them. But the evaluation requirement had a laundering effect. By borrowing the tools of clinical evaluations, such as randomly assigned treatment and control groups, evaluators made the programs seem highly scientific and, by definition, apolitical. Yet they were not apolitical. The experimental language used in the evaluations thus obscured as much of the truth about the pilots as it illuminated.

The contemporary aversion to acknowledging that politics matter in evaluation and that the "effects" of a policy cannot always be cleanly and objectively determined grows out of the history of social science and public policy described in Chapter Two. In the 1970s, evaluators wanted to stake out professional territory for social science research in policymaking. They wanted to break the association of policy-oriented research with advocacy. Breaking away from advocacy research was an important step. There is, however, a clear difference between using social science research for political reasons, as many in the Progressive Era did and many Washington think tanks do today, and using the most rigorous social science methods—both qualitative and quantitative—to assess social policy in all of its dimensions, including the political. In their zeal to lift evaluation above politics, evaluators may have left behind much of reality—the political and administrative reality—of social policy.

I am emphatically not arguing against the use of randomized studies in social policy. They do provide information about the differences between "treatment" and "control" groups that is profoundly important. Researchers must, however, understand that viewing pilot programs as "experiments" is a useful fiction and not a descriptive truth. In a true experimental design, the researchers are able to control the experiment to a high degree. There is a stringent effort to ensure that the treatment is applied consistently and that there are as few confounding variables as possible. Social experiments can never duplicate a laboratory setting. This is both a positive and a negative aspect of studying actual social programs. The inability fully to control for external circumstances is an advantage of social experiments—they provide "real-world tests" of a policy. It is hard to argue that the artificial setting of a clinical laboratory is the best place to gauge the effect of a policy that will be implemented in the messy and complex real world. After all, researchers are trying to assess how a policy will work out if it is actually implemented; they are not trying to gauge the total possible impact of a policy in an artificial context.

The experimental method, however, assumes a high level of control over the "experiment." This simply does not exist in social experiments. For example, in the Florida welfare experiment, the "treatment" given in the experiment changed midcourse from being a work-trigger time limit to being a benefit-termination time limit. In a laboratory experiment, the treatment would never be changed midcourse because of shifting political winds. More strikingly, in a clinical experiment any change of "treatment" would be clearly documented in the articles and reports on the experiment. It would be considered a shocking breach of ethics not to highlight such a change. In social policy evaluation, however, changes in treatment are often relegated to the political and subjective realm and thus not seen as falling within the proper domain of "hard" science.

This is a simple misapplication of the experimental method. A researcher *must* prominently report any changes to the treatment that might effect the outcome. Otherwise, it is impossible to understand the meaning of the outcomes. Returning again to Florida, the fact that no participants in the FTP qualified for a public job at the time limit is indisputable. The meaning of that fact, however, changes dramatically depending on what the "treatment" was that produced that outcome. If one assumes that the program operated as written, and thus included a job guarantee for all participants who "complied" with the program, then that fact suggests that everyone who really tried to find a job in the program succeeded. If, however, you know that the program made it impossible to be "compliant" and unemployed at the time limit in order to transform a work-trigger time limit into a benefit-termination time limit, then that fact has a very different meaning. It reflects more on the program and the political context in which it operated than on the participants and the effects of the policy. It does not tell us that people were unfairly denied public jobs. Perhaps they were and perhaps they were not. It only tells us that the system was set up in such a way that it was impossible to qualify for such benefits. Thus, this participant "outcome" tells us nothing about the participants.

In the early years of social experimentation, evaluation companies often designed pilot programs specifically for evaluation purposes. They exercised greater control over what actually happened in the programs. For this reason, the early experiments did not violate the assumptions of experimentation as much as later experiments would. The boom of waiver-authorized pilot programs in the early 1990s marked a loosening of evaluator control over the pilot programs. Policy innovation was led by the states. This development was not necessarily bad for social policy, but it did further erode the assumptions of clinical experimentation. In the 1990s, evaluators were imposing an experimental design over raucous, politically engaged programs. They were trying to extract the objective truth about a policy idea by focusing exclusively on areas that they could measure and quantify with some reliability, areas such as labor force participation by welfare recipients and duration of welfare use. The issues that they measured were important, and they took great pains to ensure that the measurements were accurate. But the impeccable methodological techniques that they used could not change the fact that these programs were not true experiments. The outcomes were not only a product of the treatment; they also reflected administrative procedures and political choices, such as those outlined in Chapters Four and Five.

In short, the fundamental flaw of bringing only an experimental approach to pilot programs is that most pilot programs do not meet the assumptions of experimental design. The challenge for evaluators is to bring a political and administrative context into policy evaluation without permitting it to disintegrate into advocacy science. There are two preliminary steps that need to be taken to begin to meet that challenge. First, the structural conflicts of interest faced by evaluation corporations must be removed. States should not contract their own evaluators. As ethically as evaluation corporations may have handled the issue of evaluating people on whom their livelihood depends, the structural conflict is too great. Freed from the need to generate contracts from the states themselves, evaluators could speak more freely to the political and administrative issues that shape the outcomes they report. Second, the fiction that policies are objective "treatments" that produce definitive outcomes in recipients needs to be replaced with an understanding that policy implementation, particularly in high profile pilot programs, is a part of the political process and not outside of it. Evaluators can keep methodological rigor and political credibility without obscuring the reality of that which they study. But to do so, they must acknowledge the political context in which pilot programs operate and not assume that random assignment washes politics away.

Pilot Programs as Policy-Making Institutions

The waiver process created a new institutional channel for policymaking. To view the demise of AFDC as simply the triumph of the Republican Congress and the acquiescence of a Democratic president who could not say "no" to a political opportunity, as many liberals do, is to misunderstand the path and depth of the change. Conventional conservative wisdom, which points to politicians "catching up" to public sentiment against welfare and in favor of work, is equally wrong. President Clinton's temperament did matter in the passage of PRWORA, but his willingness to let the governors do what they wanted with the waiver programs pushed reform forward arguably as much as his ultimate willingness to sign the bill. Without the waivers, the momentum for reform would not have existed to the degree that it did by the summer of

1996. The states would not have been in the process of tearing down their AFDC programs and building new, state-specific programs, many of which had time limits on benefits. According to public opinion polls, TANF did not fit with what the public wanted. The public wanted a program more in line with the president's proposal. TANF fit with what the governors wanted, state run programs that did not contain provisions—such as the job guarantee—that could jeopardize state budgets. The governors began welfare reform through the waivers and therefore had a tremendous advantage in defining it. This created the context in which the Republican Congress could successfully push for such a radical restructuring of welfare.

It is important to understand the institutional role that the pilot programs played in welfare reform, not only to enrich our understanding of that particular political event, but also to develop a stronger theoretical understanding of how policy can be "made" and entitlements eroded through waiver demonstration projects. It would be a bitter irony if the form and language of policy experimentation, promoted by academics and intellectuals to make policy choices more rational and transparent, created a back channel though which the American welfare state could be fundamentally altered with little public notice or debate. Yet that may be exactly where we are going. In 2002, as a part of the debate to reauthorize the 1996 welfare law, President George W. Bush proposed the establishment of "superwaivers" that would cut across numerous programs for the poor, some of which are currently entitlements. The House of Representatives approved the "superwaivers" in its reauthorization bill. If the provision becomes law, the legacy of the waivers will have gone far beyond a "shadow" institution and become a formal channel for policymaking in America.

"Superwaivers"

The TANF reauthorization bill passed by the House of Representatives on May 16 contains a proposal to grant sweeping authority to the Executive Branch to override, at the governor's request, nearly all provisions of federal law that govern a range of low income and other domestic programs. Under this "Superwaiver" proposal, Executive Branch officials would have virtually unfettered authority to approve waivers that effectively rewrite federal laws and alter the fundamental nature of affected programs.

> Robert Greenstein, Shawn Fremstad,
> and Sharon Parrott, 2002[1]

We are providing states even further flexibility in the form of broader waiver authority, a "superwaiver," that streamlines many federal work and assistance programs, giving the states more latitude to mold these programs to meet the unique needs of their citizens.

> Tommy Thompson, 2002[2]

By 2002, when PRWORA came up for reauthorization, the issue of welfare had receded in importance. The booming economy of the late 1990s was over. The attacks on the World Trade Center and the Pentagon of September 11, 2001, had shattered America's privileged isolation from the world's conflicts. Reauthorization was buried by other political priorities. PRWORA was scheduled to expire on September 30, 2002, weeks before the critical 2002 midterm elections. It continued through short-term extensions as Congress failed to act on long-term reauthorization.[3] The Republicans controlled the House of Representatives by a slim margin. The Senate was closely divided between Democrats and Republicans. Historically, the president's party loses seats in Congress during the midterm elections. Democrats saw the election as an opportunity to regain the House and strengthen their control of the Senate. Republicans saw a chance to take back the Senate, maintain control over the House, and strengthen the president's mandate by bucking historical trends. Key issues included the economy, homeland security, and the threat of war with Iraq. In 1996, welfare routinely ranked in the top ten issues that voters cared about. By 2002, welfare reauthorization would have been lucky to make a top one hundred list. The September 30 deadline for reauthorization expired and virtually no one noticed. A few weeks later, the Republicans won additional seats in the House and recaptured the Senate with historical gains for a sitting president's party in midterm elections.

Despite the electoral irrelevance of reauthorization, there were still important policy issues at stake. Arguably the most important was the superwaiver provision in President George W. Bush's reauthorization proposal, which was later passed largely intact, by the House of Representatives as the Personal Responsibility, Work, and Family Promotion Act of 2002. A seemingly minor and technical provision, superwaivers have the potential to fundamentally alter the balance of power between the executive branch and Congress.[4] They codify and expand the informal policy-making powers that the governors obtained through the Clinton era waiver process, and bring the governors into policymaking in unprecedented ways. The superwaiver provision originated in the Bush White House, perhaps not surprisingly, under the guidance of Secretary of Health and Human Services Tommy Thompson.

The White House described the rationale for the superwaiver provision in the following way: "Other major Federal assistance programs serving low-income populations provide similar assistance to TANF. Yet the potential effectiveness of all these programs combined is greatly compromised by differences in administrative practices and rules. This makes serving low-income populations more difficult than need be and hampers state efforts to help individuals and families escape government dependency."[5] To address the problem of too much diversity of rules and procedures, perhaps paradoxically, the White House suggested increasing state flexibility in creating programs for the poor that do not conform to federal law. "The Administration proposes new waiver authority that will allow states to build stronger, more integrated and effective services across a broad range of public assistance and training programs. State and local areas will find it easier to plan and enter into partnerships with businesses, community-based organizations, and faith-based organizations to help those who are seeking work, struggling to retain their jobs, or trying to climb the career ladder."[6] Specifically, the new waiver authority would permit the states to negotiate with the administration to restructure major programs that target the poor without going through the legislative process. The White House described the process in the following way.

States will submit waiver applications detailing their plans to the Federal Government. The Cabinet Secretaries of each Federal Department with jurisdiction over the affected programs will be able to negotiate specific terms and conditions related to their programs and waive any rules that are inconsistent with the proposal. These programs include but are not limited to: TANF, Food Stamps, The Workforce Investment Act, The Wagner-Peyser Act, Federal Housing and Homeless Assistance Programs, and GED and post-secondary education programs.[7]

In other words, the cabinet secretaries would renegotiate the effective terms of federal legislation on a case-by-case basis.

The superwaiver provision would give considerable policy-making power to cabinet secretaries and to the governors and would considerably weaken the strength of federal law in antipoverty programs. Interestingly, however, the superwaivers cannot be seen purely as devolving power to the states. The executive branch's role in policymaking would expand as much or more than the governors' role. It is the Congress that would be circumvented. As Robert Greenstein and his colleagues at the Center for Budget and Policy Priorities (CBPP) have noted, "Under the superwaiver, Executive Branch officials would have virtually unfettered authority to approve waivers that effectively rewrite federal laws and alter the fundamental nature of federal programs."[8]

Aside from constitutional concerns about the legitimacy of such a large role for the executive branch in policymaking, the proposed process would place many critical policy issues outside of the public discourse by rendering them technical issues to be negotiated by official actors rather than policy choices to be made by the polis. As Greenstein and his colleagues note, "Democratic processes would be weakened. Superwaiver authority would replace what are largely transparent Congressional legislative processes with largely behind closed-doors Executive Branch deliberations."[9] In much the same way that I have argued the waiver process took welfare reform out of the public debate in the middle 1990s, the superwaiver provision could provide an official institutional channel for policymaking by the executive branch and the governors that would be largely outside of the public's view.

Superwaivers and Evaluation

The superwaiver provision proposed by the Bush White House would have dropped the facade of social research. Testifying before the Subcommittee on Human Resources of the House Committee on Way and Means in a hearing on welfare reform reauthorization, former Clinton official Wendell Primus noted: "Unlike past waiver policies which allowed states to operate demonstration projects to test the efficacy of new initiatives or alternate approaches, there would be no requirement that these waivers have a research objective or even be subject to an independent evaluation. Rather than being designed to encourage states to test new approaches, this waiver policy would simply allow waivers of any program rule a state did not like."[10]

There is a serious argument to be made that permitting the states to innovate and, in return, demanding rigorous policy evaluation is a very positive outcome for public policy. From this perspective, superwaivers that do not contain evaluation requirements would be a loss for policy, politics, and social research. I disagree, however. Although I think that the superwaiver provision is dangerous to the democratic process because it would remove critical policy issues from public debate, removing the evaluation requirements would at least have the merit of not further obscuring policy choices with the language of social experimentation. Thompson, to his credit, was always clear about his desire to use the waivers to change social policy, and he rebelled against the overlay of social science that the Clinton administration wanted him to put on his waiver programs.

As of this writing, the 108th Congress has curtailed some of the power of the superwaivers as proposed by the Bush administration and in the original House bill to bring them more in line with the Clinton era waivers.[11] Evaluation requirements now appear likely to be attached to the demonstration projects. Evaluation requirements, however, have the potential to do more harm than good. I want to be clear that my argument is not against policy evaluation, which I strongly believe in, but rather it is against framing political choices as social experiments, as I believe the superwaivers could do. With or without an evaluation requirement, the superwaivers, should they pass, would be the most important and underrecognized provision of the TANF reauthorization. They would change not only the content of social policy but also the process of policymaking.

Although welfare reauthorization received relatively little public attention, it is worth taking a moment to look at the substantive issues that did arise and how they are likely to affect future welfare debates and legislation. The 107th Congress, not having come to an agreement over reauthorization in time, authorized TANF to continue under temporary spending authority into the 108th Congress.[12] The temporary spending authority had to then be extended again by the 108th Congress. For the states, the patchwork funding of TANF created considerable problems. Without a long-term federal commitment, it is difficult for states to budget and operate social service programs. On February 13, 2003, the House approved H.R. 4, a bill virtually identical to H.R. 4737, which had passed on May 16, 2002. The superwaiver provision remains more controversial in the Senate—even in the Republican-controlled 108th Congress—than it was in the House. The superwaiver provision was omitted from the version of the bill approved by the Senate Finance Committee in the 107th Congress. However, the Senate in the 108th Congress appears likely to include the superwaiver provision.[13]

At the federal level, the debate over reauthorization in 2002 and 2003 has been partisan, but far less heated than it had been in the middle 1990s. Some scholars and social commentators even argued that, with the political heat receding from welfare, research could play an important role in reauthorization. This was wishful thinking for the most part. Less political heat simply translated into less political attention; it did not provide space for cool analytical assessment of what worked and what did not in welfare. In fact, if anything, the cooling of the political debate around welfare reduced the influence of research. Arguably, the low intensity of the reauthorization debate made it unnecessary for political actors to use research as a source of legitimation and cover for otherwise controversial political choices. As controversy receded, so did the institutional role of experimentation.

In the foreword to *The New World of Welfare*, an excellent collection of essays by leading researchers on issues pertinent to the reauthorization of welfare reform, Michael Armacost (Brookings Institution), Michael Laracy (Casey Foundation), and Jennifer Phillips (Mott Foundation) wrote that a post 1996 detoxification of the debate on welfare made them hopeful that research in general would influence policymaking.[14] Although this is an appealingly optimistic vision of the role of welfare research in reform, it overstated the level of consensus in the welfare policy debates, perhaps misconstruing a dramatic and powerful new political alignment for consensus. Armacost, Laracy, and Phillips conceded this point implicitly when they observed, "The playing field— the realm of politically feasible debate—has narrowed considerably making consensus more possible."[15]

The political importance of welfare reform as an issue receded, in fact almost disappeared, after the 1996 reform. But the lack of heated or wide-ranging public debate is not the same as consensus. The only area in which there is consensus in welfare reform is on the issue of work, and that too has its limits. Women, even those with small children, now routinely work in this country. By the mid-1990s, it was politically untenable to maintain a policy, such as AFDC, built on the assumption that they should not. With that salient exception, we have nothing resembling consensus on welfare and poverty in the United States. What we do have, however, is the political ascendance of theoretically oriented, politically conservative scholars, and liberal research-oriented policy experts. This has created well-defined areas of specialization and minimized conflict among prominent researchers and academics.

Much as the "end of history" proclaimed after the demise of the Soviet empire reflected a moment of relative world stability, the post 1996 "detoxification" of welfare policy reflected a confluence of an economic boom and political specialization. It is highly unlikely that the old battles will resurface; no one will fight to restore the discredited AFDC. Yet, just as the cold war gave way to ethnic and religious brutality, the end of "welfare as we knew it" will unleash its own hostilities, particularly as we face economic recession and fully implemented time limits. A foreshadowing of these issues began to emerge in the reauthorization debates.

Marriage

In the 2002 welfare reauthorization debate, the social conservatives, who had lost out to the work-oriented fiscal conservatives in 1995 and 1996, had a second chance. President George W. Bush appointed Wade Horn, a prominent advocate of marriage, as assistant secretary for children and family services early in his presidency, signaling his commitment to a socially conservative position on the role of marriage in government programs aimed at reducing poverty. Most of the Bush administration's attempts to promote marriage as a solution to poverty were symbolic. The Bush TANF reauthorization plan contained relatively few policies that would directly promote marriage but the rhetorical focus did bring marriage back to the center of the welfare debate.

If there was ever a turn of events that supported the argument that research does not guide policy, the focus on marriage and out-of-wedlock childbearing in the 2002 welfare reauthorization debate is it. In an essay defending the "promarriage" initiatives, prominent social conservative Charles Murray concluded that the 1996 welfare reform has had little to no impact on out-of-wedlock births. Yet he still argued that reducing single-parent families should be a prime goal of American social policy. The central theme of welfare reauthorization—increasing two-parent families and decreasing out-of-wedlock childbirth—was an area in which the strongest advocates admitted that they had thus far had virtually no empirically verifiable success.

The government's promotion of marriage raised a number of issues that went beyond the state's ability to affect change in marriage rates and went to the more fundamental issue of the appropriate role of the state in private matters. In a House Ways and Means Subcommittee on Human Resources hearing on welfare and marriage issues, May 22, 2001, Chairman Wally Herger summed up Congress's interest in marriage as a social policy matter: "[A]s legislators charged with overseeing government programs to help poor families with children, this Subcommittee cannot turn a blind eye to the negative effects family breakdown can have on children. . . . The logic [in TANF] was clear. If States discourage out of wedlock childbearing and encourage marriage, welfare dependence will shrink and children will be better off. . . . However, only a few States have taken up this challenge."[16]

Herger went on to note the core dilemma for the Congress: "Americans rightly are concerned about government involvement when it comes to sensitive issues like childbearing and family formation. I am concerned about that, as well." Yet, he concluded that the state should play a role in promoting, or at least not discouraging, marriage. He argued, "[J]ust as we agree on removing marriage penalties in the tax code, we should also think about removing marriage penalties in public benefit programs."[17] Opponents of the marriage initiatives feared that the state would discriminate against nontraditional families. Gay and lesbian groups in particular argued that the state should not officially endorse some family forms over others. However, the debate over marriage incentives was largely symbolic. The funding amounts proposed were trivial. There was little to no evidence that social policy could increase marriage rates in low-income families even if such an outcome were universally deemed desirable. And yet, the debate was important. The definition of family and the appropriate role of government in promoting particular family forms over others are political questions that need to be openly debated. These are issues of social values rather than of program impacts and outcomes.

Work

A second area on which there is likely to be continued debate is the role of work in welfare programs. Although there was widespread agreement in the late 1990s that women on welfare—like the majority of their nonwelfare-receiving counterparts—should work, there was less agreement on how heavy those work demands should be and even what constitutes work. The debate over work requirements raises some interesting issues.

From a political perspective, there is a sound argument to be made that women on welfare should be expected to work at the same levels as their nonwelfare receiving counterparts. This builds on the New Paternalist argument that in order to retain their social citizenship, welfare recipients must fulfill broadly held social expectations. Yet women with children, particularly small children, are not routinely expected to work forty hours a week. Many women do work that much or more, but, for good or ill, this is neither the norm nor the ideal. Americans remain ambivalent about mothers working long hours. Therefore, if the goal of welfare is to bring women on welfare into the mainstream, the extended work hours may be counterproductive. They may make it difficult for these women—who are often raising children alone—to uphold other social expectations, such as active participation in their children's education. On the other hand, one can make a pragmatic argument that in a time-limited welfare system women should be encouraged to work long hours in order to prepare them for the demands that they will face once they exhaust their benefits. Here again, the core issues involve social values, not program impact.

Funding

Finally, no legislative discussion would be complete without mentioning funding. TANF was originally funded through block grants to the states—a fixed annual amount (about 16.5 billon dollars per year) that was calculated based on the average amount of money received by each state in the mid-1990s. Because the number of people receiving assistance had dropped by nearly half between the mid-1990s and 2002, the block grants provided more than enough money to the states to cover welfare recipients during that period. Some observers worried that this relative abundance would lead to poaching of money from TANF to other programs.

Rebecca Blank, dean of the Gerald R. Ford School of Public Policy at the University of Michigan, and Ron Haskins, arguably the most important congressional staff member involved in TANF, noted that viewing the unspent money as a permanent surplus would be a dangerous misreading of the conditions facing the states as they implement welfare reform. First, TANF should be more expensive per person than AFDC because it focuses on getting people into jobs and providing support services such as child care. Moreover, as the caseloads decline, the population still receiving benefits will be more disadvantaged and thus likely to need intensive and costly services to become self-sufficient before reaching the time limit on their benefits. Pure cash assistance is much cheaper. Second, because the block grant funding caps the money that the states can receive, a budget based on the caseload levels during the unprecedented boom of the late 1990s is very likely to result in a shortfall to the states during an economic downturn. Haskins and Blank recommended that Congress consider ways to provide greater cyclicality to the funding, through response to cyclical indicators or, more conservatively, inflation adjustments.[18]

There was a danger that a block grant level would be set based on the very low needs of the early reform/boom years. Even more distressingly, inflation could severely erode the real dollar values of that already low starting point.[19] The House bill proposed to set the block grant level at 16.5 billon dollars annually until 2007.[20] This fixed level does not address the concerns of inflation, which was quite low in 2002 and 2003, or of increased demand, which appeared to be a potential problem as a number of states began to report higher caseloads.[21] In the end, however, the House bill did not decrease the block grant level, as some had feared.

Conclusion

Welfare reauthorization barely stirred the passions of even those paid to care about every item on the legislative agenda. But it contained within it the seeds for a profound change in how policy is made in the United States. The superwaiver provisions are akin to Section 1115 of the Public Welfare Amendments of 1962; as minor and technical as they may look, they provide the tools to restructure social policy outside of the legislative process. The 1962 waiver provisions, unlike the superwaivers, however, were not intended to shift the policy-making process. By all appearances, Section 1115 was a genuine attempt to bring social experimentation into the policy-making process. It was an attempt to *learn* about social policy and to inform policymakers.

In the 1990s, the waiver process began to serve policy-making functions. The waivers provided the state legislatures and governors with the opportunity to create programs that otherwise would not have been permitted under federal law. These programs often served direct political functions. Florida's FTP, for example, helped Lawton Chiles to position himself as a "New" Democrat in his successful 1994 gubernatorial race against Jeb Bush. Tommy Thompson of Wisconsin and John Engler of Michigan similarly made good use of their pilot programs to garner media attention for themselves and the policies that they advocated. Bill Clinton routinely pointed to the waiver programs as evidence of his personal success in reforming welfare.

The waiver programs also served an indirect political function by changing the political dynamics of the federal welfare debate. Approval of a given policy idea in an experimental waiver program put that policy idea into the political mainstream. Replication of those ideas across the states increased their political legitimacy. Finally, the research and evaluation components of the programs created the appearance that the programs were being carefully observed and that any negative or unexpected consequence of note would be reported. This created a distinctive political dynamic; the experimental framework made a wider range of policy ideas politically viable.

The waiver process and the pilot programs also changed the state-level political and organizational dynamics around welfare reform. The competition among states to lead in welfare reform gave governors and legislators incentives to create bold welfare reform programs. In order to successfully create and implement them, the states then had to create networks of political actors who were committed to particular types of reform. In Wisconsin, these networks extended out of the state to policy think tanks and foundations across the country. Within the states, the waiver programs centralized and rewarded administrators and staff who actively participated in building the new state-based programs. They restructured the welfare bureaucracies themselves.

The Legacy of the 1990s-Era Waivers

The superwaivers would take a policy-making channel that developed out of opportunity and accident and formalize it. The legacy of the waiver programs in the 1990s may therefore go beyond the 1996 welfare reform to include a superwaiver process that fundamentally restructures the policy-making process, particularly for programs that target the poor. The dilemma for those who believe in state flexibility and policy experimentation is whether it is better for waiver programs to constitute an official policy-making channel or if they should remain a shadow institution that can, as with welfare reform in the 1990s, become powerful under the right circumstances.

I remain skeptical about the wisdom of permitting governors and cabinet secretaries to rewrite laws aimed at the poor. Legislative functions should remain with the legislative branch and should be given as much air and light as possible. It is difficult, therefore, to support the use of superwaivers as an official policy-making channel. Yet part of what made the welfare waivers of the early 1990s so powerful and dangerous to the transparency of the political process was their apolitical veneer. Arguably, it would be better for the democratic process to make the latent functions of waiver programs manifest. That, however, would lead us back to superwaivers without evaluation requirements, as initially proposed by the Bush administration, and all of their attendant perils. There is, I believe, an alternative.

Superwaivers should not become a part of the official policy-making process. Nor should political actors be expected not to make use of any (legal) opportunities that come their way, including those that are meant to remain outside of the political process. Tommy Thompson was not wrong to make political use of the waiver process. He was elected as a political actor and he very effectively took advantage of the political opportunities that presented themselves. Nor was the Bush administration wrong to try to wrest power from the Congress through the superwaivers. It is Congress's responsibility not to give up its own authority. Similarly, the responsibility for maintaining transparency in waiver programs does not rest with the political actors involved. It rests with the academic and evaluation communities.

If there is to be reciprocity between social science research and policymaking, then researchers must uphold their responsibilities to the democratic process. The well-intentioned attempt to depoliticize evaluation research through the use of randomized experimental methods, and the bracketing off of politics as outside the research mandate, helped to create the shadow institution of pilot programs in policymaking. It arguably even laid the groundwork for the formalization of this process through the superwaivers.

Researchers must now move beyond the fiction of evaluation without politics and begin to assess how to evaluate programs in ways that do not obscure the politics of their origins or administration. This is not an easy task. The risk is that the credibility of evaluation that was gained in the 1970s and 1980s as it staked out its apolitical territory will be lost as researchers and evaluators attempt to bring politics back into their domain. Even more intractably, how will policymakers be able to determine who is right? Once subjective issues of politics and administration enter into evaluation, reasonable people will disagree. It is inevitable. Yet, this does not provide sufficient justification to ignore the realities of pilot programs and to pretend that they can be extracted from politics.

Mixing politics and research must be done with care or it will corrupt them both. The Clinton-era waivers permitted states to move beyond federal law under the guise of objective social research. In doing so, it jeopardized both the integrity of the political process and the integrity of social research. If policy research becomes so focused on minute details of client outcomes that it misses the fundamental restructuring of the welfare state that is occurring as a result of the very programs it studies, then it risks looking obsolete. Equally, if policy evaluation comes to be seen as a tool used by political actors, then the hard-fought legitimacy of social science in public policy may be lost. The challenge for social scientists is to bring politics into evaluation research in order to reflect the world as it is and not only as we wish it to be. If demonstration programs are going to remain a channel for reform, then policy researchers should not study them as if they were objective experiments. They should be studied for what they are—political actions with consequences, both for the recipients in the form of "outcomes" and for the body politic in the form of a restructured welfare state and altered democratic processes.

Methodology

My methodological approach to this study, befitting the subject, was a kind of triangulation. Social policy cannot fully be understood using one level of analysis. The legislative debates and direct political maneuvering involved in shaping legislation are, of course, important. The content of a policy, which may or may not directly reflect the political debates that brought it to fruition, also matters. Finally, a policy is not actualized until it is implemented on the street level. When we use the term "social policy," therefore, we are actually talking about many different things. At minimum, social policy contains three facets: the policy as publicly debated and understood, the policy as written, and the policy as experienced at the street level.

Street-level research, therefore, should play a central role in in-depth policy research. I agree with Evelyn Brodkin's description of the process of street-level research. "At its essence, street-level research combines the techniques of organizational analysis with Ethnography. It uses intensive case studies to explore complex processes and patterns that cannot be adequately understood through experimental or quantitative research design. It adopts an ethnographic perspective in the sense that it studies street-level bureaucrats at work, and makes explicit the links between organizational structures, the individuals interacting with them and the policy 'product.'"[1] This approach is at the core of my research on Florida's Family Transition Program. As important, and I think underutilized, as this approach is, it has limits. First, practical constraints make it impossible to do a number of these in-depth studies. The time and resources necessary to conduct in-depth field research are far greater than with most other research methods. Second, conceptually, in-depth case studies do not address other critical dimensions of public policy—policy debates and legislation.

Studying policy debates is important because one of the manifest functions of social policy is to define social boundaries. For example, in the welfare reauthorization debate of 2002, the issue of fatherhood and marriage received considerable public attention even though the policy proposals actually did very little to encourage either. In fact, there was considerable skepticism among experts at the time over whether public policy could affect family formation to a significant degree. The fact that the policy as written contained little to back up the rhetoric of the policy debate did not diminish the importance of the public discussion. The public debate over the definition and importance of family had a social impact beyond its codification in social policy.

How people understand a policy can also have a tremendous effect on the utilization of that policy. A social program that is stigmatized will have a considerably lower uptake rate than a program that is not stigmatized. How a policy is understood, however, does not wholly define it. Anyone who has ever been appalled at the use of loopholes or the redefinition of a policy by the courts knows that what is written in law matters, too. Finally, however, neither public perception nor written law fully determines public policy as a lived experience. The street-level actions of those who implement social policies bring the policies to life and, in very critical ways, ultimately define social policy.

Each of these levels is a part of public policy, and, I would argue, no one level can be privileged above the others in policy analysis without risking a skewed view of the total policy, its roots, and its effects. Nor can one aspect of social policy be understood in isolation from the others. Policy is made by political actors within discourses reported in, and arguably shaped by, the media. Policy is then implemented by administrators within specific organizational and political contexts. The administration of a policy can then have feedback effects on the policy-making process itself. Policy feedback loops between existing programs and new policy directions are well-documented facts of politics. What is often overlooked is the effect that policy debates can have on implementation and administration. I have argued that in the case of welfare reform in the 1990s the policy feedback loops between existing programs (pilots) and political debates were immediate and strong. Every new pilot program expanded the definition of what was politically possible for federal reform and for the other states. At the same time, the national debates shaped what the administrators, at least in the Family Transition Program, viewed as legitimate action and thus shaped the pilot, which in turn shaped the national debate.

I have used multiple methods to address these various aspects of welfare reform. My research consisted of interviews, participant observation, content analysis of media reports, waiver requests, and reviews of official documents (outlined in the later part of this chapter), and secondary analysis of research on various state waiver programs. The next section of this chapter outlines how I came to do this research and which elements were strategic and which were fortuitous. Finally, I detail the Florida case study and other major elements of the research.

THE HISTORY OF THE RESEARCH

I began this project in 1993, when murmurs of putting time limits on welfare were beginning to grow undeniably loud. What fascinated me in particular was the idea that some welfare recipients would be exempted from the proposed time limit. I wondered if we were about to witness the birth of a new class of the "deserving poor" and who might be in it. How would welfare agencies determine whom to exempt from the time limit? It struck me immediately that the exemptions might be used to cover the most difficult people to employ in the caseload. Would the exemptions be used as "rewards" for the "deserving" or would they be used to support the most troubled and unemployable on the caseload? These questions struck me—naively in retrospect—as being exactly what the experimental pilot programs were set up to answer.

With startlingly little success, I spent much of 1994 trying to gain access to a waiver program where I could conduct research. At that point, the policy idea behind time limits still called for a public jobs program for those who "played by the rules." I was interested in the social construction of "playing by the rules." I thought that the final research would speak to issues of moral worthiness, particularly as it is differentially defined by race, gender, and marital status. I was not specifically interested in administration and not remotely interested in the politics of evaluation.

I understood intuitively—or perhaps empirically after so many unreturned phone calls—that welfare reform was profoundly political and that, lacking political connections, I was unlikely to gain access to a welfare program. Fortunately, in 1995 I received a congressional fellowship on women and public policy. As a congressional fellow, I assisted Congressman Charles Rangel at congressional hearings on welfare reform. There were five hearings during my tenure, a remarkably large number. At one hearing, I met Judith Gueron, the president of MDRC. For several months I had been pitching the idea of my conducting field research for MDRC in Florida—the first pilot program in which welfare recipients reached a time limit—with little progress. With Judith Gueron's support, I became a consultant to MDRC. The relationship with MDRC provided me with the access to Florida's FTP and MDRC with a field researcher on site. This association also introduced me to the unexpectedly complex world of evaluation politics.

While in Florida, I spent time in Tallahassee interviewing state-level political actors who gave me insights into the political origins of the Family Transition Act. Florida has sunshine laws, which facilitated my research by permitting me access to all internal state documents. When I returned to Washington, D.C., from Florida, I was able to interview Wendell Primus, who gave me a glimpse of the politics within the Clinton administration. Later, Mary Jo Bane and David Ellwood graciously agreed to be interviewed for this book. Through my experience on Capitol Hill and interviews with leading officials in the Clinton administration, I was able to obtain information on the federal welfare debate and the Clinton administration's process of granting waivers to the states. It was particularly interesting to interview participants in the Florida waiver negotiations from both the administration and the state. In addition, through Florida's sunshine laws, I had access to the correspondence between the two parties during the waiver process. I later had the good fortune to work, briefly, with Andy Bush when Jason Turner brought Bush and his colleagues from Wisconsin to New York to assist Rudolf Giuliani in his welfare reform efforts. Though not directly related to this research, this contact gave me an opportunity to see the philosophy and style of the Wisconsin reformers up close.

Once I had concluded the case study of Florida, I began to research the patterns of media accounts on welfare reform. Newspaper articles on welfare pilot programs and politics in the early 1990s were easily accessible through Lexis-Nexis. The Family Transition Program also generously lent me its media file, which contained a comprehensive set of articles on the program. The review of elite media accounts of welfare reform, therefore, was systematic, although the review of local press was more ad hoc.

The key moment in qualitative research is when everything fits together, when each document and each interview confirms the findings. This book contains my findings from Washington, D.C., to Tallahassee to Pensacola to Cambridge, Massachusetts. The pieces fit together. I leave it to the readers to judge my conclusions in light of the evidence I provide. The remainder of this appendix contains the details of the data, particularly those used in the FTP case study, for readers who are so inclined.

THE FTP CASE STUDY

The case study method offered the best approach to understand both the process by which post-time-limit benefits were granted in the FTP and the reasons why the FTP post-time-limit benefits were administered as they were. Focusing strictly on the statistics of participant outcomes, archival materials, or interviews and fieldwork would have provided only a partial view of the implementation of post-time-limit benefits in the FTP. This research therefore draws from a variety of data sources, both quantitative and qualitative. In the following pages, I first outline the Family Transition Program and how it differed from the traditional AFDC program. I then discuss the selection of the research site. Next, I review the data sources used in the research and discuss some of their strengths and weaknesses. To conclude, I briefly discuss the significance of the research.

I have not used fictitious names for the program, county, or city. Because the FTP was the first program in the country in which welfare recipients reached a time limit—a piece of information critical to understanding its implementation and importance—it would have been disingenuous to pretend that confidentiality could be maintained by the use of a pseudonym. Anyone who cared to know could have identified the program by looking at the research dates. Instead, I have focused on assuring the confidentiality of the people within the program who spoke with me. I have not identified staff, administrators, or review panel members by pseudonym, number, or demographic characteristics. With a program as small as the FTP, it would have been possible to identify the respondents by piecing together information from a few quotes. Therefore, I have tried to preserve the anonymity of the respondents by letting each quote stand on its own without any identifier beyond the person's relationship to the program (e.g., staff member or administrator). The drawback of this approach is that it creates somewhat disembodied voices for the reader.

THE RESEARCH SITE: WHY ESCAMBIA COUNTY
AND NOT ALACHUA?

The Family Transition Act established two models of the Family Transition Program, one in which client participation was voluntary and the other in which client participation was mandatory. The voluntary model was implemented in Alachua County, a midsized county in which Gainesville is the largest city. The mandatory model was implemented in Escambia County, also a midsized county, in which Pensacola is the largest city. Both counties had caseloads of approximately ten thousand cases.[2]

In Alachua County, welfare recipients had the option to sign up for the Family Transition Program or to receive traditional AFDC benefits. Once a client signed up for the FTP in Alachua County, however, she could not change her mind. Therefore, although participation in the program was voluntary at the outset, once a client enrolled in the program her participation was mandatory. In Escambia County, from May 1994 through October 1996, when individuals applied for AFDC or were recertified to receive AFDC, they were randomly assigned to the FTP program group or to the control group (which received standard AFDC benefits), provided that they did not meet exemption criteria.[3] The program and control groups each contained about twenty-seven hundred people. Persons assigned to the FTP were subject to the FTP rules, including the time limit. Control group participants received traditional AFDC benefits, which were not time limited.[4] Once assigned to the control or treatment group, participants could not switch to the other program, although they had the right to decline cash assistance altogether.

The voluntary program attracted few participants and was abandoned by Florida as a model for welfare reform.[5] Because of the small size and political marginality of the voluntary model, the federally mandated evaluation of the FTP conducted by the Manpower Demonstration Research Corporation chose to focus on the mandatory model. For the same reasons, this research also focused on the mandatory model of the FTP implemented in Escambia County.

RESEARCH MATERIALS

The field research was conducted from June to mid-September 1996 in Escambia County. Two research days were also spent in Tallahassee. I worked in cooperation with the Manpower Demonstration Research

Corporation (MDRC), a nonprofit private company contracted by the state of Florida to evaluate the Family Transition Program.[6] I collected data on the benefit-termination and extension procedures both for my own research and for MDRC's evaluation. The benefit-termination process outlined in this research was published in MDRC's report *The Family Transition Program: Implementation and Early Impacts of Florida's Initial Time-Limited Welfare Program*, which I coauthored with Dan Bloom and James Kemple.[7]

REVIEW OF CASE STUDY DATA SOURCES

Observations of review panel hearings held in June, July, and August 1996

There were two welfare offices in Escambia County, both located in Pensacola. Each office held its own review panel hearings. Panel members were drawn from a common pool. The last week of every month the review panel hearings were held. These hearings were not open to the public, but individuals from the Family Transition Program and other organizations were allowed to observe. I observed all of the hearings, which involved more than one hundred clients, at both locations in June, July, and August 1996. I was allowed to observe all parts of the hearings except the panel deliberations, which were closed to everyone but panel members and the review panel liaison. These deliberations were very brief, usually five to ten minutes long. Though I did not observe the deliberations, I was able to piece together what happened in them through my interviews with review panel members and a sample of review panel Findings and Recommendations.[8] Also, it was not difficult to find out what the review panel members had been discussing during the deliberations from their informal conversations after the hearings.

In-depth interviews with thirty out of fifty-two review panel members

After sending a letter of introduction to all members of the review panel, I telephoned each one to arrange an interview. The response was overwhelmingly positive. Only one out of the fifty-two members refused to speak with me; several others expressed concern that they had not been active on the panel and therefore might not have much to tell me. Because I was interested in how the panel was functioning, I focused on interviewing active review panel members. In June, July, and

August 1996, I interviewed thirty review panel members, roughly the number that the panel liaison claimed was active. By August, I knew almost all of the panel members that I had seen reviewing cases and had interviewed most of the active panel members.

Interviews were structured but open-ended, and typically lasted between one and two hours. I let the respondents choose where the interviews would be held: their homes, offices, or a room that I would provide. I conducted most of the interviews in respondents' homes. I preferred interviewing in respondents' homes because doing so enabled me to learn more about the community and the panel members. The respondents also tended to be open and talkative in a familiar environment. About a third of the interviews were conducted in a conference room in a district building. The room was isolated and quiet, but by virtue of being in a county building a bit formal. These interviews tended to be a little bit shorter and more formal than those held in private homes. Panel members also frequently forgot to attend these interviews.[9] A few interviews were held in respondents' offices. These interviews were the shortest and most formal of all.

The interviews were a very good source of information. Respondents were generally eager to talk about the FTP and their service on the review panel. Most felt that they were playing an important role in helping FTP participants turn their lives around. The only area that I felt was a weak point in the review panel interviews was respondents' answers to questions about race. I found it nearly impossible to get the panel members, particularly white panel members, to talk about race in any context. My assumption is that, because I am a (white) northerner and was affiliated with the federally mandated evaluation of the FTP, the panel members feared that their comments on race might be misinterpreted or used against them.

Self-administered surveys of review panel members

Based on the issues that had come up in the interviews, I designed a review panel member survey in September 1996. I received an initial response rate of approximately 45 percent. I resent the survey later in the fall of 1996 and received more responses, for a total response rate of 63 percent. Between interviews and the survey, I received information from 88 percent of the review panel members.[10] The survey was 15 pages long and contained a variety of question types, including multiple choice, yes / no, rank ordering, and open questions.

*Formal and informal interviews with the FTP
administrators and staff*

During the field research period, I spent much of my time in the welfare offices and the district office. I spoke with FTP administrators and staff almost daily. Because of my association with MDRC and the small size of the program, nearly everyone involved in the FTP knew me and many went out of their way to make me feel at home and to answer any questions that I had. In addition to having these informal contacts, I also scheduled formal interviews with three of the six supervisors and most of the FTP administrators. The most valuable information, however, came from informal contacts as I pulled members of the staff aside and asked them to explain how parts of the program worked. The formal interviews were used primarily to confirm or reject information that I had already acquired.

Observations of "prestaffings"

Each month, FTP line staff and supervisors held "prestaffing" meetings to decide which participants would be sent to the review panel.[11] At these meetings, staff and supervisors discussed whether they felt that particular participants had been compliant with the program. Other circumstances, such as the time a participant had left in the program, were also factored into the decision to bring a participant to the panel. I observed several prestaffing meetings and discussed the process of identifying "noncompliant" participants with both supervisors and staff.

Review of case files and computer files on FTP participants

I spent a little over a week reviewing a random sample of case files and computer files. With the exception of sanction rates and the percentage of cases sent to the review panel, none of the information gathered during this review was directly relevant to this research.[12] The review, however, provided me with important background material. From the case files, I could see how FTP staff handled the paperwork involved in the cases and get an idea of what most cases looked like, both those that went to the panel and those that did not.

*Interviews with Florida State House of Representatives
committee staff involved in drafting the Family Transition Act*

I interviewed two House committee staff involved in drafting the Family Transition Act. I was primarily interested in learning about the tone of the debate in the legislature and who supported or opposed the bill. The interview lasted about two hours and confirmed what I had heard from other sources, including press reports: The bill was broadly supported and there was relatively little controversy over its provisions.

Tapes of the Florida House and Senate debates over the Family Transition Act

I obtained tapes of the House and Senate debates over the Family Transition Act from the Florida State Archives. I transcribed quotes from these tapes to address the legislative intent behind the Family Transition Act.

Interview with a Tallahassee-based Department of Children and Families official involved in negotiating the federal waiver

I interviewed (in Tallahassee) a Department of Children and Families official who was involved, on behalf of the state of Florida, in negotiating with the federal government for the waivers necessary to implement the Family Transition Program. The focus of this interview was on the negotiation process itself—over which issues were in conflict between the state of Florida and the federal government and what the tone of the negotiation was.

Sample of review panel Findings and Recommendations for 51 (out of 306) cases sent to the review panel, supplemented by data on Basic Information Forms (BIFs) obtained through the Manpower Demonstration Research Corporation

I obtained a list of all FTP participants who had been to the review panel by the summer of 1996, slightly over three hundred participants. Starting with the first name on the list, I marked the first of every six names, which yielded a total of fifty-one names. Although not a true random sample, this group gave me a reasonable sample. I then asked for and received the information on these cases from the review panel liaison. This information consisted of the "activity summaries" prepared by the FTP staff before each hearing and the Findings and Recommendations by the panel. The activity summaries were the primary source of information for review panel hearings; they were sent out to panel members in advance. The Findings and Recommendations were the written determinations of the panel. In other words, the activity summaries were the records that went into the hearing and the Findings and Recommendations were the records that came out of the hearings.

Activity summaries contained background information on participants, such as their age, number of children, length of time on welfare, work history, marital status, family history of welfare use, education level, and so forth. The only piece of information that was conspicuously absent was race. In order to fill in that missing piece, I requested copies of the Background Information Form (BIF), collected by MDRC, on the fifty-one people in the sample, and received BIFs on forty-five cases. (Four people from my sample were not in the MDRC sample and two BIFs could not be located.) A BIF was filled out by FTP staff when an individual became a part of the group used for research, control or treatment. These forms were then used to provide descriptive, baseline statistics.

I used the random sample of review panel cases for two separate purposes. First, I reviewed the differences between the activity summaries and Findings and Recommendations within cases. I looked to see if the Findings and Recommendations (the information coming out of the hearings) were substantially different from the summaries of activities (information going into the hearings). In other words, was the review panel building on or challenging any of the information presented by the FTP, or was it simply ratifying the information that it was given by the Family Transition Program? The panel recommendations consistently agreed with the activity summaries on all but the most trivial points. Second, I used the background information from the activity summaries, supplemented by information from the BIFs, to construct a picture of who was being sent to the review panel—their age, race, marital status, education level, etcetera. I compared this subgroup to the population of FTP participants as a whole, using statistics collected by MDRC.

A 1992 report on welfare in Florida that was the basis for the
Family Transition Program (FTP)

A copy of this report was given to me in Tallahassee. I reference it in discussions of the origins of the Family Transition Program.

The Family Transition Act, which established the FTP

The Family Transition Act provided information on the program structure intended by the Florida legislature. This original structure was modified in the federal waiver negotiations and, of course, in the program's implementation. The FTA, however, provides the clearest indication of the Family Transition Program as it was envisioned by the state legislature.

Florida House and Senate committee reports on the
Family Transition Act

I obtained Florida House and Senate committee reports from the Florida State Archives. I used information from these reports to discuss legislative intent.

Florida's application for a federal waiver to implement the FTP,
comments made about the waiver application during the public
comment period, and the waiver approval

I received these through the U.S. Department of Health and Human Services in Washington, D.C. Information from the public comment period was used to highlight concerns about the review panel as it was outlined in the waiver application. The waiver approval itself outlines how the FTP was to operate in principle and was contrasted with the FTP as implemented.

Fax communications between Florida and the federal government
regarding provisions in the waiver

These communications were obtained from the Department of Children and Families in Florida. They were used in the discussion of conflicts over policy between Florida and the federal government and how they were resolved.

Local (Pensacola) and national press on the FTP and
welfare reform

Press information came from the FTP press files and a Lexis-Nexis search of the *New York Times* and the *Washington Post*.

Documents obtained on Capitol Hill during my
congressional fellowship

In 1995 / 96, I collected documents relevant to this research on Capitol Hill. These included: internal letters from members of Congress regarding welfare reform, documents distributed by witnesses at welfare hearings, and reports from the Congressional Research Service. This information was used in discussions of the national welfare reform debate and the politics of welfare reform in the 1990s.

Who Was Compliant?

I used two sources of information to determine differences between compliant and noncompliant participants: Background Information Forms (BIFs) and review panel records. When each participant entered the FTP, the Manpower Demonstration Research Corporation compiled a BIF. On these forms, caseworkers recorded information such as the participant's race, sex, and marital status. Information on the participant's prior use of welfare was also recorded. These forms were then used to compile a demographic profile of program participants. BIFs were the most systematic and reliable source of information on FTP participants. Because they were compiled when the participants entered the program, however, they did not contain information on the participants' compliance.

To obtain information on participants' compliance, FTP records were used. The FTP kept a file of all cases that went before the review panel. This file included the information sent to the review panel and the review panel's recommendations. A sample from these records showed that all of the clients sent to the panel were found to be "noncompliant."[1] Everyone who went to the review panel was, by the FTP's informal definition, "noncompliant." Although in theory the panel could have found any one of these participants compliant, in practice it never did. Therefore, the review panel records provided a list of all "noncompliant" participants.

A sample of fifty-one review panel records was obtained by selecting every sixth name on an alphabetized list of participants sent to the review panel. The BIFs from MDRC were obtained on forty-five of these cases. I was unable to obtain BIFs for six of the cases. Four of these six cases were enrolled in the FTP before MDRC began collecting BIF forms.[2] The BIFs for two other cases were missing for unknown reasons. In the six cases for which BIF data were not available, the information from the review panel cases files was used. The n on the demographic statistics ranged from forty-five (for race, which did not appear on any of the review panel records) to fifty-one (for duration of the time limit, which appeared on all of the review panel records).

Data on the "noncompliant" cases were collected primarily from the review panel records. Information on race was supplemented with data from the BIFs. Unlike the BIFs, not all of the review panel records contained the same kinds of information. The n for these variables ranged from twenty-eight to fifty-one. Most review panel records contained information on the participants' ages, marital status, number of children, and history of welfare receipt. Some also contained information on the clients' functional ability, including the Test of Adult Basic Education (TABE) scores discussed below, whereas others did not. References to claimed and documented disabilities also appeared in some of the panel records, but not in others. It was impossible to know when a record in which there was no reference to a disability reflected a case in which disability was not an issue and when it reflected an omission by the caseworker. I used these data cautiously, and these results should not be overinterpreted. Nonetheless, the results from these data do show some interesting and counterintuitive patterns.

THE BIF RESULTS: WHO WAS NONCOMPLIANT?

The only two statistically significant differences between the "noncompliant" group and the FTP population were in race and age. The "noncompliant" participants were disproportionately likely to be black and under 25 years. The FTP population was 51 percent black, whereas blacks comprised 69 percent of the "noncompliant" group. This difference was significant at the .05 level. This difference mirrors estimates made by Greg Duncan, Kathleen Harris, and Johanne Boisjoly of the characteristics of the welfare population likely to reach the time limit under TANF and the TANF population as a whole.[3] Using data from the Panel Study on Income Dynamics, Duncan, Harris, and Boisjoly estimated that although blacks made up only 50 percent of all welfare recipients, they would be likely to make up 68 percent of the families that reached the time limit.

Given the parallel between the projected national data from the mid-1990s and the FTP data, it is difficult to argue that the disproportionate representation of blacks in the "noncompliant" group was necessarily the result of racism within the FTP. I make this point because, historically, welfare programs in the South were administered in clearly discriminatory ways. Chapter Three notes that "moral fitness" rules in southern states were used almost exclusively against black recipients in a clear, regionally distinct pattern of discrimination.

"Noncompliant" participants were also more likely than FTP participants as a whole to be under 25 years. Of the "noncompliant" participants, 52 percent were under 25, whereas 33 percent of the FTP population were under 25. This difference was significant at the .05 level. Duncan, Harris, and Boisjoly also projected that young mothers (those under 22 years when they started their first welfare spell) were particularly likely to reach the time limit under the new welfare law.[4]

A number of factors that might be expected to be correlated with "noncompliance" were not. Expectations of who will fail under time-limited welfare are primarily shaped by ideological assumptions about the nature of poverty and the roots of welfare use. The traditional conservative assumption has been that poverty and welfare use result primarily from ill-advised personal choices. The liberal assumption has been that poverty and welfare use result more from personal disadvantage, structural deprivation, or personal inability. Therefore, a conservative commentator might predict that behavioral factors would be correlated with "noncompliance." In this case, never-married women, women with many children, or women with no consistent work history would be more likely to be "noncompliant" than other women. The "noncompliant" participants in the FTP however, were not significantly more likely to be single (never married) than the FTP population as a whole. A chi square test of the distribution of marital statuses (as opposed to the binomial distribution of ever married vs. never married) was not statistically significant, either. Furthermore, the number of children in a family was not correlated with "noncompliance."

Whether a recipient had ever held a job for more than six months was not significantly correlated with "noncompliance," either. The finding that there was no significant difference between the work histories of the "noncompliant" participants and the general FTP population is interesting because it goes against the assumption, common among both liberals and conservatives, that those who "fail" at welfare have less attachment to the workforce. It is still possible that the "noncompliant" participants had a different relationship to the labor market than the other FTP participants, but no difference was shown using this measure.

Another pervasive assumption in the FTP was that the "noncompliant" were typically the product of multigenerational welfare dependency. This idea echoes the prevalent concern that over several generations welfare use creates a hard-core group of welfare-dependent recipients. In the FTP, the "noncompliant" group was no more likely to report growing up on welfare, and there was no statistically significant difference between the "noncompliant" group and the FTP population as a whole in the length of prior welfare use.

Looking at the "noncompliant" from a structural point of view, one also sees few differences with the FTP population. Forty-four percent of the "noncompliant" participants did not have a high school degree. An additional 16 percent had a GED. Among FTP participants, in comparison, 39 percent did not have a high school diploma, and an additional 10 percent had a GED. Overall, the differences in educational attainment were not statistically significant. The abysmally low levels of formal education found in the "noncompliant" cases were common among all FTP participants.

I compared the differences in compliance rates between participants who were assigned twenty-four-month time limits and those assigned thirty-six-month time limits for use as a proxy for other forms of disadvantage. As noted earlier, the FTP assigned two different time limits: twenty-four months (two years) and thirty-six months (three years). The rationale behind the two time limits was that some welfare recipients were more disadvantaged, and therefore likely to need more time to become self-sufficient. Two groups of people were assigned a thirty-six-month clock: first, long-term welfare recipients, defined as those who have received AFDC for at least thirty-six out of the past sixty months; and, second, people who were under twenty-four years, had no high school diploma (and were not enrolled in high school or GED classes), and had not worked in the past year. Early on, some case managers assigned thirty-six-month time clocks to recipients who met any of these criteria. By 1995, it was clarified that a recipient must meet all three criteria to qualify for a thirty-six-month time clock. All other participants received twenty-four-month time clocks.

The allocation early on in the program of longer time clocks to recipients who met only one of the criteria may mean that FTP participants with thirty-six-month time clocks were not actually as disadvantaged as the law had expected. Nonetheless, the thirty-six-month group was defined as more disadvantaged than the twenty-four-month group. The difference in compliance between the two groups was not statistically significant. "Disadvantage," at least as predicted by the assignment of time limits, did not appear to be an important factor in who was labeled "noncompliant."

Data from the review panel were more detailed and offered an opportunity to examine who was "noncompliant" in more detail. The BIF data showed no significant difference between the educational attainment levels of "compliant" and "noncompliant" participants. This finding suggests that "noncompliant" participants had basic skill levels that were comparable to the FTP participant population as a whole. The review panel records, however, open the question of whether years of education and degrees attained are accurate measures of an individual's ability to read and write. The TABE scores of "noncompliant" clients were notably low, with a full 74 percent scoring below the ninth-grade level.[5]

It is possible that these scores reflected an overly low estimate of the functional ability of "noncompliant" participants. Only a little more than half (60 percent) of the "noncompliant" group took a TABE. It is likely that caseworkers sent highly functioning participants to be tested less frequently than they sent those who appeared to have some difficulties. But even if we assume that the FTP participants in the sample who were not tested would score higher than those who were tested, the TABE scores still reveal that a sizable portion of the "noncompliant" population may have had serious functional difficulties.

A look at TABE scores by education level showed that many FTP participants with high school diplomas still scored below the ninth-grade level, with 10 percent scoring below the sixth-grade level. In fact, only two participants in the sample with a high school diploma scored at the post-high-school level. The same number of "noncompliant" participants *without* a high school diploma scored at this level. In fact, there was relatively little relationship between educational attainment and functional ability, as measured by TABE scores. Education level, however, may reflect other factors, such as a participant's ability to consistently show up at a given place. In fact, there did appear to be a relationship between education level and consistent work history. This evidence suggests that educational attainment reflected a participant's ability to sustain an effort and not cause trouble more than it reflected reading and math skills.

One concern voiced by some of the administrators and staff was that a few of the participants also had disabilities that were not severe enough to make them eligible for Supplemental Security Insurance (SSI) but that might make them unable to sustain self-sufficiency. Of the review panel records, 28 percent refer to the client having or claiming to have either a mental or physical disability. One administrator noted:

I think we sat in on enough [review panel hearings] to see that there are some participants whose mental health problems more than physical problems [make it hard for them to get a job], because you can get beyond that and find some other job where their physical limitations won't, you know, deter [them] from working, and so you have a desire to work. But these symptoms with mental health problems is a major issue even if they wanted to comply. They can't always act appropriately and behave right on the job to maintain it.[6]

A substantial portion of the "noncompliant" FTP population was, or considered itself to be, disabled.

It is possible that some of the "noncompliant" participants were incapable of sustaining work and perhaps needed some form of public assistance. Traditional disability programs such as SSI require that a person be totally unable to work before receiving benefits. It is highly conceivable that AFDC had been serving as a public assistance program for the more marginally disabled who may have been able to work intermittently, and thus not qualified for SSI, yet been incapable of sustaining a family. It is also possible that some of these participants sought to be labeled "disabled" because disability is the last culturally accepted reason for nonelderly adults to be dependent on the state.

Notes

CHAPTER 1

1. David T. Ellwood, "Welfare Reform as I Knew It: When Bad Things Happen to Good Policies," *American Prospect* 26 (May-June 1996): 22–29.

2. Evelyn Z. Brodkin and Alexander Kaufman, *Experimenting with Welfare Reform: The Political Boundaries of Policy Analysis*, Working Paper No. 1, Chicago: Joint Center for Poverty Research, 1998, 29.

3. Steven M. Teles, *Whose Welfare? AFDC and Elite Politics* (Lawrence: University of Kansas Press, 1996), chap. 7.

4. Brodkin and Kaufman, *Experimenting*, 29.

5. As discussed in Chapter Two, this is an oversimplification of the process. Technical and value questions are often inseparable. However, it is useful as a starting point for a discussion of public policy issues to separate them.

6. Deborah A. Stone, *Policy Paradox and Political Reason* (New York: Harper-Collins, 1988). 4.

7. Ibid., 305.

8. Brodkin and Kaufman, *Experimenting*.

9. The very limited impact of the 1988 Family Support Act is often attributed to the fact that the welfare bureaucracy did not accept the changes and very few of them were ever implemented.

10. Carol H. Weiss, *Evaluation*, 2d ed. (Saddle River, New Jersey: Prentice-Hall, 1998); and Daniel Callahan and Bruce Jennings, *Ethics, the Social Sciences, and Policy Analysis* (Hastings-on-Hudson, New York: Plenum Press, 1983).

11. I borrow the use of this very apt term from Evelyn Brodkin and Alexander Kaufman.

12. Alice O'Connor, *Poverty Knowledge: Social Science, Social Policy, and the Poor in Twentieth-Century U.S. History* (Princeton: Princeton University Press, 2001).

13. Theda Skocpol, *Protecting Soldiers and Mothers: The Political Origins of Social Policy in the United States* (Cambridge, Massachusetts: Harvard University Press, 1992); and Paul Pierson, *Dismantling the Welfare State: Reagan, Thatcher, and the Politics of Retrenchment* (New York: Cambridge University Press, 1994).

14. David T. Ellwood, interview with author, Cambridge, Massachusetts, October 8, 2002, in author's files.

15. Mary Jo Bane, interview with author, Cambridge, Massachusetts, October 8, 2002, in author's files.

16. Ellwood, interview.

17. Bane, interview.

18. Ibid.

19. Teles, chap. 7.

20. R. Kent Weaver, *Ending Welfare as We Know It* (Washington, D.C.: Brookings Institution Press, 2000), 195.

21. Kaiser/Harvard Program on the Public and Health Social Policy, Social Policy Survey, January 1995, 3.

22. Geoffrey Garin, Guy Molyneux, and Linda DiVall, "Public Attitudes Toward Welfare Reform," *Social Policy* 25, no. 2 (winter 1994): 47.

23. Lawrence M. Mead, *The New Paternalism: Supervisory Approaches to Poverty* (Washington, D.C.: Brookings Institution Press, 1997).

24. I thank Lawrence Mead for making this point after reading an earlier draft of the manuscript.

25. John W. Kingdon, *Agendas, Alternatives, and Public Policies* (New York: HarperCollins College Publishers, 1995 [1984]), 132–37.

26. Skocpol, *Protecting Soldiers*, 16.

27. See Charles Murray, *Losing Ground: American Social Policy, 1950–1980* (New York: Basic Books, 1984).

28. Kaiser/Harvard Program, 24.

29. Ellwood, interview.

30. Teles, 132.

31. Carol S. Weissert, ed., *Learning from Leaders: Welfare Reform Politics and Policy in Five Midwestern States* (New York: Rockefeller Institute Press, 2000), 7.

32. What I have termed "a waiver" is technically a package of waivers submitted together. As long as waiver requests were submitted at the same time and as a part of the same program, I count them as being a part of the same "waiver."

33. U.S. Department of Health and Human Services, "HHS Fact Sheet: State Welfare Demonstration," October 7, 1996.

34. The majority of these articles (twenty-seven) were in 1987, right before the passage of the 1988 Family Support Act, a moderate reform of AFDC.

35. I omit 1996 because the passage of PRWORA makes that year incomparable to the others.

36. Judith Gueron and Edward Pauly, *From Welfare to Work* (New York: Russell Sage Foundation, 1991), 26.

CHAPTER 2

1. Aaron Wildavsky, *Speaking Truth to Power* (New Brunswick, New Jersey: Transaction, 2002), xxxi.

2. I was one of the congressional fellows.

3. Herbert A. Simon, *Administrative Behavior: A Study of Decision-Making Processes in Administrative Organizations* (New York: Free Press, 1997 [1949]), 92.

4. June Axinn and Herman Levin, *Social Welfare, A History of the American Response to Need*, 3d ed. (New York: Longman, 1992), 135–36.

5. Ibid., 142–43.

6. Contemporary ethnographers have identified, for example, social interactions on a street corner that convey social dominance, ways in which children are taught gender roles through school yard play, and how class advantage is transmitted to children in their everyday lives. See Elijah Anderson, *Streetwise: Race, Class, and Change in an Urban Community* (Chicago: University of Chicago Press, 1990); Gary Alan Fine, *With the Boys: Little League Baseball and Preadolescent Culture* (Chicago: University of Chicago Press, 1987); and Annette Lareau, *Home Advantage: Social Class and Parental Intervention in Elementary Education* (Philadelphia: Falmer Press, 1989).

7. Elizabeth Fee and Dorothy Porter, "Public Health, Preventive Medicine and Professionalization: England and America in the Nineteenth Century," in Andrew Wear, ed., *Medicine in Society: Historical Essays* (Cambridge, England: Cambridge University Press, 1992), 256.

8. Michael B. Katz, *Improving Poor People* (Princeton: Princeton University Press, 1995), 38.

9. Ibid.

10. Walter Channing, quoted in "'Underclass' as a Metaphor," by Michael B. Katz, in Michael B. Katz, ed., *The "Underclass" Debate* (Princeton: Princeton University Press, 1993), 6.

11. Wildavsky, xxxi–xxxiii.

12. Ibid., xxxvii.

13. Carol H. Weiss, *Evaluation* 2d ed. (Saddle River, New Jersey: Prentice-Hall, 1998), 11.

14. Axinn and Levin, 234–37.

15. Henry J. Aaron, *Politics and the Professors: The Great Society in Perspective* (Washington, D.C.: Brookings Institution Press, 1978), 167.

16. See Weiss; and Wildavsky.

17. Michael Harrington, *The Other America* (New York: Penguin, 1981), 135.

18. Axinn and Levin, 242.

19. Ibid., 243.

20. R. Shep Melnick, *Between the Lines: Interpreting Welfare Rights* (Washington, D.C.: Brookings Institution Press, 1994).

21. Steven M. Teles, *Whose Welfare? AFDC and Elite Politics.* (Lawrence: University Press of Kansas, 1996), 124.

22. James T. Patterson, *America's Struggle Against Poverty 1900–1985* (Cambridge, Massachusetts: Harvard University Press, 1986), 133.

23. Richard A. Cloward and Lloyd E. Ohlin, *Delinquency and Opportunity: A Theory of Delinquent Gangs* (Glencoe, Illinois: Free Press, 1960).

24. Aaron, 17.

25. Ibid., 167.

26. Harrington, 135.

27. Cloward and Ohlin.

28. Patterson, 142.

29. Duncan MacRae, Jr., and Dale Whittington, *Expert Advice for Policy Choices* (Washington, D.C.: Georgetown University Press, 1997).

30. Weiss, 12.

31. Wildavsky, xxiv.

32. Ibid., xxiv.

33. Judith M. Gueron and Edward Pauly, *From Welfare to Work* (New York: Russell Sage Foundation, 1991), ix.

34. Regarding MDRC, see Alice O'Connor, *Poverty Knowledge: Social Science, Social Policy, and the Poor in Twentieth-Century U.S. History* (Princeton: Princeton University Press, 2001), 231–41.

35. Weiss, 315.

36. Rebecca M. Blank and Lucie Schmidt, "Work, Wages, and Welfare," in Rebecca M. Blank and Ron Haskins, eds., *The New World of Welfare* (Washington, D.C.: Brookings Institution Press, 2001), 70–102.

37. I agree that there are serious ethical concerns with randomized experiments conducted on vulnerable populations. The families involved in the welfare experiments, for example, could have technically opted out of participating in the experiments by choosing not to receive welfare, but given their financial situations, this was not a viable choice for many. I have often wondered what the odds are of determining a new pension system by randomly assigning taxpayers to different social security plans and then identifying who fared best.

38. Lawrence M. Mead, *Beyond Entitlement: The Social Obligations of Citizenship* (New York: Free Press, 1986).

39. R. Kent Weaver, *Ending Welfare as We Know It* (Washington, D.C.: Brookings Institution Press, 2000).

40. Aaron, 33.

41. Weaver, *Ending Welfare*, 152.

42. Charles Murray, "Family Formation," in Rebecca M. Blank and Ron Haskins, eds., *The New World of Welfare* (Washington, D.C.: Brookings Institution Press, 2001), 137–60.

43. Weaver, *Ending Welfare*, 152.

44. Ibid., 162.

45. Weiss; and Weaver, *Ending Welfare*, 135–68.

46. U.S. Department of Health and Human Services, "HHS Fact Sheet: State Welfare Demonstration," October 7, 1996.

47. Evelyn Brodkin and Alexander Kaufman, "Policy Experiments and Poverty Politics," *Social Service Review* 74, no. 4 (2000): 507–32.

48. "Reform that Values Families," press release from Clinton / Gore campaign, May 21, 1996.

CHAPTER 3

1. David T. Ellwood, *Poor Support: Poverty in the American Family* (New York: Basic Books, 1986), 4.

2. Linda Gordon, *Pitied but Not Entitled: Single Mothers and the History of Welfare 1890–1935* (New York: Free Press, 1994), 4–5.

3. Most recipients of AFDC also received other assistance programs, including Medicaid and Food Stamps.

4. There are many outstanding books on the history of welfare in America. I particularly recommend Michael B. Katz's *In the Shadow of the Poorhouse: A History of Welfare in America* (New York: Basic Books, 1986); James T. Patterson's *America's Struggle Against Poverty* (Cambridge, Massachusetts: Harvard University Press, 1986); and Mary Jo Bane and David T. Ellwood's *Welfare Realities: From Rhetoric to Reform* (Cambridge, Massachusetts: Harvard University Press, 1994).

5. Regarding origins: June Axinn and Herman Levin, *Social Welfare: A History of the American Response to Need*, 3d ed. (New York: Longman, 1992), 144. Also see Gwendolyn Mink, "The Lady and the Tramp: Gender, Race, and the Origins of the American Welfare State," in Linda Gordon, ed., *Women, the State, and Welfare* (Madison: University of Wisconsin Press, 1990).

6. Ibid., 95.

7. Ibid., 93.

8. Ibid., 110.

9. Ibid.

10. Mimi Abramovitz, *Regulating the Lives of Women: Social Welfare from Colonial Times to the Present* (Boston: South End Press, 1988), chap. 6.

11. Katz, *In the Shadow*, 91–99.

12. R. Shep Melnick, *Between the Lines: Interpreting Welfare Rights* (Washington, D.C.: Brookings Institution Press, 1994), chap. 5.

13. Michael S. Sosin, "Legal Rights and Welfare Change, 1960–1980," in Sheldon Danzinger and Daniel H. Weinberg, eds., *Fighting Poverty: What Works, What Doesn't* (Cambridge, Massachusetts: Harvard University Press, 1996), 273.

14. Bane and Ellwood, 12.

15. Ibid., 12–13.

16. Joel Handler and Ellen Hollingsworth, *The "Deserving Poor": A Study of Welfare Administration* (Chicago: Markham, 1971), 28.

17. Nancy Fraser and Linda Gordon, "A Genealogy of Dependency: Tracing a Key Word of the U.S. Welfare State," *Signs* 19, no. 2 (1994): 309–36.

18. Lawrence M. Mead, *Beyond Entitlement: The Social Obligations of Citizenship* (New York: Free Press, 1986), chap. 3.

19. *Women, the State, and Welfare* (Madison: University of Wisconsin Press, 1990), edited by Linda Gordon, is an excellent collection of essays by feminist scholars on the welfare state.

20. Kaiser/Harvard Program on the Public and Health Social Policy, Social Policy Survey, January 1995, 3.

21. Katz, *In the Shadow.*

22. Piven and Cloward.

23. Jill Quadagno's *The Color of Welfare* provides an excellent analysis of the role that race has played in the American welfare state, particularly during the War on Poverty.

24. Theda Skocpol, "The Limits of the New Deal System and the Roots of Contemporary Welfare Dilemmas," in Margaret Weir, Ann Shola Orloff, and Theda Skocpol, eds., *The Politics of Social Policy in the United States* (Princeton: Princeton University Press, 1988), 303.

25. Ibid.

26. Quadagno, 117.

27. Piven and Cloward, 135.

28. Ibid.

29. Melnick, 71.

30. Cohabitation was often very loosely defined, and critics argued that it was used in a punitive and uneven manner.

31. Melnick, 85.

32. Ibid., 86.

33. Ibid., 83.

34. Ibid., 102.

35. Bane and Ellwood, 9.

36. Ibid., 16.

37. Ibid., 19.

38. Ibid.

39. Handler and Hollingsworth, 28.

40. Charles Murray, *Losing Ground: American Social Policy, 1950–1980* (New York: Basic Books, 1984), 18.

41. See Katz, *Undeserving Poor*; Mink; and Skocpol, *Protecting Soldiers.*

42. The FSA was the second piece of legislation aimed at moving welfare recipients into the workforce. Congress passed the Work Incentives Program (WIN) in 1967. WIN is significant because it was the first major piece of legislation aimed at increasing work for families on welfare. In practical terms, however, it was not a far-reaching program.

43. Carmen D. Solomon, *The Family Support Act of 1988: How It Changes the Aid to Families with Dependent Children (AFDC) and Child Support Enforcement Programs* (Washington, D.C.: Congressional Research Service, 1988).

44. U.S. Government Accounting Office, *Welfare to Work: Participants Characteristics and Services Provided in JOBS* (Washington, D.C.: GAO, 1995).

45. Lyn Hogan, *Jobs, Not JOBS* (Washington, D.C.: Progressive Policy Institute, 1995).

46. Ibid.

47. Geoffrey Garin, Guy Molyneux, and Linda DiVall, "Public Attitudes Toward Welfare Reform," *Social Policy* 25, no. 2 (winter 1994): 44–49.

48. Katz, *In the Shadow*, 9.

49. Melnick, 54–55.

50. Federal programs, for example AFDC and SSI, may come to be seen as serving the "undeserving." This, as noted, undermines support for these programs. No federal program that I know of has ever targeted groups considered to be "undeserving" at the time it was legislated.

51. Handler and Hollingsworth, 16.

52. Ibid.

53. Michael Lipsky, *Street-level Bureaucracy: Dilemmas of the Individual in Public Services* (New York: Russell Sage, 1980), 13.

54. The actions of the review panel were not closely monitored by political actors. Yet had the panel expressed concern or begun granting participants public jobs when they reached the time limit, it is very likely that this would have served as an "alarm bell," signaling that the panel did not find that the assumptions of benefit termination time limits held up in the first time-limited welfare experiment.

55. Steve Savner and Mark Greenberg, *The CLASP Guide to Welfare Waivers 1992–1995* (Washington, D.C.: Center for Law and Social Policy, 1995).

56. Steven M. Teles, *Whose Welfare? AFDC and Elite Politics* (Lawrence: University Press of Kansas, 1996), 39.

57. Ibid., 122.

58. Ibid., 132.

59. Elisabeth Boehnen and Thomas Corbett, "Welfare Waivers: Some Salient Trends," *Focus* 18, no. 1 (spring 1996): 34.

60. Ibid., 37.

61. As one researcher for the Congressional Research Service said to me wryly, "Kids don't vote, but their parents sure do like 'em."

62. The higher number was based on estimates of the House version of H.R. 4; the lower number was based on the Senate version.

63. H.R. 4, 104th Cong., 1st sess. (1995): sect. 100.

64. Charles Murray is the primary intellectual proponent of this approach to welfare reform. See *Losing Ground*.

65. For example, see Robert Moffitt, "Incentive Effects of the U.S. Welfare System: A Review," *Journal of Economic Literature* 30, no. 1 (1992): 27–31.

66. "Reform that Values Families," press release from Clinton / Gore campaign, May 21, 1996.

67. Jason DeParle, "A Sharp Decrease in Welfare Cases is Gathering Speed," *New York Times*, February 2, 1997, A1.

68. Ibid., A18.

69. Ibid.

70. Florida House of Representatives Committee on Aging and Human Services, Social Economic and Development Subcommittee, Florida State Archives, Tape #1, February 9, 1993.

71. John Boli, *New Citizens for a New Society: The Institutional Origins of Mass*

Schooling in Sweden (New York: Pergamon Press, 1989); Peter A. Hall, "Policy Paradigms, Social Learning, and the State: The Case of Economic Policymaking in Britain," *Comparative Politics* 25, no. 3 (1993): 275–96; Frank Dobbin, *Forging Industrial Policy: The United States, Britain, and France in the Railway Age* (New York: Cambridge University Press, 1994).

72. Katz, *Undeserving Poor*, 7.

CHAPTER 4

1. Florida House of Representatives Committee on Aging and Human Services, Social Economic and Development Subcommittee, Florida State Archives, February 9, 1993.

2. Carol S. Weissert, ed., *Learning from Leaders: Welfare Reform Politics and Policy in Five Midwestern States* (New York: Rockefeller Institute Press, 2000).

3. Study Commission on Employment Opportunities and Self Sufficiency, "Final Report: Study Commission on Employment Opportunities and Self Sufficiency," 1992, in author's files.

4. Quoted in June Axinn and Herman Levin, *Social Welfare: A History of the American Response to Need* (New York: Longman, 1992), 242.

5. There was bipartisan support for W2 in Wisconsin as well. The fundamentals of the bill, however, were all shaped by the core group brought together by Governor Thompson.

6. The summary of the Family Transition Act (as passed) prepared by the House of Representatives Committee on Aging and Human Services.

7. Research suggests that work-oriented welfare programs are often more successful when they are mandatory. See Lawrence M. Mead, "Should Workfare Be Mandatory? What the Research Says," *Journal of Policy Analysis and Management* 9, no. 3 (summer 1990): 400–404.

8. See Geoffrey Garin, Guy Molyneux, and Linda DiVall, "Public Attitudes Toward Welfare Reform," *Social Policy* 25, no. 2 (winter 1994): 44–49; Kaiser / Harvard Program on the Public and Health Social Policy, Social Policy Survey, January 1995; Steve Farkas and Jean Johnson, *The Values We Live By: What Americans Want from Welfare Reform* (New York: Public Agenda, 1996).

9. Julie Kosterlitz, "Reworking Welfare," *National Journal* 24 (1992): 2189–92.

10. "Of Fraud, Welfare, Vouchers," *St. Petersburg (Fla.) Times*, November 8, 1994, 2B. Chiles referred to the two components of the FTP, one of which was abandoned early on in favor of the program run in Escambia County.

11. Author's interview, Washington, D.C., May 21, 1995, in author's files.

12. Greg M. Shaw and Robert C. Lieberman, "State Welfare Policies and the Shifting Ground of American Federalism," paper presented to the annual American Political Science Association meeting, San Francisco, August 1996.

13. Florida House of Representatives Committee on Aging and Human Services, Social Economic and Development Subcommittee, Florida State Archives, February 9, 1993.

14. Ibid.

15. Particularly disadvantaged was defined as having received AFDC for thirty-six out of the last sixty months, being under twenty-four without being enrolled in high school or having a high school diploma, or having little or no work history in the past year.

16. This plan would outline services and steps that were agreed upon by both the department and the participant to help the participant become self-sufficient.

17. Mary Jo Bane to James Towey, November 12, 1993, in author's files.

18. Author's interview, Washington, D.C., autumn 1996, in author's files.

19. These were 1996 dollars.

20. See Kathryn Edin and Laura Lein, *Making Ends Meet: How Single Mothers Survive Welfare and Low-Wage Work* (New York: Russell Sage Foundation, 1997) for a discussion of the survival strategies of welfare and wage reliant women under AFDC.

21. Don Winstead to Howard Rolston, December 15, 1993, in author's files.

22. FTP Handbook, November 1995, in author's files.

23. Winstead to Rolston.

24. Cecil Lanier, interoffice memorandum on extension procedures, June 18, 1996, in author's files.

25. Ibid.

26. Waiver Terms and Condition, Florida Family Transition Program, in author's files, pages 8–9.

27. Ibid., 9–10.

28. Interview with author, Tallahassee, Florida, 1995.

29. Greenberg to Bane, October 26, 1993, in author's files.

30. Elizabeth Shogren, "2 Florida Counties to Test Clinton-Style Welfare Plan," *Los Angeles Times*, January 28, 1994, A32.

31. "Florida Gets Approval for Welfare Experiment: The State Plan Will Mirror Clinton's with Employers Subsidies and Benefit Limitations," *Orlando (Fla.) Sentinel*, January 28, 1994, A1.

32. William Claiborne, "North Floridians Are Pioneers in Clinton-Like Welfare Program," *Washington Post*, February 26, 1994, A3.

33. Author's interview, Pensacola, Florida, 1996.

34. Dan Bloom, James J. Kemple, and Robin Rogers-Dillon, *The Family Transition Program: Implementation and Early Impacts of Florida's Initial Time-Limited Welfare Program* (New York: Manpower Demonstration Research, 1997).

35. Author's interview, Pensacola, Florida, summer 1996.

36. Author's interview, Pensacola, Florida, summer 1996.

37. "Dueling Candidates Series, The Race for Governor: What They're Saying," *St. Petersburg (Fla.) Times*, October 31, 1994, 5D.

38. Bloom, Kemple, and Rogers-Dillon, 20.

39. Jim Ash, "Future is Uncertain for Welfare Program," *Pensacola (Fla.) News Journal*, September 21, 1995, C4.

40. Mimi Abramovitz, *Regulating the Lives of Women: Social Welfare Policy from Colonial Times to the Present* (Boston: South End Press, 1988).

41. Jason DeParle, "In Sink-or-Swim Welfare, Pensacola Staying Afloat," *New York Times*, June 18, 1997, A1.

42. R. Kent Weaver, *Ending Welfare As We Know It* (Washington, D.C.: Brookings Institution Press, 2000), 160.

43. Ellen Debenport, "End of the Line for 8 Women on Welfare," *St. Petersburg (Fla.) Times*, June 1, 1996, 1A, 4A.

44. The number of people who potentially could have been eligible for a public job would have been very small because the program was small and the duration was short. Most people left welfare within two years even before welfare reform. What is important is that the program, for political, financial, and administrative reasons, did not permit this option.

45. As of June 11, 1997, the FTP instituted a much more stringent sanctioning policy made possible by the new welfare law. Under this policy, participants under their first sanction lost their entire cash grant. Under the second sanction, they also lost food stamps. A third sanction resulted in the loss of cash assistance, food stamps, and Medicaid for a minimum of three months.

46. There are situations where welfare recipients cannot be sanctioned. One of the most common is when a recipient is pregnant. Presumably, the idea is that the loss of money could jeopardize the health or nutritional status of the pregnant woman and have a negative impact on the fetus.

47. The staff try to make sure that noncompliant clients are brought to the review panel at least once before they are brought for benefit termination, but in some cases clients are brought to the panel for the first time for benefit termination.

CHAPTER 5

1. Quoted in Harold L. Wilensky and Charles N. Lebeaux, *Industrial Society and Social Welfare: The Impact of Industrialization on the Supply and Organization of Social Welfare Services in the United States* (New York: Free Press, 1965), 273.

2. Unless otherwise indicated, the bulk of the material quoted in this chapter is from interviews conducted in Pensacola, Florida, by the author between May and August 1996 and held in her files.

3. Wilensky and Lebeaux, 272.

4. Florida House of Representatives Committee on Aging and Human Services, Social Economic and Development Subcommittee, Florida State Archives, Tape #1, February 9, 1993.

5. Mark Greenberg to Mary Jo Bane, October 26, 1993, in author's files.

6. I was never able to find out definitively whose idea it was to institute a review panel. The rumor that I heard, but could never substantiate, was that the idea originated between two welfare department officials on a long airplane ride as something of a joke, taking the then-current vogue for community involvement to an extreme and allowing the community to terminate welfare recipients' benefits at the time limit. I have no idea if any part of this story is true, but it illustrates the connection between the review panel and the larger move-

ment toward community boards that was occurring in Florida when the legislation passed.

7. Florida *Family Transition Act* (1993), sec. 408.928.

8. I received copies of the summaries at each hearing I attended.

9. Participants were permitted to request a copy of the summary from the case manager in advance. This information, however, was not included in the letter sent to participants informing them of the review panel hearing, and I saw no evidence that the clients were aware that they had this option. As a result, the clients tended to spend much of the hearing reviewing the summaries.

10. Although the question asked respondents to select the main role of the review panel, implying one response, six (out of thirty-one) selected more than one option. Including these respondents who picked more than one option, three viewed determining benefit termination and extensions as being one of the main roles of the panel. Only one of the respondents who selected only one answer to the question viewed determining benefit termination and extensions as being the main role of the panel.

11. FTP memo, in author's files.

12. As discussed in Chapter Four, there were a very few cases in which the panel found the participant to be compliant, but nonetheless recommended that she come into compliance with the program. In one of these cases the participant was warned that her benefits were going to be terminated, as if she were noncompliant. Because a participant must be *fully* in compliance with the FTP to receive any post-time-limit benefits, in my judgment, these cases would be considered to be noncompliant if they reached the time limit without earning at the "self-sufficiency" level.

13. Six percent of review panel members reported incomes between $0 and $9,999.

14. For respondents who reported that they were currently working, I coded their job titles. A ranking of one indicates a blue-collar job, for example truck driver or beautician, which does not require education beyond high school. A ranking of two indicates a job, such as administrative assistant or social worker, which is likely to require some education beyond high school. A ranking of three indicates a high-level professional job, such as doctor or agency head, that is likely to require some postgraduate education or considerable work experience. This coding system is not precise and is only meant to give a rough generalization as to the nature of review panel members' employment.

15. Lawrence M. Mead, *The New Paternalism: Supervisory Approaches to Poverty* (Washington, D.C.: Brookings Institution Press, 1997).

16. R. Kent Weaver, *Ending Welfare as We Know It*. (Washington, D.C.: Brookings Institution Press, 2000), 181–83. See also, Steve Farkas and Jean Johnson, *The Values We Live By: What Americans Want From Welfare Reform* (New York: Public Agenda, 1996); Kaiser/Harvard Program on the Public and Health Social Policy. Social Policy Survey, January 1995; Geoffrey Garin, Guy Molyneux, and Linda DiVall, "Public Attitudes Toward Welfare Reform," *Social Policy* 25, no. 2 (winter 1994): 44–49.

17. Weaver, *Ending Welfare*, 178–80.

18. Michael Katz, *In the Shadow of the Poorhouse* (New York: Basic Books, 1986), 103–5.

19. This is not to say that the program would not admit an error. The program staff actually did so frequently. By emphasizing what was being done to address the error and the newness of the program, they were able to admit to mishandling aspects of particular cases without causing the panel to question the competence of the program administrators and staff.

20. There is one exception: Short-term benefit extensions approved by the department were given to the panel for approval. However, the clients did not appear in these cases. Clients requesting a short-term benefit extension whose requests were not supported by the department were brought before the panel in person.

21. Philip Selznick, *Leadership in Administration: A Sociological Interpretation* (New York: Harper and Row, 1957), 58.

22. Ibid., 14.

23. Deborah A. Stone, *The Disabled State* (Philadelphia: Temple University Press, 1984).

CHAPTER 6

1. Text of Clinton's weekly radio address to the nation, May 18, 1996, http://www.presidency.ucsb.edu/docs/satradio/clinton/1996/051896.htm.

2. HHS News, "Florida Welfare Demonstration," January 27, 1994, http://www.hhs.gov/news/press/pre1995pres/940127c.txt.

3. Ibid.

4. Susan Kellam, *Welfare Experiments*, *CQ Researcher* (Washington, D.C.: Congressional Quarterly Press, 1994), 2.

5. This was true with the exception of a few experimental programs in Wisconsin, California, and a handful of other states.

6. Jill Quadagno, *The Color of Welfare: How Racism Undermined the War on Poverty* (New York: Oxford University Press, 1994), 119–20.

7. Ibid., 71.

8. Quoted in Frances Fox Piven and Richard A. Cloward, *Regulating the Poor: The Functions of Public Welfare* (New York: Vintage, 1972), 134.

9. Undoubtedly, disparate impact and outright discrimination intermingled in most policies.

10. R. Shep Melnick, *Between the Lines: Interpreting Welfare Rights* (Washington, D.C.: Brookings Institution Press, 1994), 23.

11. Ibid., 26.

12. Ibid., 75.

13. Piven and Cloward, 134.

14. Steven M. Teles, *Whose Welfare? AFDC and Elite Politics* (Lawrence: University Press of Kansas, 1996), 122.

15. Michael Wiseman, "State Strategies for Welfare Reform: The Wisconsin Story," *Journal of Policy Analysis and Management* 15, no. 4 (fall 1996): 525–26.

16. Greg M. Shaw, "The Role of Public Input in State Welfare Policymaking," *Policy Studies Journal* 28, no. 4 (2000): 712.

17. Ibid., 709.

18. Carol S. Weissert, "Learning from Midwestern Leaders," in Carol S. Weissert, ed., *Learning from Leaders: Welfare Reform Politics and Policy in Five Midwestern States* (New York: Rockefeller Institute Press, 2000), 8.

19. Ibid.

20. Steve Savner and Mark Greenberg, *The CLASP Guide to Welfare Waivers 1992–1995* (Washington, D.C.: Center for Law and Social Policy, 1995), 58A.

21. Thomas Kaplan, "Wisconsin's W2 Program: Welfare as We Might Come to Know It?" in Carol S. Weissert, ed., *Learning from Leaders: Welfare Reform and Politics and Policy in Five Midwestern States* (New York: Rockefeller Press, 2000), 87.

22. Wiseman, "State Strategies," 531.

23. Ibid., 532.

24. Ibid.

25. HHS News, "Wisconsin Welfare Demonstration," November 1, 1993, http://www.acf.dhhs.gov/news/press/1993/welfdewi.html.

26. Ibid.

27. Office of the Assistant Secretary for Evaluation and Planning, "Approaches to Evaluating Welfare Reform: Lessons from Five State Demonstrations," http://aspe.os.dhhs.gov/hsp/isp/waivers/intro.htm, 6.

28. Author's interview with David T. Ellwood, Cambridge, Massachusetts, October 8, 2002, in author's files.

29. Ibid.

30. HHS News, "HHS Releases President's Fast-Track Welfare Reform," August 17, 1995, http://www.acf.dhhs.gov/news/press/1995/fastck.html.

31. Ibid.

32. Ibid.

33. HHS News, "Clinton Administration Makes Award to Change the Culture of Welfare," November 6, 1995, http://www.acf.dhhs.gov/news/press/1995/culture.html.

34. Months in which income was earned were not counted toward the time limit. Additional children born after assignment to the program did not change the time limit.

35. Office of the Assistant Secretary.

36. Author's interview with Mary Jo Bane, Cambridge, Massachusetts, October 8, 2002, in author's files.

37. Elisabeth Boehnen and Thomas Corbett, "Welfare Waivers: Some Salient Trends," *Focus* 18, no. 1 (spring 1996): 34.

38. Institute for Research on Poverty, "Informing the Welfare Debate: A Conversation with State Officials," *Focus* 18, no. 1 (1996): 30–33.

39. The original movement away from decentralization resulted from racial

discrimination by the states and local offices. So far, there has been little evidence that a return to decentralization has increased discrimination. It may be that the United States does not currently have the ingrained racism of the previous period. It is also possible that the research has not focused enough on this issue to document it. At this point it is too soon to know whether racial discrimination will become an issue in welfare again.

40. Savner and Greenberg, 1.

41. Jennifer Neisner, *State Welfare Initiatives* (Washington, D.C.: Congressional Research Service, 1995), 3.

42. Ibid.

43. Michael Wiseman, "Welfare Reform in the United States: A Background Paper," *Housing Policy Debate* 7, no. 4 (fall 1996): 595–648.

44. R. Kent Weaver, *Ending Welfare as We Know It* (Washington, D.C.: Brookings Institution Press, 2000), 195.

45. Regarding the percentage, see Kaiser/Harvard Program on the Public and Health Social Policy Survey, January 1995, table one.

46. Barbara Vobejda, "Clinton Signs Welfare Bill Amid Division," *Washington Post*, August 23, 1996, A1.

47. Ibid.

48. Author's interview, Washington, D.C., fall 1996, in author's files.

49. I stop short of arguing that the pilot programs were a necessary condition for the passage of PRWORA because it is impossible to prove that, in the absence of the pilot programs, the other factors that contributed to the passage of PRWORA might not have produced a similar bill. Having said that, I do think that the explicit use of the pilot programs for political purposes by key actors in welfare reform, notably Tommy Thompson and Bill Clinton, the high levels of media attention that the programs received, and the public's interest in "testing" welfare policies documented in the Kaiser Foundation's 1995 poll, suggest that the pilots played a critical role in welfare reform.

50. Chicago: University of Chicago Press.

51. Paul J. DiMaggio and Walter W. Powell, "Introduction," in Walter W. Powell and Paul J. DiMaggio, eds., *The New Institutionalism in Organizational Analysis* (Chicago: University of Chicago Press, 1991), 10.

52. Richard Scott, and John W. Meyer, "The Organization of Societal Sectors," in Walter W. Powell and Paul J. DiMaggio, eds., *The New Institutionalism in Organizational Analysis* (Chicago: University of Chicago Press, 1991), 108.

53. Bane, interview.

54. John W. Meyer and Brian Rowan, "Institutionalized Organizations: Formal Structure as Myth and Ceremony," in Walter W. Powell and Paul J. DiMaggio, eds., *The New Institutionalism in Organizational Analysis* (Chicago: University of Chicago Press, 1991), 50.

55. See Shanto Iyengar and Donald R. Kinder, *News that Matters: Television and American Opinion* (Chicago: University of Chicago Press, 1987).

56. Eric Pianin, "Tenet of Clinton Plan Faces Test," *Washington Post*, May 20, 1994, A6.

57. Local papers were not a part of the research that Brian Gran and I conducted. I collected and reviewed numerous local newspaper stories in my own research. The following quotes are drawn from them in addition to the national papers.

58. Diane Hirth, "Welfare Reform is Taking Shape in State," *Orlando (Fla.) Sentinel*, December 26, 1994.

59. Jason Deparle, "The Difficult Math of Welfare Reform," *New York Times*, December 5, 1993, 30.

60. Eric Pianin, "Similarities, Conflicts Arise At Welfare Reform Hearings," *Washington Post*, July 28, 1994, A9.

61. Bane, interview.

62. Ellwood, interview.

63. Ibid.

CHAPTER 7

1. Daniel P. Carpenter, "State Building Through Reputation Building: Coalitions of Esteem and Program Innovation in the National Postal System 1883–1913," *Studies in American Political Development* 14 (2000): 124.

2. Ron Haskins, "Effects of Welfare Reform on Family Income and Poverty," in Rebecca M. Blank and Ron Haskins, eds., *The New World of Welfare* (Washington, D.C.: Brookings Institution Press, 2001), 104.

3. Douglas Besharov, "Waivers Change the Face of Welfare," *Albany (N.Y.) Times Union*, June 29, 1996, A7.

4. See Edwin Amenta, *Bold Relief: Institutional Politics and the Origins of Modern American Social Policy* (Princeton: Princeton University Press, 1998); Nancy K. Cauthen and Edwin Amenta, "Not for Widows Only: Institutional Politics and the Formative Years of Aid to Dependent Children," *American Sociological Review* 61, no. 3 (1996): 427–48; Robert Lieberman, *Shifting the Color Line: Race and the American Welfare State* (Cambridge, Massachusetts: Harvard University Press, 1998); Theda Skocpol, "Bringing the State Back In: Strategies of Analysis in Current Research," in Peter B. Evans, Dietrich Rueschemeyer, and Theda Skocpol, eds., *Bringing the State Back In* (New York: Cambridge University Press, 1985), 3–37; Theda Skocpol, *Protecting Soldiers and Mothers: The Political Origins of Social Policy in the United States* (Cambridge, Massachusetts: Belknap Press of Harvard University Press, 1992); Margaret Weir, Ann Shola Orloff, and Theda Skocpol, "Introduction: Understanding American Social Politics," in Margaret Weir, Ann Shola Orloff, and Theda Skocpol, eds., *The Politics of Social Policy in the United States* (Princeton: Princeton University Press, 1988), 3–35; Margaret Weir, Ann Shola Orloff, and Theda Skocpol, "The Future of Social Policy in the United States: Political Constraints and Possibilities," in ibid., 421–45; Paul Pierson, *Dismantling the Welfare State: Reagan, Thatcher, and the Politics of Retrenchment* (New York: Cambridge University Press, 1994).

5. Peter A. Hall, *Governing the Economy: The Politics of State Intervention in Britain and France* (New York: Oxford University Press, 1986), 19.

6. See Kathleen Thelen and Sven Steinmo, "Historical Institutionalism in Comparative Politics," in Sven Steinmo, Kathleen Thelen, and Frank Longstreth, eds., *Structuring Politics: Historical Institutionalism in Comparative Analysis* (New York: Cambridge University Press, 1992), 2; and Arthur L. Stinchcombe, *Theoretical Methods in Social History* (New York: Academic Press, 1978), 57.

7. Antonia Maioni, *Parting at the Crossroads: The Emergence of Health Insurance in the United States and Canada* (Princeton: Princeton University Press, 1998).

8. Evelyne Huber, Charles Ragin, and John D. Stephens, "Social Democracy, Christian Democracy, Constitutional Structure, and the Welfare State," *American Journal of Sociology* 99, no. 3 (1993): 711–49.

9. Besharov, A7.

10. David T. Ellwood, interview with author, Cambridge, Massachusetts, October 8, 2002, in author's files.

11. Michael Lipsky, "Bureaucratic Disentitlement in Social Welfare Programs," *Social Service Review* 58, no. 1 (1984): 3–27.

12. Ibid., 3.

13. Mary Jo Bane, interview with author, Cambridge, Massachusetts, October 8, 2002, in author's files.

14. Ellwood, interview.

15. Carpenter, 122.

16. Ibid.

17. Ibid.

18. Ibid., 148.

19. Ibid., 141.

20. I would like to thank Steven M. Teles for his insights into the role of policy evaluation in the new welfare regime.

21. Lois M. Quinn and Robert S. Magill, "Politics Versus Research in Social Policy," *Social Service Review* (1994): 503–20.

22. Ibid., 504.

23. Manpower Demonstration Research Corporation, "Final Results from the Nation's First Test of Welfare Time Limits," November 21, 2000, http://www.mdrc.org/PressReleases/FTP-PR.htm.

24. Quoted in Michael Winerip's "What Some Much-Noted Data Really Showed About Vouchers," *New York Times*, May 7, 2003, B12.

25. Ibid., B12.

26. Ibid.

27. Ibid.

28. Ibid.

AFTERWORD

1. Robert Greenstein, Shawn Fremstad, and Sharon Parrott, *"Superwaiver" Would Grant Executive Branch and Governors Sweeping Authority to Override Federal Laws* (Washington, D.C.: Center for Budget and Policy Priorities, 2002), 1.

2. Tommy Thompson, "Continuing to Transform Welfare: The Next Bold—and Compassionate—Step," http://www.hhs.gov/news/speech/2002/020523.html.

3. Karen Spar, *"Superwaiver" Proposals in Current Welfare Debate* (Washington, D.C.: Congressional Research Service, 2003), 1.

4. Greenstein, Fremstad, and Parrott, 1.

5. "Working Toward Independence," February 2002, http://www.white-house.gov/news/releases/2002/02/print/welfare-book-11.html.

6. Ibid.

7. Ibid.

8. Greenstein, Fremstad, and Parrott, 1.

9. Ibid., 3.

10. Testimony of Wendell Primus at House Subcommittee on Human Resources hearing on welfare reauthorization proposals, April 11, 2002, http://waysandmeans.house.gov/hearings.asp?formmode = archive&hearing = 27.

11. Spar, 3.

12. Vee Burke, *Welfare Reform: An Issue Overview* (Washington, D.C.: Congressional Research Service, 2002), 1.

13. Spar, 3.

14. Michael Armacost, Michael Laracy, and Jennifer Phillips, preface to Rebecca M. Blank and Ron Haskins, eds., *The New World of Welfare* (Washington, D.C.: Brookings Institution Press, 2001), v—ix.

15. Ibid., vii.

16. Testimony of Wally Herger at the Subcommittee on Human Resources hearing on welfare and marriage issues, May 22, 2001, http://waysand-means.house.gov/legacy/humres/107cong/5-22-01/107–28final.htm.

17. Ibid.

18. Ron Haskins and Rebecca Blank, "Welfare Reform: An Agenda for Reauthorization," in Rebecca M. Blank and Ron Haskins, eds., *The New World of Welfare* (Washington, D.C.: Brookings Institution Press, 2001), 3–32.

19. Ibid.

20. Congressional Research Service, *TANF: Brief Comparison of Reauthorization Bills* (order code RL31393) (Washington, D.C.: Library of Congress, 2002), 18.

21. Burke, 3.

APPENDIX 1

1. Evelyn Brodkin, "Assessing Welfare Reform at the Street Level: What Policy Makers Need to Know," *Poverty Research News, Joint Center for Poverty Research* 5, no. 4 (July-August 2001): 16.

2. Dan Bloom and David Butler, *Implementing Time-Limited Welfare Reform: Early Experiences in Three States* (New York: Manpower Demonstration Research, 1995), 19.

3. In order to control the intake of participants into the FTP and keep the

evaluation manageable, random assignment was sometimes slowed or stopped. During that period, individuals applying or being recertified were placed into the traditional AFDC program.

The following groups were exempted from the FTP: disabled or incapacitated adults, full-time caretakers of disabled dependents, guardians not included in the AFDC grant, people under eighteen who were in school or working thirty hours or more per week, parents with children six months or younger, and recipients who were sixty-two years old or older. The exemption for individuals with children under six months was valid only at the time of random assignment. If a participant had an infant after she was assigned to the FTP, she was not exempted from the time limit, though she was exempted from participation in other activities.

4. Control group participants continued to receive "AFDC" benefits even after AFDC was ended by the federal government and replaced with a time-limited program, TANF. This was done to maintain, as much as possible, the experimental design of the evaluation research. Obviously, it is a little bit odd to have a control group in a program that no longer exists. For the research presented here, however, this is not an issue. AFDC ended in October 1996, one month after this research was completed.

5. Research suggests that work-oriented welfare programs are much more successful when mandatory. See Lawrence M. Mead, "Should Workfare Be Mandatory? What the Research Says," *Journal of Policy Analysis and Management* 9, no. 3 (summer 1990): 400–404.

6. An external evaluation of the FTP was a federal requirement for the program.

7. New York: Manpower Demonstration Research Corporation, 1997.

8. Findings and Recommendations is the document produced by the panel based on its deliberations. These go to clients and case managers and are official records of the panel's decisions.

9. The review panel liaison and I often joked about panel member no-shows, because at review panel hearings panel members often lectured FTP participants about the importance of showing up for appointments or at least calling to cancel. Apparently, it was not unusual for panel members to miss the hearings without contacting the liaison. The same turned out to be true of my interviews when I held them at the county building.

10. The review panel gained and lost members continually. These percentages are based on the list of panel members that I received in June 1996, and therefore cannot be considered absolute.

11. Project Independence (PI), a JOBS-funded employment program, also had staff attend these meetings. A PI career advisor and an FTP case manager were assigned as a team to work with each participant. Because these PI staff were working with the FTP, I include them when I use the term "FTP staff." Although technically incorrect, for the sake of simplicity I collapse the two groups into one.

12. These rates were calculated by MDRC based on the case file review conducted by the whole research team.

APPENDIX 2

1. In five of the cases, the participant was listed as being "compliant" in some places on the form and "noncompliant" in others. Because a participant must be *completely* compliant with the program to receive any post-time-limit benefits, a partial noncompliance brought to the panel is in effect a total "noncompliance."

2. There was a very small pilot group of FTP participants prior to the full implementation of the program.

3. Greg J. Duncan, Kathleen Mullan Harris, and Johanne Boisjoly, "Time Limits and Welfare Reform: How Many Families Will Be Affected?" Working Paper No. 1, Chicago: Joint Center for Poverty Research, 1997.

4. Ibid.

5. There was some controversy within the Family Transition Program over how reliable these scores were, with some of the staff feeling that clients sometimes threw the tests in the hope that if they had low scores, then little would be expected of them.

6. Author's interview, Pensacola, Florida, summer 1996, in author's files.

Bibliography

Aaron, Henry J. *Politics and the Professors: The Great Society in Perspective*. Washington, D.C.: Brookings Institution Press, 1978.

Abramovitz, Mimi. *Regulating the Lives of Women: Social Welfare Policy from Colonial Times to the Present*. Boston: South End Press, 1988.

Amenta, Edwin. *Bold Relief: Institutional Politics and the Origins of Modern American Social Policy*. Princeton: Princeton University Press, 1998.

Amenta, Edwin, and Yvonne Zylan. "It Happened Here: Political Opportunity, the New Institutionalism, and the Townsend Movement." *American Sociological Review* 56, no. 2 (1991): 250–65.

Anderson, Elijah. *Streetwise: Race, Class, and Change in an Urban Community*. Chicago: University of Chicago Press, 1990.

Armacost, Michael, Michael Laracy, and Jennifer Phillips. Preface to Rebecca M. Blank and Ron Haskins, eds., *The New World of Welfare*. Washington, D.C.: Brookings Institution Press, 2001.

Ash, Jim. "Future Is Uncertain for Welfare Program." *Pensacola (Fla.) News Journal*, September 21, 1995, C4.

Axinn, June, and Herman Levin. *Social Welfare: A History of the American Response to Need*. 3d ed. New York: Longman, 1992.

Bane, Mary Jo. Interview with author, Cambridge, Massachusetts, October 8, 2002. In author's files.

———. Letter to James Towey, November 12, 1993. In author's files.

Bane, Mary Jo, and David T. Ellwood. *Welfare Realities: From Rhetoric to Reform*. Cambridge, Massachusetts: Harvard University Press, 1994.

Baumgartner, Frank R., and Bryan D. Jones. *Agendas and Instability in American Politics*. Chicago: University of Chicago Press, 1993.

Belz, Herman. *Equality Transformed*. New Brunswick, New Jersey: Transaction, 1991.

Bernstein, Marver H. *Regulating Business by Independent Commission*. Princeton: Princeton University Press, 1955.

Besharov, Douglas. "Waivers Change the Face of Welfare." *Albany (N.Y.) Times Union*, June 29, 1996, A7.

Blank, Rebecca M., and Lucie Schmidt. "Work, Wages, and Welfare." In Rebecca M. Blank and Ron Haskins, eds., *The New World of Welfare*, pp. 70–102. Washington, D.C.: Brookings Institution Press, 2001.

Blank, Rebecca M., and Ron Haskins, eds. *The New World of Welfare*. Washington, D.C.: Brookings Institution Press, 2001.

Blau, Peter, and Marshall W. Meyer. *Bureaucracy and Modern Society*. New York: Random House, 1987 [1956].

Bloom, Dan, and David Butler. *Implementing Time-Limited Welfare Reform: Early Experiences in Three States*. New York: Manpower Demonstration Research Corp., 1995.

Bloom, Dan, James J. Kemple, and Robin Rogers-Dillon. *The Family Transition Program: Implementation and Early Impacts of Florida's Initial Time-Limited Welfare Program*. New York: Manpower Demonstration Research Corp., 1997.

Bloom, Dan, James Kemple, Pamela Morris, Susan Scrivener, Nandita Verma, and Richard Hendra. *The Family Transition Program: Final Report on Florida's Initial Time-Limited Welfare Program*. New York: Manpower Demonstration Research Corp., 2000.

Boehnen, Elisabeth, and Thomas Corbett. "Welfare Waivers: Some Salient Trends." *Focus* 18, no. 1 (spring 1996): 34–37.

Boli, John. *New Citizens for a New Society: The Institutional Origins of Mass Schooling in Sweden*. New York: Pergamon Press, 1989.

Booth, William. "In Florida's Welfare Experiment, Mothers' Ambition Is the Catalyst." *Washington Post*, December 28, 1994, A3.

Broder, John M. "Keeping Score: Big Social Changes Revive the False God of Numbers." *New York Times*, August 17, 1997, Section 4, 1.

Brodkin, Evelyn. "Assessing Welfare Reform at the Street Level: What Policy Makers Need to Know." *Poverty Research News, Joint Center for Poverty Research* 5, no. 4 (July-August 2001).

Brodkin, Evelyn Z., and Alexander Kaufman. *Experimenting with Welfare Reform: The Political Boundaries of Policy Analysis*. Working Paper No. 1. Chicago: Joint Center for Poverty Research, 1998.

———. "Policy Experiments and Poverty Politics." *Social Service Review* 74, no. 4 (2000): 507–32.

Burke, Vee. *Welfare Reform: An Issue Overview*. Washington, D.C.: Congressional Research Service, 2002.

Callahan, Daniel, and Bruce Jennings. *Ethics, the Social Sciences, and Policy Analysis*. Hastings-on-Hudson, New York: Plenum Press, 1983.

———. "Social Science and the Policy-Making Process." *Hastings Center Report* 13 no. 1 (February 1983, special supplement): 3–8.

Carpenter, Daniel P. "State Building Through Reputation Building: Coalitions of Esteem and Program Innovation in the National Postal System 1883–1913." *Studies in American Political Development* 14 (2000): 121–55.

Cauthen, Nancy K., and Edwin Amenta. "Not for Widows Only: Institutional Politics and the Formative Years of Aid to Dependent Children." *American Sociological Review* 61, no. 3 (1996): 427–48.

Claiborne, William. "North Floridians Are Pioneers in Clinton-Like Welfare Program." *Washington Post*, February 26, 1994, A3.

Cloward, Richard A., and Lloyd E. Ohlin. *Delinquency and Opportunity: A Theory of Delinquent Gangs.* Glencoe, Illinois: Free Press, 1960.

Congressional Research Service. *TANF: Brief Comparison of Reauthorization Bills* (order code RL31393). Washington, D.C.: Library of Congress, 2002.

David, Paul. "Clio and the Economics of QWERTY." *American Economic Review* 75 (1985): 332–37.

Debenport, Ellen. "End of the Line for 8 Women on Welfare." *St. Petersburg (Fla.) Times*, June 1, 1996, 1A, 4A.

DeParle, Jason. "The Difficult Math of Welfare Reform." *New York Times*, December 5, 1993, 30.

———. "A Sharp Decrease in Welfare Cases is Gathering Speed." *New York Times*, February 2, 1997, Section 1, 1.

———. "In Sink-or-Swim Welfare, Pensacola Staying Afloat." *New York Times*, June 18, 1997, A1.

Detlefsen, Robert. *Civil Rights Under Reagan.* San Francisco: ICS Press, 1991.

DiMaggio, Paul J., and Walter W. Powell. "Introduction." In Walter W. Powell and Paul J. DiMaggio, eds., *The New Institutionalism in Organizational Analysis*, pp. 1–38. Chicago: University of Chicago Press, 1991.

Dobbin, Frank. "Cultural Models of Organization: The Social Construction of Rational Organizing Principles." In Diana Crane, ed., *Sociology of Culture: Emerging Theoretical Perspectives*, pp. 117–41. Cambridge, Massachusetts: Basil Blackwell, 1994.

———. *Forging Industrial Policy: The United States, Britain, and France in the Railway Age.* New York: Cambridge University Press, 1994.

"Dueling Candidate Series, The Race for Governor: What They're Saying." *St. Petersburg (Fla.) Times*, October 31, 1994, D5.

Duncan, Greg J., Kathleen Mullan Harris, and Johanne Boisjoly, "Time Limits and Welfare Reform: How Many Families Will Be Affected?" Working Paper No. 1. Chicago: Joint Center for Poverty Research, 1997.

Edelman, Lauren. "Legal Ambiguity and Symbolic Structures: Organizational Mediation of Civil Rights Law." *American Journal of Sociology* 97 (1992): 1531–76.

Edin, Kathryn, and Laura Lein. *Making Ends Meet: How Single Mothers Survive Welfare and Low-Wage Work.* New York: Russell Sage Foundation, 1997.

Ellwood, David T. Interview with author, Cambridge, Massachusetts, October 8, 2002. In author's files.

———. *Poor Support: Poverty in the American Family.* New York: Basic Books, 1986.

———. "Welfare Reform as I Knew It: When Bad things Happen to Good Policies." *American Prospect* 26 (May–June 1996): 22–29.

Farkas, Steve, and Jean Johnson. *The Values We Live By: What Americans Want from Welfare Reform.* New York: Public Agenda, 1996.

Fee, Elizabeth, and Dorothy Porter. "Public Health, Preventive Medicine and Professionalization: England and America in the Nineteenth Century." In Andrew Wear, ed., *Medicine in Society: Historical Essays,* pp. 249–75. Cambridge, England: Cambridge University Press, 1992.

Fine, Gary Alan. *With the Boys: Little League Baseball and Preadolescent Culture.* Chicago: University of Chicago Press, 1987.

"Florida Gets Approval for Welfare Experiment: The State Plan Will Mirror Clinton's with Employers Subsidies and Benefit Limitations." *Orlando (Fla.) Sentinel,* January 28, 1994, A1.

Florida House of Representatives Committee on Aging and Human Services. Final Bill and Economic Impact Statement CS/HB 587. Florida State Archives, April 14, 1993.

———. Social Economic and Development Subcommittee. Florida State Archives, February 9, 1993.

———. Social Economic and Development Subcommittee. Florida State Archives, Tape #1, February 9, 1993.

Fraser, Nancy. "Gender Equity and the Welfare State." *Political Theory* 22, no. 4 (1994): 591–618.

Fraser, Nancy, and Linda Gordon. "A Genealogy of Dependency: Tracing a Key Word of the U.S. Welfare State." *Signs* 19, no. 2 (1994): 309–36.

"Of Fraud, Welfare, Vouchers." *St. Petersburg (Fla.) Times,* November 8, 1994.

Friedland, Roger, and Robert Alford. "Bringing Society Back In: Symbols, Practices, and Institutional Contradictions." In Walter W. Powell and Paul J. DiMaggio, eds., *The New Institutionalism in Organizational Analysis,* pp. 232–63. Chicago: University of Chicago Press, 1991.

FTP Handbook. November 1995. In author's files.

Galbraith, John Kenneth. *The Affluent Society.* Boston: Houghton Mifflin, 1958.

Garin, Geoffrey, Guy Molyneux, and Linda DiVall. "Public Attitudes Toward Welfare Reform." *Social Policy* 25, no. 2 (winter 1994): 44–49.

Gordon, Linda. *Pitied but Not Entitled: Single Mothers and the History of Welfare 1890–1935.* New York: Free Press, 1994.

———, ed. *Women, the State, and Welfare.* Madison: University of Wisconsin Press, 1990.

Gould, Stephen Jay. *The Mismeasure of Man.* New York: W.W. Norton, 1981.

Greenberg, Mark. Letter to Mary Jo Bane, October 26, 1993. In author's files.

Greenstein, Robert, Shawn Fremstad, and Sharon Parrott. *"Superwaiver" Would Grant Executive Branch and Governors Sweeping Authority to Override Federal Laws.* Washington, D.C.: Center for Budget and Policy Priorities, 2002.

Gueron, Judith M., and Edward Pauly. *From Welfare to Work.* New York: Russell Sage Foundation, 1991.

Hall, Peter A. *Governing the Economy: The Politics of State Intervention in Britain and France*. New York: Oxford University Press, 1986.

———. "Policy Paradigms, Social Learning, and the State: The Case of Economic Policymaking in Britain." *Comparative Politics* 25, no. 3 (1993): 275–96.

Handler, Joel, and Ellen Hollingsworth. *The "Deserving Poor": A Study of Welfare Administration*. Chicago: Markham, 1971.

Harrington, Michael. *The Other America*. New York: Penguin, 1981.

Haskins, Ron, and Rebecca Blank. "Welfare Reform: An Agenda for Reauthorization." In Rebecca Blank and Ron Haskins, eds., *The New World of Welfare*, pp. 3–32. Washington, D.C.: Brookings Institution Press, 2001.

Heclo, Hugh. *Modern Social Politics*. New Haven, Connecticut: Yale University Press, 1974.

Herger, Wally. Testimony at U.S. House of Representatives Subcommittee on Human Resources hearing on welfare and marriage issues. May 22, 2001. http://waysandmeans.house.gov/legacy/humres/107cong/5-22-01/107–28final.htm.

HHS News. "Clinton Administration Makes Award to Change the Culture of Welfare." November 6, 1995. http://www.acf.dhhs.gov/news/press/1995/culture.html.

———. "Florida Welfare Demonstration." January 27, 1994. http://www.hhs.gov/news/press/pre1995pres/940127c.txt.

———. "HHS Releases President's Fast-Track Welfare Reform." August 17, 1995. http://www.acf.dhhs.gov/news/press/1995/fastck.html.

———. "Wisconsin Welfare Demonstration." November 1, 1993. http://www.acf.dhhs.gov/news/press/1993/welfdewi.html.

Hilgartner, Stephen, and Charles L. Bosk. "The Rise and Fall of Social Problems: A Public Arenas Model." *American Journal of Sociology* 94 (1988): 53–78.

Hirth, Diane. "Welfare Reform is Taking Shape in State." *Orlando (Fla.) Sentinel*, December 26, 1994.

Hogan, Lyn. *Jobs, Not JOBS*. Washington, D.C.: Progressive Policy Institute, 1995.

Horwitz, Morton J. *The Transformation of American Law 1870–1960: The Crisis of Legal Orthodoxy*. New York: Oxford University Press, 1992.

Huber, Evelyne, Charles Ragin, and John D. Stephens. "Social Democracy, Christian Democracy, Constitutional Structure, and the Welfare State." *American Journal of Sociology* 99, no. 3 (1993): 711–49.

Immergut, Ellen. *Health Politics: Interests and Institutions in Western Europe*. New York: Cambridge University Press, 1992.

Institute for Research on Poverty. "Informing the Welfare Debate: A Conversation with State Officials." *Focus* 18, no. 1 (1996): 30–33.

Iyengar, Shanto, and Donald R. Kinder. *News that Matters: Television and American Opinion*. Chicago: University of Chicago Press, 1987.

Kaiser/Harvard Program on the Public and Health Social Policy. Social Policy Survey. January 1995.

Kaplan, Thomas. "Wisconsin's W2 Program: Welfare as We Might Come to Know It?" In Carol S. Weissert, ed., *Learning from Leaders: Welfare Reform and Politics and Policy in Five Midwestern States*, pp. 77–118. New York: Rockefeller Institute Press, 2000.

Katz, Michael B. *Improving Poor People*. Princeton: Princeton University Press, 1995.

———. *In the Shadow of the Poorhouse: A Social History of Welfare in America*. New York: Basic Books, 1986.

———. *The Undeserving Poor: From the War on Poverty to the War on Welfare*. New York: Pantheon, 1989.

———, ed. *The "Underclass" Debate*. Princeton: Princeton University Press, 1993.

Kellam, Susan. *Welfare Experiments, CQ Researcher*. Washington, D.C.: Congressional Quarterly Press, 1994.

Kingdon, John. *Agendas, Alternatives, and Public Policies*. New York: HarperCollins College Publishers, 1995 [1984].

Knoke, David, Franz Urban Pappi, Jeffrey Broadbent, and Yutaka Tsujinaka. *Comparing Policy Networks: Labor Politics in the U.S., Germany, and Japan*. New York: Cambridge University Press, 1996.

Kosterlitz, Julie. "Reworking Welfare." *National Journal* 24 (1992): 2189–92.

Krasner, Stephen. *International Regimes*. Ithaca, New York: Cornell University Press, 1984.

Lanier, Cecil. Interoffice memorandum on extension procedures. June 18, 1996. In author's files.

Laumann, Edward, and David Knoke. *The Organizational State: A Perspective on National Energy and Health*. Madison: University of Wisconsin Press, 1987.

Lareau, Annette. *Home Advantage: Social Class and Parental Intervention in Elementary Education*. Philadelphia: Falmer Press, 1989.

Levin-Epstein, Jodie. *CLASP Update*. Washington, D.C.: Center for Law and Social Policy, 1995.

Lieberman, Robert. *Shifting the Color Line: Race and the American Welfare State*. Cambridge, Massachusetts: Harvard University Press, 1998.

Lieberman, Robert, and Greg Shaw. "Looking Inward, Looking Outward: The Politics of State Welfare Innovation Under Devolution." *Political Research Quarterly* 53, no. 2 (2000): 215–40.

Lipsky, Michael. "Bureaucratic Disentitlement in Social Welfare Programs." *Social Service Review* 58, no. 1 (1984): 3–27.

———. *Street-level Bureaucracy: Dilemmas of the Individual in Public Services*. New York: Russell Sage, 1980.

Lowi, Theodore J. *The End of Liberalism*. New York: W.W. Norton, 1969.

MacRae, Duncan, Jr., and Dale Whittington. *Expert Advice for Policy Choices*. Washington, D.C.: Georgetown University Press, 1997.

Maioni, Antonia. *Parting at the Crossroads: The Emergence of Health Insurance in the United States and Canada*. Princeton: Princeton University Press, 1998.

Manpower Demonstration Research Corporation. "Final Results from the Nation's First Test of Welfare Time Limits." November 21, 2000. http://www.mdrc.org/PressReleases/FTP-PR.htm.

Mead, Lawrence M. *Beyond Entitlement: The Social Obligations of Citizenship*. New York: Free Press, 1986.

―――. *Government Matters: Welfare Reform in Wisconsin*. Princeton: Princeton University Press, forthcoming.

―――. *The New Paternalism: Supervisory Approaches to Poverty*. Washington, D.C.: Brookings Institution Press, 1997.

―――. "Should Workfare Be Mandatory? What the Research Says." *Journal of Policy Analysis and Management* 9, no. 3 (summer 1990): 400–404.

Melnick, R. Shep. *Between the Lines: Interpreting Welfare Rights*. Washington, D.C.: Brookings Institution Press, 1994.

Meyer, John, and Brian Rowan. "Institutionalized Organizations: Formal Structure as Myth and Ceremony." In Walter W. Powell and Paul J. DiMaggio, eds., *The New Institutionalism in Organizational Analysis*, pp. 41–62. Chicago: University of Chicago Press, 1991.

Mink, Gwendolyn. "The Lady and the Tramp: Gender, Race, and the Origins of the American Welfare State." In Linda Gordon, ed., *Women, the State and Welfare*, pp. 92–122. Madison: University of Wisconsin Press, 1990.

Moffitt, Robert. "Incentive Effects of the U.S. Welfare System: A Review." *Journal of Economic Literature* 30, no. 1 (1992): 27–31.

Morill, Calvin, and Cindy McKee. "Institutional Isomorphism and Informal Social Control: Evidence from a Community Mediation Center." *Social Problems* 40 (1993): 445–63.

Murray, Charles. "Family Formation." In Rebecca M. Blank and Ron Haskins, eds., *The New World of Welfare*, pp. 137–60. Washington, D.C.: Brookings Institution Press, 2001.

―――. *Losing Ground: American Social Policy, 1950–1980*. New York: Basic Books, 1984.

Myles, John, and Paul Pierson. "Friedman's Revenge: The Reform of 'Liberal' Welfare States in Canada and the United States." *Politics and Society* 25, no. 4 (1997): 443–73.

Neisner, Jennifer. *State Welfare Initiatives*. Washington, D.C.: Congressional Research Service, 1995.

O'Connor, Alice. *Poverty Knowledge: Social Science, Social Policy, and the Poor in Twentieth-Century U.S. History*. Princeton: Princeton University Press, 2001.

Office of the Assistant Secretary for Evaluation and Planning. "Approaches to Evaluating Welfare Reform: Lessons from Five State Demonstrations." http://aspe.os.dhhs.gov/hsp/isp/waivers/intro.htm.

Orloff, Ann Shola. "Farewell to Maternalism: Welfare Reform, Ending the Entitlement for Poor Single Mothers and Expanding the Claims of Poor Employed Parents." Paper presented at Harvard Seminar on Inequality and Social Policy, February 26, 2001.

―――. "Gender and the Social Rights of Citizenship: The Comparative Analysis of Gender Relations and Welfare States." *American Sociological Review* 58, no. 3 (1993): 303–28.

Osborne, David. *Laboratories of Democracy.* Boston: Harvard Business School Press, 1988.

Parrott, Sharon, Heidi Goldberg, and Shawn Fremstad. *Recycling an Unwise Proposal: State Concerns and New State Fiscal Realities Ignored in House Republican Welfare Bill.* Washington, D.C.: Center for Budget and Policy Priorities, 2003.

Patterson, James T. *America's Struggle Against Poverty 1900–1985.* Cambridge, Massachusetts: Harvard University Press, 1986.

Pianin, Eric. "Similarities, Conflicts Arise At Welfare Reform Hearings." *Washington Post,* July 28, 1994, A9.

———. "Tenet of Clinton Plan Faces Test." *Washington Post,* May 20, 1994, A6.

Pierson, Paul. *Dismantling the Welfare State: Reagan, Thatcher, and the Politics of Retrenchment.* New York: Cambridge University Press, 1994.

———. *The New Politics of the Welfare State.* Working Paper Series #57. New York: Russell Sage Foundation, 1994.

Piven, Frances Fox, and Richard A. Cloward. *Regulating the Poor: The Functions of Public Welfare.* New York: Vintage, 1972.

Powell, Walter W., and Paul J. DiMaggio. *The New Institutionalism in Organizational Analysis.* Chicago: University of Chicago Press, 1991.

Pressman, Jeffrey L., and Aaron B. Wildavsky. *Implementation.* Berkeley: University of California Press, 1973.

Primus, Wendell. Interview with author, Washington, D.C., autumn 1996. In author's files.

———. Testimony at U.S. House of Representatives Subcommittee on Human Resources hearing on welfare reauthorization proposals. April 11, 2002. http://waysandmeans.house.gov/hearings.asp?formmode = archive&hearing = 27.

Quadagno, Jill. *The Color of Welfare: How Racism Undermined the War on Poverty.* New York: Oxford University Press, 1994.

Quinn, Lois M., and Robert S. Magill. "Politics Versus Research in Social Policy." *Social Service Review* (1994): 503–20.

"Reform that Values Families." Press release from Clinton/Gore campaign, May 21, 1996.

Rogers-Dillon, Robin. "The Dynamics of Welfare Stigma." *Qualitative Sociology* 18, no. 4 (1995): 439–56.

Rogers-Dillon, Robin, and John David Skrentny. "Administering Success: The Legitimacy Imperative and the Implementation of Welfare Reform." *Social Problems* 46, no. 1 (1999): 13–29.

Savner, Steve, and Mark Greenberg. *The CLASP Guide to Welfare Waivers 1992–1995.* Washington, D.C.: Center for Law and Social Policy, 1995.

Scott, Richard. "Unpacking Institutional Arrangements." In Walter W. Powell and Paul J. DiMaggio, eds., *The New Institutionalism in Organizational Analysis,* pp. 164–82. Chicago: University of Chicago Press, 1991.

Scott, Richard, and John W. Meyer. "The Organization of Societal Sectors." In Walter W. Powell and Paul J. DiMaggio, eds., *The New Institutionalism in Organizational Analysis*, pp. 108–40. Chicago: University of Chicago Press, 1991.

Selznick, Philip. *Leadership in Administration: A Sociological Interpretation.* New York: Harper and Row, 1957.

Shaw, Greg M. "The Role of Public Input in State Welfare Policymaking." *Policy Studies Journal* 28, no. 4 (2000): 707–20.

————. "State Welfare Policies and the Shifting Ground of American Federalism." Paper presented to the annual American Political Science Association meeting, San Francisco, August 1996.

Shaw, Greg, and Robert Shapiro. "The Polls: Poverty and Public Assistance." *Public Opinion Quarterly* 66, no. 1 (2002): 105–28.

Shogren, Elizabeth. "2 Florida Counties to Test Clinton-Style Welfare Plan." *Los Angeles Times*, January 28, 1994, A32.

Simon, Herbert A. *Administrative Behavior: A Study of Decision-Making Processes in Administrative Organizations.* New York: Free Press, 1997 [1949].

Skocpol, Theda. "Bringing the State Back In: Strategies of Analysis in Current Research." In Peter B. Evans, Dietrich Rueschemeyer, and Theda Skocpol, eds., *Bringing the State Back In*, pp. 3–37. New York: Cambridge University Press, 1985.

————. "The Limits of the New Deal System and the Roots of Contemporary Welfare Dilemmas." In Margaret Weir, Ann Shola Orloff, and Theda Skocpol, eds., *The Politics of Social Policy in the United States*, pp. 3–37. Princeton: Princeton University Press, 1988.

————. *Protecting Soldiers and Mothers: The Political Origins of Social Policy in the United States.* Cambridge, Massachusetts: Belknap Press of Harvard University Press, 1992.

————. *States and Social Revolutions: A Comparative Analysis of France, Russia, and China.* New York: Cambridge University Press, 1979.

Skrentny, John David. *The Ironies of Affirmative Action: Politics, Culture, and Justice in America.* Chicago: University of Chicago Press, 1996.

Solomon, Carmen D. *The Family Support Act of 1988: How It Changes the Aid to Families with Dependent Children (AFDC) and Child Support Enforcement Programs.* Washington, D.C.: Congressional Research Service, 1988.

Sosin, Michael R. "Legal Rights and Welfare Change, 1960–1980." In Sheldon Danzinger and Daniel H. Weinberg, eds., *Fighting Poverty: What Works, What Doesn't*, pp. 260–82. Cambridge, Massachusetts: Harvard University Press, 1986.

Soss, Joe, Sanford F. Schram, Thomas P. Vartanian, and Erin O'Brien. "Setting the Terms of Relief: Explaining State Policy Choices in the Devolution Revolution." *American Journal of Political Science* 45, no. 2 (2001): 378–95.

Spar, Karen. *"Superwaiver" Proposals in Current Welfare Debate.* Washington, D.C.: Congressional Research Service, 2003.

Stack, Carol. *All Our Kin.* New York: Basic Books, 1974.

Stinchcombe, Arthur L. *Theoretical Methods in Social History*. New York: Academic Press, 1978.

Stone, Deborah A. *The Disabled State*. Philadelphia: Temple University Press, 1984.

———. *Policy Paradox and Political Reason*. New York: HarperCollins, 1988.

Study Commission on Employment Opportunities and Self Sufficiency. "Final Report: Study Commission on Employment Opportunities and Self Sufficiency," 1992. In author's files.

Teles, Steven M. *Whose Welfare? AFDC and Elite Politics*. Lawrence: University Press of Kansas, 1996.

Thelen, Kathleen, and Sven Steinmo. "Historical Institutionalism in Comparative Politics." In Sven Steinmo, Kathleen Thelen, and Frank Longstreth, eds., *Structuring Politics: Historical Institutionalism in Comparative Analysis*, pp. 1–32. New York: Cambridge University Press, 1992.

Thompson, Tommy. "Continuing to Transform Welfare: The Next Bold—and Compassionate—Step." www.hhs.gov / news / speech / 2002 / 020523.html.

Trattner, Walter I. *Social Welfare or Social Control? Some Historical Reflections on Regulating the Poor*. Knoxville: University of Tennessee Press, 1983.

U.S. Department of Health and Human Services. "HHS Fact Sheet: State Welfare Demonstration." October 7, 1996.

U.S. Government Accounting Office. *Welfare to Work: Participants' Characteristics and Services Provided in JOBS*. Washington, D.C.: GAO, 1995.

U.S. House of Representatives Ways and Means Subcommittee on Human Resources. Hearing on Illegitimacy. March 12, 1996.

———. Hearing on Welfare and Marriage Issues. May 22, 2001. http:// waysandmeans.house.gov / legacy / humres / 107cong / 5-22-01 / 107–28final .htm.

———. Hearing on Welfare Reauthorization Proposals. April 11, 2002. http:// waysandmeans.house.gov / hearings.asp?formmode = archive&hearing = 27.

Vobejda, Barbara. "Clinton Signs Welfare Bill Amid Division." *Washington Post*, August 23, 1996, A1.

Weaver, R. Kent. *Ending Welfare as We Know It*. Washington, D.C.: Brookings Institution Press, 2000.

———. "The Politics of Blame Avoidance." *Journal of Public Policy* 6, no. 4 (1986): 371–98.

Weir, Margaret. *Politics and Jobs*. Princeton: Princeton University Press, 1992.

Weir, Margaret, Ann Shola Orloff, and Theda Skocpol. "Introduction: Understanding American Social Politics." In Margaret Weir, Ann Shola Orloff, and Theda Skocpol, eds., *The Politics of Social Policy in the United States*, pp. 3–35. Princeton: Princeton University Press, 1988.

———. "The Future of Social Policy in the United States: Political Constraints and Possibilities." In Margaret Weir, Ann Shola Orloff, and Theda Skocpol, eds., *The Politics of Social Policy in the United States*, pp. 421–45. Princeton: Princeton University Press, 1988.

Weiss, Carol H. *Evaluation*. 2d ed. Saddle River, New Jersey: Prentice-Hall, 1998.

Weissert, Carol S., ed. *Learning from Leaders: Welfare Reform Politics and Policy in Five Midwestern States*. New York: Rockefeller Institute Press, 2000.

"What Will Happen to Welfare?" *St. Petersburg (Fla.) Times*, October 18, 1994.

Wildavsky, Aaron. *Speaking Truth to Power*. New Brunswick, New Jersey: Transaction, 2002.

Wilensky, Harold L., and Charles N. Lebeaux. *Industrial Society and Social Welfare: The Impact of Industrialization on the Supply and Organization of Social Welfare*. New York: Free Press, 1965.

Wilson, James Q. *Bureaucracy: What Government Agencies Do and Why They Do It*. New York: Basic Books, 1989.

Winerip, Michael. "What Some Much-Noted Data Really Showed About Vouchers." *New York Times*, May 7, 2003, B12.

Winstead, Don. Letter to Howard Rolston, December 15, 1993. In author's files.

Wiseman, Michael. "State Strategies for Welfare Reform: The Wisconsin Story." *Journal of Policy Analysis and Management* 15, no. 4 (fall 1996): 515–46.

———. "Welfare Reform in the United States: A Background Paper." *Housing Policy Debate* 7, no. 4 (1996): 595–648.

Wolfe, Alan. *One Nation After All*. New York: Viking Press, 1998.

"Working Toward Independence." February 2002. http://www.whitehouse.gov/news/releases/2002/02/print/welfare-book-11.html.

Zedlewski, Sheila, and Loprest, Pamela "Will TANF Work for the Most Disadvantaged Families?" In Rebecca Blank and Ron Haskins, eds., *The New World of Welfare*, pp. 311–28. Washington, D.C.: Brookings Institution Press, 2001.

Zucker, Lynne. "The Role of Institutionalization in Cultural Persistence." In Walter W. Powell and Paul J. DiMaggio, eds., *The New Institutionalism in Organizational Analysis*, pp. 83–107. Chicago: University of Chicago Press, 1991.

Index